Globalization and American Popular Culture

GLOBALIZATION AND AMERICAN POPULAR CULTURE

FOURTH EDITION

LANE CROTHERS

Illinois State University

ROWMAN & LITTLEFIELD
Lanham • Boulder • New York • London

Executive Editor: Susan McEachern
Assistant Editor: Rebeccah Shumaker
Senior Marketing Manager: Deborah Hudson

Credits and acknowledgments for material borrowed from other sources, and reproduced with permission, appear on the appropriate page within the text.

Published by Rowman & Littlefield
A wholly owned subsidiary of The Rowman & Littlefield Publishing Group, Inc.
4501 Forbes Boulevard, Suite 200, Lanham, Maryland 20706
www.rowman.com

Unit A, Whitacre Mews, 26-34 Stannary Street, London SE11 4AB, United Kingdom

British Library Cataloguing in Publication Information Available

Library of Congress Cataloging-in-Publication Data
Names: Crothers, Lane.
Title: Globalization and American popular culture / Lane Crothers, Illinois
  State University.
Description: Fourth edition. | Lanham : Rowman & Littlefield, 2017. | Series:
  Globalization | Includes bibliographical references and index.
Identifiers: LCCN 2017030224 (print) | LCCN 2017034996 (ebook) | ISBN
  9781538105320 (electronic) | ISBN 9781538105306 (cloth : alk. paper) |
  ISBN 9781538105313 (pbk. : alk. paper)
Subjects: LCSH: Popular culture—United States. | Mass media—Social
  aspects—United States. | Globalization—Social aspects—United States. |
  Civilization, Modern—American influences. | United States—Foreign
  economic relations. | United States—Foreign public opinion.
Classification: LCC E169.12 (ebook) | LCC E169.12 .C74 2017 (print) | DDC
  306.0973—dc23
LC record available at https://lccn.loc.gov/2017030224

Printed in the United States of America

For Austin and Gigi, because someday
I get to try to explain all this to you,
probably like you'll try to explain it all to me

CONTENTS

ACKNOWLEDGMENTS FOR THE FOURTH EDITION

In 2007, when the first edition of this book was published, Facebook had only been open to the public for a year. Apple released its iPhone, the first of the so-called smartphones, at nearly the same time as this book became available for purchase. As impossible as this may seem, since both Facebook and smartphones seem so central to so many of our lives today, it turns out that Americans have had the opportunity to use and enjoy Facebook on their iPhones (and, I hope, this book!) for fewer years than the nation has been in combat in Afghanistan (since 2001).

Yet, unlike the war in Afghanistan, both Facebook and the iPhone can be seen to have wrought massive changes in American life and life around the world as well. Entire industries have been turned upside down as gig economy platforms like Uber and Lyft provide ad hoc services once reserved for taxi companies, and Airbnb opens people's homes to serve as hotels all over the world. A wirelessly connected world has fueled both the revolutions of the Arab Spring and the phenomenon of cute cat videos uploaded to YouTube's seemingly inexhaustible server banks. It has turned "viral" into a digital rather than a medical concept and has pushed ever more of our lives into the public sphere.

For a time, as earlier versions of this book have suggested, it appeared that the new, digital, interconnected world order might disrupt the American popular culture industry, just as it had the taxi and hotel markets. It turned out to be relatively easy to "rip" movies, music, and television programming from DVDs and CDs and spread them around the globe. This in turn allowed for the illegal use and sales of American popular culture products like music—meaning that, as a practical matter, the companies and producers who made a given piece of music might well never get paid for creating it. Had users gone on to not pay for things like movies and television programs the way they weren't (and aren't) paying for music, the core of the American popular culture industry as represented by the image of Hollywood, California, might well have been destroyed.

Yet, as I write these acknowledgments to the fourth edition of this book in late spring 2017, American popular culture products dominate the world. People watch American movies and television programs. They listen to American music. They dress in American fashions, eat at American restaurants, and at least to some extent enjoy American sports. Notably, they do all this even though the recently elected president of the United States, Donald Trump, has made anti-immigrant, xenophobic comments and demonstrated anti–free trade attitudes in his policies. Nonetheless, American popular culture seems ever more, well, popular, everywhere around the world.

In part, as I discuss later in this book, the rise of social media platforms like Facebook, linked wirelessly together through devices like the iPhone (and other smartphones), helps explain the continued pervasiveness of American popular culture. Social media and wirelessly linked devices now serve as both drivers of and engines for the spread of American popular culture globally. Facebook and other social media platforms, after all, provide a venue to host video clips and other artifacts from American popular culture sources. Friends and others can view and link to these clips, sometimes driving millions of eyes to them. The obscure can go viral in an instant and become an object of worldwide attention in less time than it takes to brush one's teeth.

Social media and wireless devices also provide means through which users can create content as well—through which they can drive the expansion of American popular culture. Users are no longer wholly dependent on major corporations to create entertainment content. Now they can create their own—which may nonetheless be derivative or duplicative of existing, established forms. In other words, in creating content users might be reinforcing dominant styles as well. Turkish hip-hop, for example, is surely Turkish. As is discussed in chapter 3, it is also hip-hop—and thus, at least to some extent, American.

With such thoughts as context, I am pleased to be able to offer this fourth edition of *Globalization and American Popular Culture*. In the ten years since the first edition was published, much has changed—from the way entertainment is delivered to our homes to increased global access to McDonald's restaurants in China. Yet much has remained the same: American popular culture products remain preeminent in global attention. It is a wonderful thing to be able to offer these thoughts and updates in a dynamically developing field.

As always, some thanks. I owe thanks to the different editors who have reviewed, commented on, and otherwise nurtured this book from its earliest imagining: Susan McEachern at Rowman & Littlefield and series editors Manfred B. Steger and Terrell Carver. The book is stronger for their work. Tammy Johnson of Illinois State University provided invaluable research support for the first edition of this project. I owe Manfred Steger special thanks for the many conversations, discussions, and words of encouragement he shared with me regarding this project and many others. His early insights into the project profoundly shaped its outcome, and he deserves special credit for this. The conversations continue, which is a good thing.

My experiences of living outside the United States for extended periods have also made this a better book. From September 2007 through February 2008, I served as the Eccles Centre Visiting Professor in North American Studies at the British Library in London. Although I was not working on this project there, living in London for six months gave me unique insights into the ways American popular culture engages with cultures around the world. While there, I took advantage of opportunities to travel to Amsterdam, Rome, and Istanbul and thereby broaden my experience in invaluable ways. I thank the Eccles Centre for its support. (I recently had a chance to return to Istanbul and revisit my experiences there, and I thank the faculty and students at Kadir Has University for this opportunity.) I also want to thank the Illinois State University donor who supported my time in the wonderful but remarkably expensive city of London.

Then, from August 2015 to the end of May 2016, I lived with my family in Helsinki, Finland, where I served as the Fulbright Bicentennial Chair in American Studies at the University of Helsinki. The remarkable Fulbright program allows scholars and students from around the world the chance to live and learn outside the United States (for Americans) or in it (for international students and faculty). In addition to performing my regular duties in Helsinki, I traveled with my family extensively in Finland and visited Stockholm, St. Petersburg, Munich, Heidelberg, Salzburg, and Copenhagen. More, as a father of two young children, I had a special opportunity to see how children are socialized in an environment different from my "normal" one, the United States. This time abroad improved the book, and its pages reflect several of my experiences. I thank Fulbright for their support.

Finally, a special thanks to Dr. Martha Horst, who gives the time and the energy and the love that make all of life exciting and challenging, leaving me anxious to explore more of the world every day.

As I have noted in the acknowledgments of every edition of this book, the life of an academic is a privileged one. We are given the freedom to think about things we like to think about, to talk about things we like to talk about, and to write about things we like to write about. This is a rare gift in the modern world, and I appreciate the many teachers, family members, and friends who have supported me over the years as I have worked to fully inhabit life as an academic. It is a rare thing to know one is doing what one is meant to do. I have the privilege of living with that knowledge every day.

Thanks to you all. This book would not have been possible without you. Any errors and weaknesses are mine alone.

TABLES

CHAPTER 1

AMERICAN POPULAR CULTURE AND GLOBALIZATION

This book examines the ways that American movies, music, and television programs shape and are shaped by contemporary globalization. It also examines other features of American pop culture in this light, including fast food, clothing, sports, and social networking. As will be seen, audiovisual media like movies, music, and television provide a significant means by which images of the "American" way of life, whether political, social, or economic, are transmitted around the world. Likewise, fast-food restaurants like McDonald's, drink companies like Coca-Cola and Pepsi, sports like basketball and baseball, and clothing like Levi's jeans are global cultural icons. Facebook and sites like it serve as hubs through which American popular culture reaches ever-widening parts of the world. It is through these artifacts (and many others) that the rest of the world sees American values and lifestyles.

POPULAR CULTURE AND GLOBAL POLITICS

At first glance, the idea of writing—or, for that matter, reading—a book on the relationship between the profound economic, social, political, and cultural changes going on in the modern world, collectively labeled "globalization," and the movies, music, and television programs (among other features) that compose American popular culture may seem a bit odd. Globalization, after all, seems "heavy": it is the result of numerous powerful forces and is fundamentally remaking the way the world works. Popular culture, by contrast, seems "light": whether in theme or in impact, it is intuitively hard to see how even a movie megahit like *Guardians of the Galaxy* could play a meaningful role in such a profound thing as globalization.

Yet popular cultural entertainments have been central to the new era of globalization. For example, in 1998 movies, music, and television programming were the leading U.S. export.[1] In other words, American producers of TV shows, films, and music sold more programming overseas than the United States sold in agricultural products or weapons. This was true even without factoring in the economic and cultural power of American brands like McDonald's, Levi's, and Starbucks. Whatever one thinks of its products, American pop culture is clearly a global phenomenon.

The end of the Cold War and the emergence of new technologies like the Internet, mobile phones, and small-dish satellite television systems have allowed American popular culture access to an ever-growing global market. This spread has served both to enhance the profits of U.S. corporations and to highlight and augment cultural tensions that exist between the United States and the nations and communities into which American popular culture has expanded. After all, most people around the world will never visit the United States or meet an American in person. They will never have a Peace Corps volunteer work in their town, village, or city. They may work in factories that produce goods intended for the American market, but their managers will probably be local, and the rules that govern the factory will be imposed by the native government, not the United States. And despite the increased U.S. global military presence after the terrorist attacks of September 11, 2001, most people live in countries and communities that will never be attacked, much less occupied, by U.S. forces. Accordingly, what people are likely to see of and know about America will be filtered through the lens of American popular culture. As sociologist Todd Gitlin has put it, American popular culture is "the latest in a long succession of bidders for global unification. It succeeds the Latin imposed by the Roman Empire and the Catholic Church, and Marxist Leninism."[2] As a consequence, the global spread of American popular culture is at the heart of the contemporary era of globalization, and it is simply not possible to fully understand the ways in which globalization is reshaping the contemporary world without understanding the role that American popular culture plays in this emerging global era.

The linkage—and tensions—of American popular culture and global politics can be illustrated with brief analyses of three cases in which American popular culture and global politics have intersected. The first is the Cold War, the nearly fifty-year political and military standoff between the United States and the Soviet Union from 1945 to 1991. The second is the controversial U.S. Global War on Terror (GWoT), launched after the terrorist attacks on New York City and Washington, D.C., on September 11, 2001—typically referred to as 9/11. The third is the recent rise of anti-globalist, nativist/populist movements in many nations that previously pursued globalization aggressively.

During the Cold War, for example, the United States and the Soviet Union established vast international coalitions that promoted their interests, and each tried to check the actions of the other. The U.S.-led coalition was centered in the Americas, Western Europe (which came into being only because of post–World War II policies), and the Pacific area of Australasia. The Soviet coalition consisted of the Eurasian landmass on which the Soviet Union was located, Eastern Europe, and at times China. (China was allied with the Soviet Union after the former's Communist revolution in 1949; however, it subsequently developed an independent agenda as a Communist nation outside the control of the Soviet Union.) The two sides promoted dramatically different social, political, and economic philosophies: capitalism and liberal representative democracy in the Western, U.S.-led coalition, and communism and state control in the Soviet, Eastern bloc. These coalitions occasionally engaged in armed struggle, usually through proxies, as happened in wars in Korea (1950–1952), Vietnam (1964–1975), and Afghanistan (1979–1989). More often, their fights were at the level of propaganda. Each side insisted its way of life was superior.

Global trade and immigration patterns, social and political ideas, security systems, and even popular culture practices were profoundly shaped by the Cold War. The Western bloc advocated relative freedom in personal choice, economic trade, and immigration, while the Eastern bloc practiced state control, limitation of personal freedom, and government ownership of factories and other productive enterprises. The West insisted that personal liberty promoted maximum happiness and growth, benefiting most people even if others suffered from problems like poverty, crime, and lack of opportunity. The East insisted that government control would allow the products of society to be distributed among all people equally, thereby limiting some people's economic and individual freedoms to ensure that everyone had the basics of life.

At least part of this struggle was linked to popular culture. Soviet leaders and their ideological allies regularly referred to the West as culturally corrupt. By this they meant that Western—usually American—cultural products like movies, music, television, fast food, clothing, and the like were insubstantial and meaningless or, worst of all, promoted poor moral values. (Why this might be the case is addressed in detail in chapter 2.) While Westerners insisted that popular entertainment and performers like the singer-superstar Elvis Presley or television shows like *Leave It to Beaver* provided individuals with opportunities to create, invent, and provide joy and pleasure to others, Soviet leaders argued that the values expressed in these acts and programs tended to erode public morals and social order. Soviet rulers, accordingly, worked hard to keep Western-style pop culture away from the Soviet people.

Yet, in working to exclude Western entertainment from their societies, the leaders of the Soviet-Communist bloc (including the People's Republic of China) ended up creating interest in American popular culture among their citizens. By making the fruit of American popular culture forbidden, the leadership made it attractive. As a result, a vigorous black market developed across the Soviet Union and its allies as people smuggled or otherwise brought Western popular culture commodities like books, magazines, food, clothes, and other products into their lives. Western popular culture was thus present in the Communist bloc well before the Soviet Union finally collapsed in 1991.

Western leaders exploited the lure of their popular culture during the Cold War. They created radio and television stations such as Radio Free Europe/Radio Liberty to broadcast as much popular culture material into the Soviet bloc as could be programmed. This programming was done to achieve the very purpose the Soviets accused it of: to westernize the values of those who watched or listened to it. In addition, the U.S. Central Intelligence Agency (CIA) funded efforts to introduce anti-Soviet literature into Russia, promoting Russian-language works of literature like Boris Pasternak's *Doctor Zhivago* and a translation of George Orwell's *Animal Farm*.[3] Its efforts led to the smuggling of something like 10 million books into the Soviet Union. Western leaders thus used the power and appeal of American popular culture to help win the hearts and minds of people inside the Communist bloc.

In using American pop culture as a tool of the Cold War, Western policymakers were exploiting what political scientist Joseph Nye has referred to as "soft power."[4] The notion of soft power refers to cultural, social, intellectual, and ideological ideas, values, attitudes, and behaviors that influence human life. Nye distinguishes these soft forms of power from "hard power," which is typically associated with the use of violent, coercive tools of social action like armies and economic sanctions. Soft power is a significant factor in global politics, Nye argues, because it is subtle and indirect and thus less likely to promote resentful, angry reactions to its use. As such, it provides a way for one people—in the case of the Cold War, people in the political West—to change the attitudes and behaviors of other cultures without resorting to war or other forms of coercion that inevitably lead the loser to hate and resent the winner. Soft power can achieve these results because those who experience soft power may not even be aware they are subject to its effects, so they never think to grow resentful or angry as they see their societies change around them. Indeed, they may change their ideals, values, and practices to align with those favored by an enemy or alien government willingly.

It would be too much to argue that the Soviet Union fell apart because of the corrupting appeal of American popular culture—although former Romanian dictator Nicolae Ceaușescu apparently regretted allowing the 1980s soap opera *Dallas* to be shown in his country, where it inspired viewers to wish for the kind of economic and personal freedom the show depicted.[5] The forces that led to the dissolution of the Soviet Union were complex and diverse. It is, however, fair to say that in denying their citizens access to the Western movies, music, and television programs and other artifacts they desired, the governments of the Soviet bloc undermined their own legitimacy.

Humorist P. J. O'Rourke offered a pithy insight into the power of American popular culture during the Cold War when he wrote, in 1989, "In the end we beat them with Levi 501 jeans. Seventy-two years of Communist indoctrination and propaganda was drowned out by a three-ounce Sony Walkman. A huge totalitarian system has been brought to its knees because nobody wants to wear Bulgarian shoes."[6] Put another way, a government afraid of popular American television programs, music, or movies, as well as of things like clothing styles, fast-food chains, and sports franchises, is probably inherently weak and, in time, likely to fail for a variety of reasons.

American popular culture's role in international affairs has become even more important in the years following the Soviet Union's collapse. New patterns of trade, security, information, investment, ideas, and even entertainment exchange have emerged. These changes, collectively labeled "globalization," appeared, at least to many early students of the topic, likely to create what President George H. W. Bush called a "new world order" grounded in universal principles of democracy and global free trade. If, for example, a region had a comparative advantage in growing rice but lacked the educational system to build a large high-tech industry, it would export rice and import computers from a region with lots of software engineers but limited land for rice growing. Similar patterns would emerge in every industry, including the popular culture industry. If one country or culture held a comparative advantage in the production of some consumer good over other countries or cultures, its products would rise to global dominance. No country would produce everything it needed within its borders (or the borders of its coalition), at least not efficiently, and everyone would benefit from the lower prices and enhanced choices that would emerge with an integrated global economy.

Advocates insisted that free trade would do more than just create a globally integrated market, however. It would also promote the spread of democracy around the world. Theorists and political leaders insisted that the pressures of competing in a global market would force repressive societies to open to unleash the creative, productive power of their people. In turn, engaged, excited, and creative individuals would pressure their governments to open and become responsive to the needs of their citizens. In time, this would lead to the formation of new democratic governments around the globe. Democracy would inevitably emerge from a global regime of free trade. A new era of economic and political freedom was soon to arrive.

Of course, we have not realized the promise of a fully democratic world freely trading goods, services, ideas, cultures, and freedoms. Indeed, there are good reasons to suppose we never will. The reason for this skepticism is simple. As a practical matter, few people care where their rice is grown or where their computer is built. The exchange of rice for computers is generally understood to take place with little moral impact on either society. There may be long-term economic consequences that derive from the imbalance of trade that exists when one society is rich and developed and capable of designing and programming computers while others are poor and underdeveloped, of course. Moreover, these imbalances may be the result of historical forces like colonialism, racism, repression, and violence that were and remain immoral. Regardless of these problems, however, the specific exchange of some rice for a computer is rarely invested with ethical significance.

By contrast, the exchange of cultural goods is almost always laden with moral meaning. People care where their cultural artifacts come from, what values they express, and how they shape the lives of the people who use them. This is true even of cultural products like movies, music, and television programs, since, as is shown in chapter 2, they reflect their makers' culture and values. American cultural artifacts, for example, inevitably bring the ideas, values, norms, and social practices embedded in American popular culture into contact—and often tension—with those of other cultures around the world. Consequently, the dramatic expansion in the global dissemination of American popular culture that accompanied the end of the Cold War increased rather than decreased the potential points of cultural friction between the United States and its global neighbors.

The fact that cultures resist change also makes the notion of a global market in free trade unlikely. When their norms are challenged, people rarely adopt the "new" point of view easily or quickly (if at all). Instead, as is discussed later in this chapter, they tend to resist, reject, or dismiss the different ideas as wrong, immoral, or false. This reaction is particularly intense when the new point of view seems to attract children, who are generally seen as culturally vulnerable, naïve, and manipulable. This reaction is also likely when the source of such cultural changes is distant, alien, and seemingly beyond one's ability to influence—something that is certainly true of Hollywood-made popular culture, for example. People almost always become concerned when they perceive that their friends, families, neighbors, and children are adopting new, different, and even alien rituals, behaviors, norms, and values. Cultural power may be "soft," in Joseph Nye's phrase, but it is power nonetheless. Simply calling it "soft" does not mean that people will easily or readily adopt the values, ideals, practices, and rituals of a cultural "other." Soft power simply does not guarantee peaceful contacts among people.

The boundaries of cultural conflict in the modern world came into horrific view after the terror attacks of September 11, 2001. By destroying the two towers of the World Trade Center in New York City and severely damaging the Pentagon outside Washington, D.C., the terrorists set in motion a series of events that led the United States to undertake two wars, one in Afghanistan that started in October 2001 and one in Iraq that began in March 2003. Insisting that its actions were necessary as acts of self-defense, the United States deployed hundreds of thousands of soldiers to these two countries, ultimately leading to the overthrow of each nation's government. It additionally established a global effort to track and detain suspected terrorists, often without trial or recourse to courts either in the United States or elsewhere in the world. The ongoing U.S. post-9/11 operations remain both highly controversial and central to contemporary international relations.

As was the case with the Cold War, the U.S. GWoT has several cultural dimensions. For example, the 9/11 hijackers rejected both American foreign policy and Western norms, values, and cultural practices. They were advocates of a specific form of Islam that calls for an overturning of modernity and a return to values and behaviors they insist were dominant in the earliest days of the emerging Islamic world. Their actual and apparent targets highlight this rejection: The World Trade Center towers stood as symbols of global free trade. The Pentagon is the headquarters of the most powerful military in the world. And while the fourth plane did not hit a target, it was apparently aimed at either the White House or the U.S. Capitol, each a powerful symbol of American power, democracy, and culture. That the hijackers used arguably the most potent symbols of the modern world—jet airliners capable of crossing vast distances and cultural contexts in brief periods—as the tools of their terror only serves to highlight the cultural disconnect between their goals and the world they were attempting to change. Any assault on the United States was thus, at least in part, an attack on the relatively secular, tolerant, human rights–seeking, and capitalist values that Americans sense are central to their political and social lives. (The nature of American political culture is addressed in detail later in this chapter.) Thus, while the strikes of 9/11 were not *only* an assault on American culture, they were in part such an attack.

As they did during the Cold War, American policymakers used cultural tools after 9/11. They recognized the need to win hearts and minds across the world as they sought to deflate international concerns that the United States was simply engaging in a Christian crusade against Arab and Islamic enemies. For example, the United States funded the creation of a new television network, Alhurra, aimed at the Arab world to counter what it asserted was biased coverage of the United States and its policies in media like Al Jazeera, an international Arabic-language television network. It also established a public diplomacy project to promote the "good news" about U.S. ideals, values, culture, and people.

Cultural tensions not only lay at the heart of the attacks on the United States and the U.S. responses to them but also shaped global reaction to both. Whatever the intent of U.S. public diplomacy, the global public image of the United States declined dramatically in the months and years after 9/11. The world rapidly shifted from sympathy for the United States and Americans shortly after September 11—for example, in its editorial of September 13, 2001, the French newspaper *Le Monde* famously stated, "Today we are all Americans"—to concern, doubt, and fear about how the United States responded to 9/11. A 2002 study of attitudes in twelve countries regarding Americans and American culture found that respondents believed that U.S. popular culture made Americans "selfish, domineering, violent, and immoral." In 2003, *Time* magazine asked 250,000 people across Europe which country posed the greatest threat to world peace: Iraq, North Korea, or the United States. Only 8 percent of respondents chose Iraq, while another 9 percent chose North Korea. A BBC poll taken in eleven countries later that same year supported these findings. Pollster John Zogby found that popular support for U.S. leadership and actions dropped dramatically across the Arab world between 2002 and 2004. Much of the planet's population seemed to agree with the title of an editorial that mystery writer John le Carré published in the London *Times* in 2003: "The United States of America Has Gone Mad."[7]

Yet, even as the world seemed to resist U.S. policy and leadership, it continued to embrace American popular culture. The invention and distribution of wirelessly connected devices like iPods, tablets, and smartphones, all capable of delivering streaming video and music content directly to users wherever they were (assuming access to a wireless or cellular signal), led to explosive growth in international access to American popular culture. Likewise, high-speed Internet drove the spread of American popular culture even after the GWoT began.

For example, after 9/11 a Russian version of *Married with Children*, a U.S. sitcom popular in the 1980s, became so popular its producers hired the show's original writers to create new episodes for the Russian market.[8] Hollywood movies now generate more ticket sales in the global market than in the domestic one.[9] Hours of U.S.-produced television programming on European television screens jumped from 214,000 in 2000 to 266,000 in 2006. Despite—or perhaps because of—the U.S. war in and occupation of Iraq, that nation has a booming hip-hop subculture.[10] So does Japan.[11] Hip-hop music has also been shown to have played a role in the Arab Spring, the uprisings that led to the overthrow of numerous dictators in the Arab world from winter 2010 to spring 2012.[12] (The Arab Spring is discussed in chapter 5.) American popular culture's power and appeal in the world community clearly transcend short-term variations in support for the United States' international policies. It became a ubiquitous part of the global order even as U.S. politics led many people to resist or challenge U.S. economic, diplomatic, and military preeminence.

More recently, in the last few years, even the so-called developed nations (relatively wealthy, relatively democratic countries like those in North America and Europe, Asian nations like Japan and South Korea, and Australia and New Zealand) have experienced the rise of political movements seeking to resist, reset, and otherwise challenge the notion that globalization is either inevitable or laudable. Voters in the United Kingdom, for example, recently voted to pull out of the European Union (EU), a coalition of twenty-eight countries that have tried to link their political and economic systems together in a relatively unified whole. France, another EU member, has a large anti-immigrant movement represented by the National Front party led by Marine Le Pen; Germany has a similar party, and Austria recently reimposed travel restrictions throughout that nation to curb immigration across its territory. Even the United States, which has been among the most active supporters of contemporary globalization (discussed later in this chapter), has a large population of people seemingly resisting and resenting the kinds of political and cultural linkages across societies that lie at the core of globalization as a phenomenon. (Aspects of this resistance will be addressed in chapter 5.)

Fear of immigration and the economic and social changes that can occur during periods of high migration appear to be central to these recent efforts to resist globalization. To the degree that globalization encourages the (relatively) free movement of people around the world (something discussed later in this chapter), immigration and globalization are bound together. When people move, however, they bring with them their languages, values, and religious practices—in short, their cultures. This is true whether immigrants come legally or without the proper papers; whether they seek economic opportunity or religious freedom; whether they hope to enter a new society and embrace its norms and values or to replicate their "home" values in a new land.

Popular culture—movies, music, and television, of course, but also styles of dress, modes of social interaction, food preferences, and much more—constitute an obvious point on which immigrants and "natives" might clash. Immigrants, after all, regularly seek to continue living as they always have: eating foods they know and love, wearing clothes in which they are comfortable, engaging in religious practices that have deep meaning to them. Such actions may, however, frighten, confuse, or simply befuddle those who have lived in a place for an extended period: for longtime residents of a given community, immigrants can appear to disrupt what has always seemed normal, right, and ordinary. Such concerns can grow more intense in conditions of economic stress: if immigrants appear to get jobs when locals struggle or are seen (fairly or not) to receive benefits not available to established residents, tensions between immigrant and host communities can flare up.

Importantly, as a practical matter the benefits (and costs) of globalization are not distributed evenly in any society—even one like the United States, where much "globalization" occurs. As is discussed later in this chapter, some people "win," while others "lose." Moreover, as discussed throughout this book, the intersections that are an inevitable component of globalization are culturally fraught: they lead to situations in which it is at least possible for one culture or community to come to dominate another. They are points of cultural contestation that some are drawn to and others fear. (Chapter 5 addresses some examples of this dynamic in light of recent anti-globalization/anti-immigrant movements shaping contemporary global politics.)

UNDERSTANDING CULTURE, AMERICAN CULTURE, AND POPULAR CULTURE

The question of what culture is and why it matters in social and political life is an old one, complicated by a literature rife with competing definitions, examples, critiques, and reassertions of culture's significance in human life. It is further complicated by the use of the term in at least two dramatically different ways: as an explanation of a "way of life" for some group or community (the anthropological approach) and as a tool for the normative evaluation of particular behaviors or forms of entertainment ("popular" versus "high" culture). Since this book uses both types of meanings throughout in different contexts, a brief discussion of the complexity of culture is appropriate before we link culture to globalization.

ANTHROPOLOGICAL CULTURE

To discuss culture in its anthropological sense is to refer to the root values, ideas, assumptions, behaviors, and attitudes that members of different communities generally share in an unexamined, automatic way. Cultures provide the context in which economic, social, and political life makes sense to their members.

Core to the notion of culture is the assertion that most human behavior is learned. For example, while most human babies are born with the innate capacity for language (barring physical disabilities), they do not speak a language at birth. Instead, they have to learn one. Sounds themselves are irrelevant; what matters is how combinations of sounds have meaning to the people who share the same linguistic repertoire. This process then continues for other aspects of human life: people, almost always as children, are socialized into the patterns of culture unique to their communities, learning the tools they need for survival and growth from the environments in which they are raised.

Among the many things that cultures teach their members are normative standards of evaluation—of dress, food, behavior, attitudes, ideas, and many other things. One learns that some things/ideas/attitudes/behaviors are appropriate, while others are not. Institutions such as laws, courts, police, parents, schools, and religions then reinforce what is learned. Because culture shapes the attitudes, behaviors, and values of children (and to a lesser extent adults and newcomers to a given community), children are seen to be especially important to every culture. Cultures, after all, are sustained by teaching each new generation of people the values and ideals of the local community. Accordingly, when different cultural values engage children, this engagement is inevitably fraught: some people worry that a "different" culture's values, ideals, and practices could be injurious to their culture—the one people want their children to adopt.

Importantly, cultural forces usually work unnoticed: just as children in the cradle never realize they are being taught language as their parents play with them, the agents of cultural socialization embed attitudes of right and wrong, normal and abnormal, moral and immoral in each generation through an array of means, like pejorative comments or facial expressions, that do not appear as explicit acts of education. Cultural socialization is deep. One simply doesn't usually think about what's right and wrong, for example, because right and wrong are deeply culturally embedded. They seem, therefore, obvious and to need no justification.

Cultures also contain self-defense mechanisms. These include the shaming of those who transgress the culture's standards, the making and enforcing of rules governing what should or should not be done in the first place, and the punishment of those who violate the culture's rules. If someone transgresses cultural norms, he or she becomes subject to an array of critical responses that can range from indignant, reproachful stares to arrest, ostracism, and even death. Cultures thereby fight back against or otherwise resist those ideas and behaviors that challenge their stability and permanence.

The formative and defensive dimensions of culture combine to make cultures generationally stable, reproducible, and relatively resistant to change. Group attitudes about right and wrong, morality and immorality, language and gibberish, or any other feature of a particular culture do not easily change. Indeed, if they did, cultures could not exist across generations. Accordingly, any idea, value, attitude, behavior, ritual, or other dimension of human life that might cross from one culture and contact another has the potential to become a flashpoint of cultural conflict. Such contact need not cause tension, but it can. The dramatic expansion in the trade in and use of American popular culture thus serves as a useful case study of the interaction of cultures in this global age.

"AMERICAN" CULTURE AS A CASE OF CULTURE

Embedded at the center of this book is a significant, perhaps unconscious, assumption. After all, a book about "American" popular culture presumes that something identifiable as "American" culture exists to then be popularized. Accordingly, we ought to spend some time identifying both the distinctively "American" elements of American culture and the kinds of values that cultural artifacts might embody.

Understanding any culture requires access points, places where it reveals itself over time. What Marc Howard Ross has called "public culture" offers a particularly useful way to gain access to American culture. Public culture encompasses the common terms of reference, symbols, rituals, and ideologies within which different groups and individuals press their claims for power, policy, and identity. Such terms are not a matter of private conscience; we find them, among other places, in public documents, speeches, campaigns, and political symbols referred to by others as they promote their agendas. Such public cultural symbols constitute a shareable language through which different groups and individuals press for their goals, define meaning, and create rules and standards of conduct. Different groups and individuals express their alternative political programs through shared cultural frames. The public culture contains the terms in which political debate and struggle can occur in different communities.[13]

For the United States, one obvious repository of public culture lies in core texts that form the touchstone against which social and public ideas are regularly tested. These include the Declaration of Independence, the Constitution and the Bill of Rights, the Emancipation Proclamation and Abraham Lincoln's Second Inaugural Address, Franklin Roosevelt's "Four Freedoms" speech, and Martin Luther King Jr.'s "Let-ter from Birmingham Jail" and "I Have a Dream" speech. While by no means exhaustive, this list of representations of American public culture provides one port of entry for understanding the kinds of values, ideas, and norms that shape American cultural life.

Viewed through the lens of public culture, American culture can be termed "civic."[14] That is, people who live in the United States usually couch the values, ideas, and expectations they refer to when explaining what they believe and why, as well as which programs they favor, in norms like democracy, individual rights, tolerance, and so on, which cumulatively constitute a civic culture. Over time, because of forces like the nation's religious founding, its colonial history, and its success in integrating millions of immigrants into the national community, this culture has come to be labeled "American." Thus, Americans are united not by a common ethnicity, language, or some other bond. Rather, they are defined by their faith in an ideology: civic nationalism. This ideology is so deeply embedded and unquestioned that some scholars have suggested it should be understood as a civic religion: a sacred text expressing eternal truths on which judgments of right and wrong, good and evil, ought to rest.[15]

As shown throughout this book, Americans typically prefer policies that reflect their civic values. They also tend to promote ideas and practices that advance these ideals. For example, Americans think of liberty in a "negative" way, meaning that they generally believe that government should leave people alone so that individuals can think, believe, and act as they please.[16] Similarly, Americans value political equality, the sense that everyone is entitled to equal political rights. Americans also advocate individualism, the idea that individuals have rights that government should protect, even as most individuals are deemed responsible for their own decisions and their own fates. Other ideas, like representative democracy (in which citizens elect others to represent them in government, with the expectation that those elected will promote the interests and values of their constituents locally, statewide, and nationally), tolerance (the idea that since individuals have rights and responsibilities, and those rights and responsibilities are the most important part of the political and social system, everyone must let everyone else practice their values in order to preserve the opportunity for themselves), exceptionalism (the idea that the United States is a special nation ordained by God to fulfill an important role in the world), and capitalism (understood as an economic system in which individuals buy, sell, and trade goods and services with the intention of making a profit determined largely by the market forces of supply and demand, which establish who gets what, when, and for how much) all feature as core elements of America's public, civic culture. Americans can also be overtly patriotic, espousing the virtues of American political and social life far more actively than members of many other societies do.

Of course, these cultural values have not been applied fairly or consistently to all Americans throughout the nation's history. Democracy, economic opportunity, and religious tolerance were not afforded to slaves in the American South, for example. Indeed, many of the men who signed the Declaration of Independence owned slaves, despite that document's insistence that "all men are created equal" and are "endowed by their Creator with certain inalienable rights." Similarly, the Constitution denied women the same rights it accorded to men. In a large sense, the history of the United States chronicles the violation of the nation's core cultural values—suggesting that these values are little more than window dressing, designed to obscure the true forces shaping American political life: class, perhaps, or structural racism and misogyny.

Despite these violations of American civic culture's promise, its very transgression in part demonstrates its influence. Many critiques of America's failures to live up to its civic values have, over time, been couched in civic terms—that is, the civic culture has provided the tools that advocates for change have used to compel the system to live up to its promises. The civil rights movement of the 1950s and 1960s, for example, rested on the insistence that the Declaration of Independence's category of "all men" included African Americans, thus entitling them to the "certain unalienable rights" that the document claims are natural to everyone. Subsequent movements have used similar rhetoric in demanding that women, LGBTQ individuals, Hispanics, the disabled, and many others be included among the "rights-bearing" people against whom majorities cannot discriminate at will. In failing to meet the promises embedded in the civic culture, then, Americans found themselves subject to movements for change that demanded that the civic culture be made inclusive of people otherwise left out or left behind.

As chapters 3 and 4 will show, the values and ideals of American public culture get expressed through American popular culture and then marketed across the planet. American public culture is inevitably embedded in the products of popular culture. Issues of culture are thus intrinsically linked to globalization in the modern era.

POPULAR CULTURE

The concept of culture has several meanings beyond its anthropological sense. One focus has been the question of what constitutes "popular" culture. While there are myriad approaches to what, exactly, might be meant by "popular" culture, it is perhaps easiest to think of it in consumerist, commercial terms. "Popular culture" encompasses anything used or engaged with by large numbers of people and created specifically for that purpose.[17] Thus, the primary purpose of a piece of "popular culture" is to be consumed by users who pay for the privilege of reading a mass-produced book or magazine or using some other product that was created to be used. Such production is essentially secular in nature, meaning that nothing is sacred or holy—everything is available for marketing and consumption.[18] Manufacturers produce popular culture to generate a profit: a book, a magazine, or—once the technology developed—recorded music, a movie, a television program, or anything else labeled popular culture got made only because of its likely sales appeal.

This conception of popular culture derives in part from an understanding of its supposed opposite: "high culture." High culture includes artifacts like works of art, which, in contrast to popular culture products, are understood to exist as conscious acts of creation with no purpose beyond their own existence. For critics like Matthew Arnold, "high culture" distinguishes people who have "taste" and pursue what he called "the best that was thought and said" from those who pursue what a character in Shakespeare's *Henry V* refers to as the "base, common, and popular."[19] Interest in things popular was base and common; pursuit of "the best of what was thought and said" was "cultured."

In the past critics of "popular" culture often argued that high culture was "good" because it was "aesthetic," while popular culture had no innate value beyond the pleasure it gave those who consumed it. Put simply, pop culture products contained nothing aesthetic or "high." As one critic put it, mass-produced popular culture was no more meaningful than chewing gum.[20] Consequently, there was no value in studying or examining the patterns and norms embedded in its products. The "real" values of society lay in its high culture, not its common one.

In the mid-twentieth century, however, scholars like Herbert Gans, Mary Douglas, and Baron Isherwood led others interested in popular culture to define the cultural meaning of popular mass-produced and mass-consumed items in new and valuable ways. Gans noted that an item did not lose its value simply because it was mass-produced; instead, the people who used it derived meaning and value from it. Douglas and Isherwood found that communities of individuals—cultures—tend to share common conceptions of what ought to be purchased, used, and consumed.[21] Mass production does not eliminate meaning. It simply provides another way for different groups of people to make meaningful choices in establishing, reinforcing, and representing particular cultural boundaries.[22]

Popular culture thus provides a way for researchers to learn about the values, needs, concerns, and standards by which different communities of people live. It offers insights into the meanings and values that its users attribute to it. The adoption or rejection of particular pop culture products is thus fraught with social and political meaning. Accordingly, such artifacts are a valuable tool for explaining patterns of belief and behavior within and among societies.

GRASPING GLOBALIZATION

So what is globalization, and how is the concept used in this book? Manfred B. Steger has offered a concise, highly usable approach to understanding globalization that both accounts for its many dimensions and informs the analysis offered in this work. Steger defines globalization as a "*set of social processes* that are thought to transform our present social condition into one of globality." Globality, in turn, is "a *social condition* characterized by the existence of global economic, political, cultural, and environmental interconnections and flows that make many of the currently existing borders and boundaries irrelevant." A combination of economic, political, and cultural factors promote globalization by (1) making it possible to create new and increased ties among people, social networks, and ideas that span traditional nation-state boundaries; (2) linking people in new ways, making it possible for work or travel or shopping or other activities to take place twenty-four hours a day around the world; (3) advancing the speed of communication and the expectation of instantaneous contact, in effect making global events and issues local ones as well; and (4) shaping and reshaping individuals' ideas and identities as they are exposed to this increasingly complex world. Hence, while globalization is dynamic, uncertain, and insecure, its goal is the state of globality—what Steger describes as "interdependence and integration."[23]

As this book addresses throughout, however, the forces shaping globalization seem to both draw people together through trade and increased cultural contacts and to anger, frustrate, and frighten many groups and individuals in various communities. Globalization may be a set of processes tending to promote a condition of globality, but it also seems to create movements and reactions in opposition to it. Political scientist James Rosenau coined the term *fragmegration* to describe the integration-fragmentation dynamic that shapes globalization today. Fragmentation and integration occur at the same time, profoundly shaping the dynamics of globalization. Moreover, fragmegration affects different individuals, groups, sectors of the economy, and communities in varying ways.[24] Thus, whether for economic, political, or cultural reasons, or some combination of these, globalization seems to drive some people apart even as it promotes new international connections among other people around the world. To understand globalization, then, it is necessary to assess how economic, political, and cultural forces that stimulate the growth of shared social institutions and values bring some people together while at the same time pushing others apart.

As this book shows, American popular culture is an agent of cultural globalization. It is a conduit by which values, ideas, and experiences in the world at large can become known to Americans, only to be adapted and reflected out into the world again. Moreover, popular culture is a business run by megacorporations and marketed across the globe. Accordingly, it has an impact on the economic dimension of globalization. This economic activity inevitably has both cultural and political effects, as the sudden intrusion of new forms and modes of communication, entertainment, and lifestyles promotes tensions in local communities. Globalization is not simply good. It is multidimensional, dynamic, and transformational in both desired and unintended ways.

ECONOMIC GLOBALIZATION

The economic dimensions of globalization are perhaps the best understood and most studied feature of contemporary globalization. In fact, so common are the assertions of those individuals and groups who favor economic globalization that Manfred Steger argues they have combined to form a powerful political ideology, globalism, to legitimate and promote their preferred policies.[25] Since economic globalization interacts with the cultural dimension of globalization, a brief accounting of this arena of globalization is appropriate here before we move on to the cultural.

One of the central features of contemporary globalization is the degree to which the economic livelihoods of people living in many different countries are now linked through world trade, international finance, and the operations of transnational corporations. This is a remarkable change from the way global economics worked even fifty years ago. For most of the last five hundred years or so, most countries (and, if they had one, their associated colonial empires) pursued their economic interests in competition with the other nations and empires of the world. For example, rather than cooperate to build ships or grow food, nations attempted to grow all the food they needed within their own borders (including the boundaries of their colonies), as well as to produce all the ships they needed. Indeed, the desire to go it alone in economic practices was one of the major stimuli that led the European powers to pursue colonies: lacking sufficient resources and markets at home to keep their industrial factories working, they conquered foreign territories from which they could extract natural resources and to which they could sell finished products. (The U.S. expansion across the continent of North America served much the same purpose in the nineteenth century.) The goal of such practices was to protect the profits and jobs of workers and owners in the home country.

Near the end of World War II, the United States and its allies (with the notable exception of the Soviet Union) decided that such go-it-alone policies were not the best way to ensure their economic futures. They decided that competition for economic resources had in part caused the horrific violence of the two world wars. They further decided that protectionist trade policies had caused and deepened the economic collapse of the Great Depression in the 1920s and 1930s. Finally, they decided that they needed to establish a new kind of economic and political alliance to counter the growing power of the Soviet Union, which espoused communism as its organizing philosophy. With this context as background, they began the process of economic globalization that shapes the world today.

The core of the economic dimension of globalization as developed by the United States and its allies rests on the ideal—if not the perfect practice—of free trade. Free trade is a principle of economic theory that holds that there should be few, if any, restraints on the flow of goods, services, and even people around the world. The theory holds that goods and services should be produced wherever they can be most efficiently made—a concept known as comparative advantage. This is held to be true whether the product in question is a pound of rice, a computer, or a television program. Restraints on trade inevitably make the prices of some goods and services artificially high and deny those areas that might make a product more cheaply the opportunity to develop. Similar problems emerge if legal or social regulations constrain the free flow of capital, people, ideas, or anything else around the planet. While there may be social and political disruptions as industries, jobs, and markets redistribute themselves around the world, free trade is expected to be good overall, at least in the long run.

The major powers of the West began the process of expanding trade and reducing barriers among themselves near the end of World War II. They agreed to stabilize their currencies in relation to the U.S. dollar, established institutions like the General Agreement on Tariffs and Trade (GATT) and the International Monetary Fund (IMF) to oversee currency exchanges and trade rules for member states, and supported treaties and organizations to enforce the rules governing free trade. In subsequent years, free trade agreements proliferated, and regional free trade zones like the North American Free Trade Agreement (NAFTA) and the European Union were set up. With the end of the Cold War in 1991, new areas of trade emerged, global financial markets were deregulated, and it became possible to invest—and compete for capital—around the world. Services, too, became global as communication technologies like the Internet and cellular phones made it possible to outsource work (e.g., customer service phone operations) formerly done in the corporation's home country. Finally, with the deregulation of financial markets and the emergence of global free trade, new institutions arose to exploit the economic opportunities afforded on a worldwide stage. This led to the emergence of transnational corporations. Companies like General Motors, Honda, or Airbus (a joint European enterprise to build commercial aircraft) are now global enterprises, spread across the world pursuing profit for investors. Relatively free trade is, as a consequence, the dominant mode of global economic exchange today.

Yet free trade has a dark side that has become increasingly evident over time. As globalization promotes greater economic integration around the world, for example, people whose skills can be replaced at lower cost often lose their jobs. This certainly happened in the case of low-skill factory jobs like those in the textile industry in the United States in the 1980s and 1990s. But people who lose their jobs lose more than just their work. They also lose their identities—the ability to perform their role as providers for their families and friends through work they imagine doing for a lifetime. They then lose connection to their extended neighbors in the national community as people move, jobs are realigned, and state policies shift to accommodate the pressures of globalization. Again, this tends to be true whether the industry or economic enterprise affected by globalization is a farm, a factory, or a music production studio. Each change may create new industries and offer new economic opportunities for some groups of people all over the world, but each of these processes, in addition to many others, inevitably transforms the economic, social, and political order of developing as well as developed nations in diverse ways with varying effects. (This dynamic process has been labeled "creative destruction.") Some people in the new global era have gotten phenomenally wealthy, but others have lost their jobs and the ability to control their lives over the same period. Economic globalization has costs as well as benefits.

In addition, while the United States is the rhetorical leader of the world's free trade movement, its behavior has not always matched its cheerleading. As it happens, the United States works to protect its domestic industries from foreign competition even as it pressures other governments to open their borders to American products. For example, for years the United States has kept in place policies like subsidies to farmers of globally uncompetitive crops like cotton because these farmers pressure their elected officials to maintain subsidy programs. Accordingly, American trade negotiators also seek to insert language into free trade agreements that favors American-produced goods on the global market. Restrictions on trade in certain kinds of computer chips or other high-tech devices serve to protect American manufacturers, as do patent and other laws governing the use of inventions created in the United States. Thus, while the United States has been the world's great free trade advocate, it, like other nations, seeks trade arrangements that are favorable to its citizens' interests.

As noted earlier in this chapter (and addressed in detail throughout this book), popular culture is a central element in contemporary international trade. As such, it has the potential to provide substantial, enjoyable, affordable entertainment and other products to literally billions of people—the ideal of free trade in general. However, American producers of popular culture have powerful advantages of capital, knowledge, and distribution networks compared to local producers in most of the rest of the world. Accordingly, American producers can drive local producers of popular culture out of business. For economic reasons alone, then, diverse groups and communities may either favor or oppose the global trade in popular culture as economically beneficial or harmful to their interests. Contemporary globalization is inevitably shaped by these choices.

POLITICAL GLOBALIZATION

Politics are central to any discussion of globalization for the simple reason that economic and political life cannot be separated to any meaningful degree, especially since the world is divided into a series of nation-states that govern people in discrete territories known as countries. Nations have historically attempted to control the economic activities that occur within their borders. Moreover, the United States and its allies made a political choice to promote free trade in the aftermath of World War II. Economic matters have political consequences, and vice versa.

The right of a nation-state to impose whatever laws it desires on its people is at the heart of any discussion of globalization. This principle, known as sovereignty, has been the central organizing principle of international relations at least since the Peace of Westphalia was adopted in Europe in 1648. The general rule by which nations conducted their relationships from 1648 through the end of World War II was that so long as one state did not threaten or otherwise interfere with another, the two had no just cause to go to war or to attempt to influence each other's internal politics. While never observed faithfully, this rule nonetheless provided international relations with an organizing principle around which states could make rules, attempt to govern their citizens, and otherwise conduct their business in ways that made sense to them.

Economic globalization, especially free trade in goods and services, poses multiple challenges to nation-states. For example, both free trade and transnational corporations are new phenomena in global politics, phenomena that test a nation's power to pass laws to control its own economic destiny. After all, if a state passes restrictive laws protecting workers' rights at home, a transnational corporation might simply relocate to friendlier shores. The state's ability to control what businesses do is seriously constrained in such an environment. In addition, the notion that government regulation of trade is harmful for consumers is a political claim that, if accepted, necessitates political changes to a nation's trade laws. It is also common for people to ask their governments to take actions that will protect their community's interests and livelihoods when they perceive an assault on their cultures, economies, and ways of life. Predictably, then, political movements intended to limit any negative consequences of globalization have emerged because of the dislocations associated with globalization and free trade.

As the global era began—or at least resumed in the aftermath of the fall of the Soviet Union—some authors argued that global free trade would herald the end of the nation-state. For these thinkers, there were few problems, if any, that the market could not solve more efficiently and fairly than governments could. Thus, the answer to almost any social problem (e.g., poverty, crime, economic inequity) was to free markets from constraints and allow them to work: as defined by the logic of comparative advantage, goods and services would be produced across the globe in those areas that could do so most productively and efficiently. States consequently needed to get out of the way—they needed to amend their policies to promote free trade since, inevitably, governments that passed policies in opposition to free trade would ultimately undermine their people's chances for a happy, full, democratic life.[26]

Empirically, however, neither politics nor states have gone away in favor of all-encompassing markets. Instead, states and state policies are adapting to the pressures of economic globalization in three ways. The first can be seen in the emergence of new forms of international political organization that transcend traditional state boundaries but have legal power over the residents of member states. For example, since globalization leads to increased contacts among people, it makes sense that it has a regional component: links of geography and culture tend to promote contacts over time.[27] Similarly, as our knowledge of human rights and other abuses around the world has grown, largely as a result of emerging communications systems like Facebook and Twitter, the work of nongovernmental organizations that focus on human rights, environmental regulation, and the like has become more prominent.[28] New political relationships, made by states to regulate both state and nonstate actors, have emerged to govern the economic and cultural consequences of contemporary globalization. The European Union stands as a key example of such regional governance systems.

A second role for states derives from their role in the creation and management of globalization in the first place. After all, the neoliberal policies of free trade and increased flows of capital that emerged in the West at the end of World War II resulted from the choices of specific nation-states made at particular moments in time. Governments set rules for trade, communication, and environmental policies (to name a few).[29] Logically, then, governments might choose to change the regulatory regimes through which they instituted free trade and market liberalization. Indeed, as discussed in chapter 5, states have proven quite willing to assert a right to protect local culture and industry despite the logic of free market globalization. As will be seen, one reason diverse states have asserted their right to protect their cultures has been the concern that American culture, even (or perhaps especially) in its popular form, has the power to corrupt and undermine local values and local producers.

The U.S. response to the terrorist attacks of September 11, 2001, has demonstrated a third means by which states can exert control over economic and social forces in the global era. The creation and deployment of the world's military forces means that states will remain an agent in world affairs for some time to come. For example, after 9/11 the United States restricted immigration and asserted its right to use military force to defend itself anywhere it perceives a threat to its interests across the globe. Other nations, some of which are discussed in a series of case studies in chapter 5, have used their power to control the laws of their societies to limit the ways in which their people interact with American popular culture. Notably, nations that have taken these actions have remained economically and politically viable, even powerful, regardless of globalists' claims that such acts violate the spirit and inevitable benefit of free trade.

Free trade and economic globalization have also promoted the rise of a loosely coordinated global movement of groups that engage in political protest activity to encourage governments to pass policies that protect people from negative effects associated with globalization. As Steger and others have shown, some of the groups and individuals involved in this movement include populist, nativist-minded people who, while living in economically advantaged countries like those in Europe or in the United States, fear the cultural exchanges inevitably embedded in globalization—particularly increased immigration across previously more rigid national borders. For such persons, globalization poses a risk that once-dominant cultures might be changed from within as new people, with new values and practices, enter the established society and take advantage of democratic opportunities to change its organization.

A different set of actors and groups oppose contemporary globalization on the grounds that it is likely to overwhelm and transform less advantaged societies. Such persons and institutions focus on questions of social justice as they worry that the unfettered global pursuit of the cheapest goods will result in outcomes that are harmful to the people who make the products (usually for very little money and with few benefits or safety protocols) and then find their local cultural values supplanted by Western, perhaps American, ones. Representatives of this movement seek to pressure governments and corporations to set and follow rules that protect jobs and livelihoods in developed countries while also protecting health, safety, environmental, and other types of standards in the rest of the world. They also insist on the right of local communities to preserve their cultures in the face of global corporate and cultural power. As chapter 5 will show, while this movement has had only a modest influence in the globalization debate, it has had its biggest successes in its efforts to limit the free trade of American popular culture. Popular culture is in fact among the most heavily regulated components of international trade, even in the modern era of globalization. Trade in audiovisual entertainment is treated quite differently under international trade agreements than is trade in cars or steel or grain. This, in turn, derives from its perceived importance in cultural affairs. Political systems act to protect local cultures and culture-producing enterprises. As such, popular culture is an element of political as well as economic globalization.

Politics is thus intrinsically bound up with the process of globalization. Political decisions facilitated the free trade movement on which the logic of globalization is founded, and politics has shaped the regulatory environment in which the move toward globality has taken place. Politics has also provided a means by which displaced and concerned persons can work to relieve the pains they believe globalization has caused them. Politics is, accordingly, at the heart of the globalization of American popular culture.

CULTURAL GLOBALIZATION

In broad terms, analysts of cultural globalization focus on the question of how Western goods, services, ideas, values, and media affect local, usually non-Western cultures once they enter the new markets opened by globalization.[30] Some analysts, relying on a view of culture as a set of fixed, rigid ideas, values, and practices that make peaceful cultural change unlikely, are pessimistic about the likely resulting effects. They see three kinds of negative effects emerging from the global spread of American popular culture in the years since the fall of the Soviet Union in 1991: (1) cultural corruption, (2) cultural imperialism, and (3) cultural homogenization. Other cultural analysts focus on the concept of cultural hybridity to offer a more hopeful sense of cultural interaction over time.

CULTURAL CORRUPTION

Many critics who are concerned that cultural corruption follows from American popular culture build on the research of the Frankfurt School. As expressed in works of scholars like Theodor Adorno, Max Horkheimer, and Jürgen Habermas, adherents of the Frankfurt School begin with the idea that the Industrial Revolution broke the traditional ties that oriented people to life in their societies. Whereas once people lived in small communities governed by rules established by religious, political, and familial authorities who lived in the same small towns, the Industrial Revolution drove people into large cities where traditional authority structures could not function. When millions of people moved from rural areas to cities to take jobs in the new factories, they were separated from the institutions and values that had previously served as the teachers and enforcers of moral behavior. This separation was significant because life in the cities, at least in contrast with the bucolic image of life on the farm offered by critics of town living, was nasty, dirty, and immoral. Brothels, crime, and disease flourished, for example, even as new forms of entertainment like dime novels and the penny press found markets peddling stories of lust, violence, and exploitation. In turn, life became dominated by new values, such as consumerism and the pursuit of entertainment and individual interests, regardless of their social effects. In such circumstances, people became profoundly isolated despite living together in large numbers: lacking traditions of trust and authority like those embedded in their rural communities, new urban migrants were often left to their own devices to survive. As a result, people's life orientations shifted from dedication to the social good of their communities to the autonomous desire to satisfy the self.

Frankfurt School analysts emphasized the way that new forms of communication, particularly mass communications and entertainment like newspapers, radio, and the movies, could promote false or harmful ideas to their mass audiences. Without historical moral anchors like local religious and community leaders to offer authoritative dicta on crucial issues of the day, people living in the mass isolation of large cities could only know or care about what they were told by newspaper publishers, radio broadcasters, movie producers, and other agents of mass communication. This shift from social to private authority made people susceptible to manipulation by outside forces. Thus, two great transformations occurring at the same time—the social and manufacturing changes associated with rapid urbanization and the Industrial Revolution and the rise of mass communication and entertainment to fill the urban market—created a world in which mass media and entertainment could lead to the undermining of moral society in favor of some corrupted new order.

Some contemporary critics of American popular culture espouse a version of Frankfurt School thought known as mass society theory.

For adherents of mass society theory, the moral decay of urban society (compared to agrarian, rural societies) is a result of the messages and meanings embedded in the communications of mass entertainment.[31] As people became separated from the rural, traditional social and political institutions that defined their lives and provided them with meaning, they were exposed to exploitative, manipulative media. The media replaced traditional forces in socializing behavior and attitudes: immoral behavior in novels and magazines was easy to mirror in lustful violence in the real world. Individuals are, essentially, helpless victims of those who control the media. This concern is particularly acute in the case of some individuals or groups, such as children, who are seen as gullible and prone to manipulation.[32] Thus critics employing mass society theory argue that people need to be protected from "bad" cultural products and messages for their own good, echoing—or perhaps foretelling—the arguments of Soviet leaders about the corrupting influence of American popular culture during the Cold War.

CULTURAL IMPERIALISM

A second group of critics of the globalization of American popular culture focus on its capacity for cultural imperialism. As a concept, cultural imperialism suggests that the interaction of different cultures will inevitably be conflictual. Members of each culture will seek to destroy or eliminate the other. They might do this using outright violence or by undermining the alien culture and installing a new, dominant culture in its place. The logic of cultural imperialism can be illustrated quickly in the work of two prominent scholars in political science, Samuel Huntington and Benjamin Barber. Huntington, for example, argued that civilizational/cultural boundaries constituted ultimate cleavages along which political conflict would inevitably arise.[33] In Huntington's model, cultural interactions would stimulate civilizational conflicts, as members of each group sought to expand or defend their cultural turf. Benjamin Barber made a similar, more nuanced argument when he noted that the values, products, and processes of globalization can and must provoke what he called "jihad"—the "bloody holy war on behalf of partisan identity that is metaphysically defined and fanatically defended."[34] Jihad was thus counterpoised against "McWorld"—the integrated, sophisticated, and even cosmopolitan world reflected in the notion of global free trade and cultural interaction. Jihad could occur between societies—the highly integrated globalized societies of the West, for example, versus those of the less developed, less linked world. But it could also emerge within nations (e.g., between coastal communities heavily dependent on trade and upland areas in the same polity that found trade issues uninteresting or not worth acting on). Under such circumstances, increased cultural contacts associated with globalization are likely to generate violence and fragmentation, not the new world order promised by globalism's proponents.

CULTURAL HOMOGENIZATION

Those critics concerned with the concept of cultural homogenization agree that American popular culture may well dominate the world; however, rather than worrying about the imposition of supposedly "American" values on local populations, these critics fear that corporate-produced mass entertainment will ultimately move everyone's values toward those associated with mass consumer capitalism. One scholar has termed this "McDonaldization."[35] Corporations like McDonald's are expected to have such advantages in economies of scale, organization, predictability, and efficiency that, combined with superior marketing, they will drive traditional providers out of business. The same logic applies if the corporation in question is Walmart, Home Depot, or Starbucks. The fear is that in time everyone everywhere will end up eating the same thing, reading the same thing, and wearing the same thing. Under such circumstances, cultural diversity would be lost forever. In its place we would have a world of soulless consumers just looking for the next thing to buy, which would be exactly like what everyone else in the world already had and wanted, until the corporations generated the next must-have item. One culture, consumer capitalism, would dominate the globe.

CULTURAL HYBRIDITY

There are, however, less skeptical analysts of cultural globalization. One group of scholars focuses on the concept of cultural hybridization.[36] Roughly defined as "mixing," hybridization has been characterized as "the ways in which forms become separated from existing practices and recombine with new forms and new practices."[37] Such mixing is common in global affairs. Christianity emerged from Judaism and retained many of its core values before being adopted by and integrated into the Roman Empire, for example; it then served as one source for the creation of Islam. Contemporary English is the result of the mixing of an array of cultural and linguistic traditions that began at least a thousand years ago. There were no horses in the Western Hemisphere until Spanish colonists brought them in the sixteenth century; accordingly, the iconic image of Native Americans chasing bison across the plains in the American West became possible only when two widely different and profoundly hostile cultures came into contact—and indeed when one quite literally tried to annihilate the other. The core dimensions of discrete cultures often turn out, on closer inspection, to be hybrid forms.

Brought into the context of contemporary globalization, scholars who focus on hybridity note that the interaction of American values, institutions, products, and services does not necessarily have to lead to the elimination of local norms and desires in favor of rational, efficient American alternatives. Instead, businesses can adapt their practices to fit the needs of their workers and the cultures of their clients.[38] Or American corporations may develop a profit interest in celebrating and protecting the diversity of the cultures in which they operate.[39] Cultural communication and hybridization can be a two-way process; Western societies can be as influenced by non-American ones as non-American communities are influenced by the United States. Jan Nederveen Pieterse has referred to the result as a global mélange.[40] Marwan M. Kraidy suggests that hybridization is the inherent end of globalization.[41]

Hybridization does not always lead to equal cultural exchange, however. Roland Robertson has coined the term *glocalization* to describe the ways globalization can change cultures in favor of the needs, interests, and values of the dominant trading partners. Paying particular attention to questions of identity—how individuals and groups define their values, ideals, and communities—Robertson sees glocalization as a "massive, twofold process involving *the interpenetration of the universalization of particularism and the particularization of universalism.*"[42] Products found in local communities can be packaged and adapted for international markets, or globally popular products can be adapted to local conditions. (As is examined in chapter 4, McDonald's does not use beef fat in its fry oil in India, for example.) Robertson thus argues, "The contemporary capitalist creation of consumers frequently involves the tailoring of products to increasingly specialized regional, societal, ethnic, class, and gender markets—so-called micro-marketing." In turn, while the broader global community experiences new products and ideas, the local community is integrated into the global economy as another group of consumers.[43]

Popular culture, as cultural artifacts and products marketed around the world, stands at the center of the glocalist/hybridized/globalist dynamic. Different groups and individuals can respond to pieces of popular culture from American sources in diverse ways. As shown in chapter 5, many groups and nations resist American popular culture as an element of globalization. However, as addressed in chapter 6, these concerns may be misaimed; globalization is a complex phenomenon, and American popular culture is both less fixed and less permanent than is often supposed.

CONCLUSION

This book examines the ways that the messages and mechanisms of American popular culture are a force for fragmegration in contemporary globalization. It focuses on the way American public culture is expressed on a global scale in movies, music, television programs, fast-food franchises, sports, and styles of clothing. As will be seen, what some find appealing about the American dream others find repellent. What one group admires about a civic culture another sees as proof that people have lost their moral values. What many see as hopeful in globalism's promise still others view as symptomatic of the end of uniqueness. What is free choice for some is petty consumerism for others. What promises a vision of inexpensive, enjoyable entertainment for some threatens others' livelihoods. Teasing out these dynamics is the task of the rest of this book.

NOTES

1. Paul Farhi and Megan Rosenfeld, "American Pop Penetrates Worldwide," *Washington Post*, October 25, 1998.

2. Farhi and Rosenfeld, "American Pop Penetrates Worldwide."

3. Darien Cavanaugh, "The CIA Battled the Kremlin with Books and Movies," *War Is Boring*, September 27, 2015, https://warisboring.com/the-cia-battled-the-kremlin-with-books-and-movies/#.vtpi2p60q (accessed May 14, 2017).

4. Joseph S. Nye, *Soft Power: The Means for Success in World Politics* (Cambridge, MA: PublicAffairs, 2004).

5. Nick Gillespie and Matt Welch, "How *Dallas* Won the Cold War," *Washington Post*, April 27, 2008.

6. P. J. O'Rourke, *Give War a Chance* (New York: Grove Press, 1992), 13.

7. Adapted from Toby Miller, "Anti-Americanism and Popular Culture" (paper prepared for the Center for Policy Studies, Central European University, 2005).

8. Except where noted, these points come from Tim Arango, "World Falls for American Media, Even as It Sours on America," *New York Times*, November 20, 2008, http://www.nytimes.com/2008/12/01/business/media/01soft.html (accessed February 29, 2012).

9. Ryan Faughnder, "$40 Billion in Box Office? Thank China and 'Star Wars,'" *Los Angeles Times*, December 31, 2015, http://www.latimes.com/entertainment/envelope/cotown/la-et-ct-global-box-office-20151231-story.html (accessed March 10, 2017).

10. Tim Arango and Yasir Ghazi, "An Embrace of the U.S., Spun and Mixed by Iraqis," *New York Times*, October 12, 2011.

11. Ian Condry, "Japanese Hip-Hop and the Globalization of Political Culture," in *Urban Life: Readings in the Anthropology of the City*, ed. George Gmelch and Walter Zenner (Prospect Heights, IL: Waveland Press, 2001), 357–87.

12. Ulysses, "Hip Hop and the Arab Uprisings," openDemocracy, February 24, 2012, http://www.opendemocracy.net/ulysses/hip-hop-and-arab-uprisings (accessed February 24, 2012).

13. Marc Howard Ross, "Culture and Identity in Comparative Political Analysis," in *Comparative Politics: Rationality, Culture, and Structure*, ed. Mark I. Lichbach and Alan S. Zuckerman (New York: Cambridge University Press, 1997), 42–80.

14. The following discussion rests on a number of works. See, for fuller discussion, James Morone, *The Devils We Know: Us and Them in America's Raucous Political Culture* (Lawrence: University of Kansas Press, 2015); Timothy Noah, *The Great Divergence: America's Growing Inequality Crisis and What We Can Do about It* (New York: Bloomsbury Press, 2012); J. David Greenstone, *The Lincoln Persuasion: Remaking American Liberalism* (Princeton, NJ: University of Princeton Press, 1993); John Kenneth White, *The Values Divide: American Politics and Culture in Transition* (New York: Chatham House, 2003); John W. Kingdon, *America the Unusual* (New York: Worth, 1999); Daniel Judah Elazar, *American Federalism: A View from the States*, 3rd ed. (New York:

Harper & Row, 1984); Richard Ellis, *American Political Cultures* (New York: Oxford University Press, 1993); Louis Hartz, *The Liberal Tradition in America* (New York: Harcourt, Brace, 1955); Richard Hofstadter, *The American Political Tradition and the Men Who Made It* (New York: Vintage, 1974); Samuel P. Huntington, *American Politics: The Promise of Disharmony* (Cambridge, MA: Belknap, 1981); Rogers Smith, *Civic Ideals: Conflicting Visions of Citizenship in U.S. History* (New Haven, CT: Yale University Press, 1997); Daniel J. Boorstin, *The Genius of American Politics* (Chicago: University of Chicago Press, 1953; Seymour Martin Lipset, *American Exceptionalism: A Double-Edged Sword* (New York: Norton, 1996); Charles Lockhart, *The Roots of American Exceptionalism: Institutions, Culture, and Politics* (New York: Palgrave Macmillan, 2003); Deborah L. Madsen, *American Exceptionalism* (Jackson: University of Mississippi Press, 1998); and Trevor B. McCrisken, *American Exceptionalism and the Legacy of Vietnam: U.S. Foreign Policy since 1974* (New York: Palgrave Macmillan, 2003).

15. Compare Sidney E. Mead, *The Nation with the Soul of a Church* (New York: Harper & Row, 1975); Sacvan Bercovitch, *The American Jeremiad* (Madison: University of Wisconsin Press, 1978); Sacvan Bercovitch, *The Puritan Origins of the American Self* (New Haven, CT: Yale University Press, 1975); Robert N. Bellah et al., *The Good Society* (New York: Knopf, 1991); Robert Putnam and David Campbell, *American Grace: How Religion Divides and Unites Us* (New York: Simon & Schuster, 2010); and Robert N. Bellah et al., *Habits of the Heart: Individualism and Commitment in American Life* (Berkeley: University of California Press, 1985).

16. Isaiah Berlin, *Two Concepts of Liberty* (Oxford, UK: Clarendon Press, 1958).

17. Holt N. Parker, "Toward a Definition of Popular Culture," *History and Theory* 50 (May 2011): 147–70. See also Stuart Hall, "Notes on Deconstructing 'the Popular,'" in *Popular Culture: A Reader*, ed. Raiford Guins and Omayra Zaragoza Cruz (Los Angeles: Sage Publications, 2005), 64–71.

18. Todd Gitlin, "Television Screens: Hegemony in Transition," in *Cultural and Economic Reproduction in Education*, ed. M. Apple (London: Routledge & Kegan Paul, 1981), 202, quoted in Robert Burnett, *The Global Jukebox: The International Music Industry* (New York: Routledge, 1996), 33.

19. David Steigerwald, *Culture's Vanities: The Paradox of Cultural Diversity in a Globalized World* (Lanham, MD: Rowman & Littlefield, 2004), 29.

20. Quoted in Steigerwald, *Culture's Vanities*, 38.

21. Compare Herbert Gans, *Popular Culture and High Culture: An Analysis and Evaluation of Taste* (New York: Basic Books, 1974), and Mary Douglas and Baron Isherwood, *The World of Goods* (New York: Basic Books, 1979).

22. Steigerwald, *Culture's Vanities*, 40.

23. Manfred B. Steger, *Globalization: A Very Short Introduction*, 3rd ed. (New York: Oxford University Press, 2013), 9–16.

24. James N. Rosenau, *Distant Proximities: Dynamics beyond Globalization* (Princeton, NJ: Princeton University Press, 2003).

25. See Manfred B. Steger, *Globalism: Market Ideology Meets Terrorism*, 2nd ed. (Lanham, MD: Rowman & Littlefield, 2005), for a full discussion of this argument.

26. Compare Peter Dicken, *Global Shift: Mapping the Changing Contours of the Global* Economy, 7th ed. (New York: Guilford Press, 2015); George Ritzer, ed., *The Blackwell Companion to Globalization* (Malden, MA: Blackwell, 2007); David Held, *Democracy and the Global Order: From the Modern State to Cosmopolitan Governance* (Stanford, CA: Stanford University Press, 2007); Lowell Bryan and Diana Farrell, *Market Unbound: Unleashing Global Capitalism* (New York: Wiley, 1996); Robert Kuttner, *Everything for Sale: The Virtues and Limits of Markets* (New York: Knopf, 1997); Harvey Cox, "The Market as God: Living in the New Dispensation," *Atlantic* (March 1999): 18–23; Edward Luttwak, *Turbo-capitalism: Winners and Losers in the Global Economy* (New York: Harper & Row, 1999); Robert Reich, *The Work of Nations* (New York: Vintage, 1992); Robert O. Keohane, *After Hegemony* (Princeton, NJ: Princeton University Press, 1984); James H. Mittelman, *Globalization: Critical Reflections* (Boulder, CO: Lynne Rienner, 1996); Roland Robertson, *Globalization: Social Theory and Global Culture* (London: Sage, 1992); Kenichi Ohmae, *The End of the Nation-State: The Rise of Regional Economies* (New York: Free Press, 1995); Kenichi Ohmae, *The Borderless World: Power and Strategy in the Interlinked World Economy* (New York: HarperBusiness, 1990); Thomas Friedman, *The Lexus and the Olive Tree: Understanding Globalization* (New York: Picador, 1999); Francis Fukuyama, *The End of History and the Last Man* (New York: Avon Books, 1992); and Lester Thurow, *The Future of Capitalism: How Today's Economic Forces Shape Tomorrow's World* (New York: Morrow, 1996).

27. Jan Nederveen Pieterse, *Globalization and Culture: Global Mélange*, 3rd ed. (Lanham, MD: Rowman & Littlefield, 2015), 12–13.

28. Steger, *Globalization*, 103–30.

29. For a fuller discussion of these points, see Craig Calhoun, *Nations Matter: Culture, History, and the Cosmopolitan Dream* (London: Routledge, 2007); Arjun Appadurai, *Modernity at Large: Cultural Dimensions of Globalization* (Minneapolis: University of Minnesota Press, 1996); Ernest Gellner, *Nations and Nationalism* (Malden, MA: Blackwell, 1983); and Hans Schatte, *Globalization and Citizenship* (Lanham, MD: Rowman & Littlefield, 2012).

30. Paul Hopper, Understanding Cultural Globalization (Cambridge, MA: Polity, 2007).

31. For a fuller discussion of each of these points, see Ralph Hanson, *Mass Communication*, 6th ed. (Thousand Oaks, CA: Sage Publications, 2017), and Stanley J. Baran and Dennis K. Davis, *Mass Communication Theory: Foundations, Ferment, and Future*, 5th ed. (Boston, MA: Wadsworth Cengage Learning, 2009).

32. Donald K. Emmerson, "Singapore and the 'Asian Values' Debate," *Journal of Democracy* 6, no. 4 (1995): 95–105.

33. Samuel Huntington, *The Clash of Civilizations and the Remaking of World Order* (New York: Simon & Schuster, 1996).

34. Benjamin R. Barber, *Jihad vs. McWorld: How Globalism and Tribalism Are Reshaping the World* (New York: Ballantine Books, 1996), 9.

35. George Ritzer, *The McDonaldization of Society 5*, 2nd ed. (Thousand Oaks, CA: Pine Forge Press, 2008).

36. Compare Marwan M. Kraidy, *Hybridity, or the Cultural Logic of Globalization* (Philadelphia: Temple University Press, 2005); Arjun Appadurai, *Modernity at Large: Cultural Dimensions of Globalization* (Minneapolis: University of Minnesota Press, 1996); Ulf Hannerz, *Cultural Complexity: Studies in the Social Organization of Meaning* (New York: Columbia University Press, 1992); Ulf Hannerz, *Transnational Connections: Cultures, People, Places* (London: Routledge, 1996); and Pieterse, *Globalization and Culture*.

37. William Rowe and Vivian Schelling, *Memory and Modernity: Popular Culture in Latin America* (London: Verso, 1991), 231.

38. James L. Watson, ed., *Golden Arches East: McDonald's in East Asia* (Stanford, CA: Stanford University Press, 1997).

39. Kraidy, *Hybridity*.

40. See Pieterse, *Globalization and Culture*, for a full discussion of this point.

41. Kraidy, *Hybridity*.

42. Roland Robertson, *Globalization: Social Theory and Global Culture* (London: Sage Publications, 1992), 100 (emphasis in original). See also Richard Giulanotti and Roland Robertson, "Culture: The Glocal Game, Cosmopolitanism, and Americanization," in *The Global Studies Reader*, ed. Manfred B. Steger, 2nd ed. (New York: Oxford University Press, 2015), 176–94.

43. Robertson, *Globalization*, 100–102.

CHAPTER 2

"AMERICAN" POPULAR CULTURE IN MOVIES, MUSIC, AND TELEVISION

To write (or read) a book on the effect(s) of American popular culture on contemporary globalization is to assume, perhaps without being aware of it, that there is something uniquely American about the popular culture made or developed in the United States and consumed around the world. Chapter 1 introduced the notion that American public culture contains an array of values, norms, and practices that distinguish it from other cultures. American public culture was shown to be "civic": members of the political community publicly declare that Americans believe in ideals and values that, taken together, are seen to promote the dignity and rights of all individuals—whether they actually practice what they preach or not. These values include specific forms of liberty, political equality, individualism, democracy, tolerance, exceptionalism, and capitalism.

Yet the global popular culture corporations that control much of the world's trade in popular culture (see chapters 3 and 4 for discussions of them) have an interest in not appearing to be agents of one culture or another. Cultures often conflict, after all, and, as discussed in chapter 1, people often resent and resist cultural products that come from foreign, distant places and seem to undermine the ideals and values of local people, especially children. Global corporations have an incentive to be as culturally neutral as possible. A cultural content producer seen to be overtly "American" may have a hard time selling its goods on the global market. Corporations might, therefore, try to avoid being labeled "American."

Despite these pressures, however, popular culture can be seen to reflect the values of the nation from which it emerges. This chapter explores the "Americanness" of American popular culture. It examines how popular culture can reflect national culture and summarizes academic studies that link popular culture and American culture. It also explores the many formulas, genres, and conventions that shape American popular culture products in specific and predictably American ways, even in a global era.

The argument developed in this chapter hinges on the notion that products created by one culture inevitably bear its imprint. As Ernest Gellner has explained, it is impossible to escape the cultural context in which an item emerges, is produced, and then is sold. This is the result of the Industrial Revolution, which made the creation of mass-produced popular culture possible in the first place. Gellner argues that achieving a goal in an industrial community requires more than walking from one end of a field to the other with a plow. Instead, running a complex machine or managing money or overseeing people as they work requires a sophisticated understanding of others' ideas, expectations, and goals. People in an industrial society need to understand how their work connects with an entire system of processes, actions, and actors if they are to create a car, balance a corporation's accounts, or coordinate the efforts of an entire factory floor. It needs, in other words, to make cultural "sense": to truly contribute to a thing's making, people need to understand what it is, why it matters, and how it works. It needs to be culturally relevant and embedded.[1] Consequently, the products of the Industrial Revolution necessarily express the values and ideals of the culture that produced them. This is true whether the product is language, a car, or popular culture artifacts like movies, music, television programs, clothes, eating establishments, or sports.

AMERICAN CIVIC CULTURE AND AMERICAN POPULAR CULTURE

There is empirical support for Gellner's theoretical linkage of national and popular cultures. For example, in "Deep Structures: Polpop Culture on Primetime Television," Allen McBride and Robert K. Toburen offer a useful and interesting explanation of how American popular culture expresses the values of American civic culture.[2] For the article, they analyzed the content of fifteen of the twenty most popular television programs from the 1992 broadcast year. (They did not examine programs that lacked a continuing story line, like news magazines or clip shows such as *America's Funniest Home Videos*.) Thirteen of the programs were situation comedies; the others were hour-long dramas of various sorts.

The specific focus of their analysis was conflict: how it arose and how, when, and by whom it was resolved. For McBride and Toburen, conflict serves as a useful indicator of the cultural values of a given community. Different cultures can be expected to both initiate and resolve conflicts differently. In a traditional community, for example, conflict would likely emerge when an individual challenged his or her assigned place in the system, and the conflict would likely be resolved through appeal to community standards and norms. In an individualist society, by contrast, simply challenging hierarchical norms would likely be insufficient to start a conflict, and an appeal to comply with group values is unlikely to resolve a conflict with a person motivated by the desire to improve his or her personal lot in life.

McBride and Toburen's central finding is consistent with the idea that the United States has a civic culture organized around the rights of individuals. They show that individualist values dominate both conflict and conflict resolution on popular American television programming. In the programs they studied, most conflicts were between individuals, at least one of whom was usually seeking some personal benefit for him- or herself or a friend or loved one. The conflict was usually resolved through interpersonal negotiation, bargaining, and cooperation—although the fact that many of the shows involved family relationships guaranteed that many conflicts were resolved through an appeal to an authority figure like a parent. In any case, McBride and Toburen show that the core civic value of individualism is omnipresent in popular American television shows.

Conrad Kottak's analysis of Brazilian television provides additional confirmation of the individualism apparent in American television programming, while adding additional insights to this finding. Kottak notes that compared to American programming, Brazilian television shows are more focused on the importance of extended traditional families. Rather than showing adults who live far away from home and have interesting or important jobs, for example, Brazilian programs show adults living at or near home and interacting with their family members instead of bosses, social leaders, or members of the broader community. Similarly, Kottak finds that Brazilians have less expectation of privacy than do Americans. Family members, servants, and others can easily walk into or out of homes or overhear personal conversations through the usually open doors and windows of Brazilian residences. Brazilian programming emerges from a web of social interdependence and accountability, while American programming derives from the deep individualism of American life.[3]

Kottak also sees the value of political equality reflected very differently in Brazilian and American television. Issues of social and economic class, for example, are largely absent from American programming (even though they certainly exist in American life), but class and status are central to Brazilian television. Few American programs make the economic class of their stars a central focus of their story lines. The characters in American programs rarely, if ever, link their social and economic status to political or financial factors beyond their control, even if the shows focus on working-class families or characters. Likewise, better-off characters like doctors and lawyers are usually seen to have achieved their status by their own hard work, not as the result of some racial, ethnic, gender, or class bias. By contrast, Kottak notes that Brazilian programming reflects the social, political, and economic inequalities in Brazilian life. The class and racial foundations of Brazilian programming stand in stark contrast to the egalitarian ethic that is one of the defining characteristics of American public culture and is usually reflected in American popular culture.

Kottak is also insightful on issues of race in both Brazilian and American societies. In the United States, race is a fairly rigid category ascribed to a person at birth. It is fixed through some combination of color, appearance, parentage, and culture. In contrast, race in Brazil is fluid. Brazilians use few, if any, markers like color, hair type, or background to ascribe racial categories to individuals. As a consequence, characters are rarely defined by race in Brazilian programming.

Yet Kottak notes that black characters have been both more common and more popular in the United States than they are on Brazilian television. This is true even though the major audience for U.S. programming is white. *The Cosby Show*, for example, was both the number one show in the United States for several years in the late 1980s and early 1990s and one of the most distributed programs worldwide. It focused on the lives of an African American family, the Huxtables. However, its story lines usually revolved around typical family situations rather than the complexities of living as a black family in a racist nation. The Huxtable parents had jobs—one as a doctor and the other as a lawyer—which they had achieved through hard work. They could provide their children with a healthy and comfortable home. They lived in a large New York City house and interacted easily and comfortably with a diverse range of Americans. In other words, the Huxtable family was self-sufficient, individualist, egalitarian, and tolerant—quintessential Americans.

Notably, white Americans celebrated this vision of an employed, educated, and successful African American family. The Huxtables reflected the broad patterns of American public culture in ways that reinforced the ideals Americans claim to value—such as hard work, tolerance, capitalist success, and so on. The correlation between the Huxtables' lives and the values of American public culture made it easy for white Americans to embrace the Huxtables as an African American version of the American dream. Put another way, it is hard to imagine a television show being as popular as *The Cosby Show* if it featured a dysfunctional family, headed by a single woman working several jobs or receiving welfare and decrying her fate as a black female in a racist America. Her story would not fit American cultural values as closely as the Huxtables' story did.

Timothy Havens has offered an extended analysis of *The Cosby Show*'s popularity as "the biggest show in the world." For Havens, *The*

Cosby Show was noteworthy for its ability to address issues of race, racism, and economic inequality in a way that was recognizable and appealing to audiences worldwide. Thus, rather than making economic hardship and social exclusion a central theme (one that would be hard to pull off given the economic and social status of the parents in the show), the program addressed questions of race and discrimination in indirect ways. For example, the Huxtables' son, Theo, had an "Abolish Apartheid" sticker on his bedroom door. Show plots included discussions of the significance of the civil rights movement both in the past and in contemporary life. African American art hung on the Huxtables' walls, while jazz and blues, musical forms often associated with black performers, played in the house. In other words, *The Cosby Show* could appeal to diverse audiences because it provided an appealing vision of a happy, integrated African American family enjoying the full promise of American life.[4]

The Huxtables do more than just express an American way of life, however. They manifest the notion of transparency. Scott Robert Olson explains that American popular culture, because of a unique mix of cultural factors addressed further in chapter 3, "has a competitive advantage in the creation and global distribution of cultural taste." This advantage is transparency, which he defines as "any textual apparatus that allows audiences to project indigenous values, beliefs, rites and rituals into imported media or the use of those devices." Thus, Olson continues, "this transparency effect means that American cultural exports, such as cinema, television, and related merchandise, manifest narrative structures that easily blend into other cultures."[5]

Havens finds transparency in the reaction of international audiences to *The Cosby Show*. Drawing on other research, he quotes a resident of Barbados as noting, "Black people in this show are not isolated, no fun is made of Blackness, and the characters are shown as leading wholesome moral lives." Similarly, a black South African viewer simply explains, "The show makes me proud of being black." Another black South African even sees hope in *The Cosby Show* for educating and persuading white South Africans to treat blacks with dignity and respect: "*The Cosby Show* . . . is saying, 'Come on, you white guys [in South Africa], the blacks are not so bad as you make them out to be. Look at us, we are having a good life and normal problems here in America. Give those guys down there a chance. Let's change for the better and live together, not apart.'" Havens even finds nonblack audiences identifying with the Huxtable family: a Lebanese Shiite man notes, "American blacks are a little like us. They have big families."[6] American stories and contexts as depicted in *The Cosby Show* are thus both American and transparent across a wide variety of cultures. This combination makes it relatively easy for American popular culture to spread across the globe—particularly when it is distributed as described in chapters 3 and 4.

At least one other study has highlighted the cultural content of American programming. Daradirek Ekachai, Mary Hinchliff-Pelias, and Rosechongporn Komolsevin examined the influence U.S. media have on the perception of the United States by regular consumers of U.S. movies, music, and television in Thailand. Thailand has a long history of showing U.S. programming. Television shows like *Dallas*, *L.A. Law*, and *Magnum, P.I.* were popular in Thailand, as were movies like *Jaws*, *Raiders of the Lost Ark*, and the *Rambo* and *Die Hard* series. Thais have also regularly been exposed to sports programming from the National Basketball Association, the National Football League, and boxing. Researchers polled Thai viewers of American programming and found results that Conrad Kottak's Brazilian audience might well recognize. Thais believe Americans are individualistic and committed to their rights to self-expression and personal development. They see Americans as pleasure loving, scientifically minded, passionate, impulsive, athletic, musical, persistent, practical, and efficient. In contrast, Thais thought Americans were not traditional, naïve, loyal to family, lazy, or quiet. The researchers also found that frequent TV viewers were 47 percent more likely to believe that the depictions of American life accurately reflected American reality than were occasional or infrequent viewers: 56 percent of those who saw four or more American movies per week believed that those films accurately captured life in the United States, compared with 43 percent of moderate viewers and 33 percent of occasional viewers.[7] At least for Thais, then, American popular culture had an explicitly American content.

"AMERICAN" STORIES

Empirical studies that examine how America's civic culture infuses popular culture products produced in the United States provide one lens to expose the way American public culture shapes American popular culture, but they are not the only way to discern such influence. A close reading of American popular culture artifacts reveals various themes or formulaic patterns—tropes—that manifest themselves repeatedly in those products. These formulae arise for at least two reasons: (1) economic success (once a formula proves successful, others mimic it), and (2) expedience—the market for American popular culture is insatiable, and replicating previous material is easier (especially when it has proven successful financially) than innovating or creating new material. In either case, any popular culture product is vulnerable to and available for duplication, repetition, and stereotyping. Examining pop culture tropes provides another way to explore the cultural values embedded in the artifacts of American popular culture.

The ubiquity of American English. One aspect of American popular culture that needs discussion is, to a native speaker of American English, perhaps so obvious as to be ignored: almost all of it is produced in American English. Throughout most of its period of dominance in world entertainment, American popular culture has been made, sold, and even consumed in American English. (There is a growing market for American-made content in Spanish, as will be discussed in chapter 5.) People worldwide have had access to programming and other cultural artifacts that are expressed in "American." And while some of that programming might be dubbed in the local language or presented with subtitles, not all of it is: I, for example, watched *Crocodile Dundee* in English (American and Australian, in this case) one rainy night in Amsterdam. (I later saw it dubbed into Italian in Rome and saw it again—in English—in Helsinki.) This simple fact—that American audiovisual entertainment is conceived and distributed in American English—helps explain the global reach of American popular culture.

Moreover, the marketing tie-ins to which the products of American popular culture are linked (discussed in chapter 3), whether Mickey Mouse's ears or a *Star Wars* T-shirt, are often recognizably and obviously both American and in English. Accordingly, American popular culture—whether consumed directly (e.g., a movie in which the dialogue is in American English) or packaged into derivative products—has a distinctively American character that, as discussed in chapters 3, 4, and 5, can provoke concerns from people who believe that the language in which movies, music, and television programs are being presented is systematically destroying indigenous cultures.

Happy endings. Another remarkably consistent feature of most American audiovisual entertainments is the happy ending. On America's televisions and movie screens, problems almost always resolve themselves in the allotted time: the situation comedy ends with a homily about family love; the cop show's bad guy goes to jail; the hero of the action-adventure movie is reunited with his or her child/family/buddies. The country group Dixie Chicks had a huge hit with "Goodbye Earl," in which the song's heroines murder an abusive husband and get away with it, improving the world as a result. Perhaps most remarkably of all, *Titanic*, one of the most popular movies of all time, manages a happy ending amid the horrors of that ship's sinking: the heroine loses her lover to the frigid waters of the North Atlantic, but she is improbably rescued as a sole survivor in a sea of corpses, escapes her hated fiancé, marries for love, and has a wonderful family—all while keeping her ship-born love in her heart forever.

Chapter 3 will address why the happy ending became a central feature of American popular culture. What matters here is that once established, this formula served as the foundation for producing the endless television shows and movies needed to fill the growing market for popular culture. The happy ending thus made both business and political sense as a central feature of American popular culture.

Triumphant individuals. The happy ending is more than a "feel good" close to an American movie or TV show, however. It also serves to emphasize the importance of the individual in determining his or her own fate and happiness. The happy ending is, in large measure, an audiovisual manifestation of the myth of the self-made man expressed in nineteenth-century tales like the Horatio Alger stories. Horatio Alger wrote hundreds of dime novels, all offering basically the same story: anyone, no matter his or her life circumstances, can succeed through hard work, perseverance, and dedication. One's class background is irrelevant: a poor person can become rich through effort. Thus, one's station in life is ultimately one's own responsibility: since everyone can succeed, failure to do so is obviously the result of laziness.

Happy endings teach Alger's lesson to contemporary audiences. Bruce Willis might have to run (improbably) across broken glass in his bare feet while fighting the heavily armed, well-trained, numerous bad guys in *Die Hard*, for example, but because he is willing to do it and committed to his task, he is able to defeat the obviously European terrorists who are holding his wife and her coworkers hostage. Similarly, Scarlett O'Hara may have had her house burned down and lost her lover by the end of *Gone with the Wind*, but "tomorrow," she says, "is another day," as she swears she will never be hungry again. No problem is too big for the individual to overcome; no limitation is determinative of one's fate. The happy ending is triumphant American individualism realized on screen.

Spectacle. Likewise, the visual spectacle of dramatic special effects offers a lure to audiovisual culture that few non-Hollywood products can offer. As a practical matter, the concentration of talent and financing available to American movie, music, and television makers allows their products to achieve a standard that far exceeds that which most global competitors can meet. The most obvious example of this phenomenon lies in big-budget, "blockbuster" films: whether *Die Hard*, *Star Wars*, or *Avatar*, American films are far more likely to be extremely expensive to make, with elaborate special effects to carry the story forward. Indeed, elaborate special effects have the additional advantage of being transparent: an exploding spaceship tracing a fiery arc as it burns up in an alien planet's atmosphere requires no culturally sensitive nuance to understand. It is its own meaning.

There is another form of spectacle evident in American audiovisual popular culture: opulent consumerism. Whether it is rap music videos filled with Cadillac Escalades, ever-larger gold crosses proclaiming the wearer's Christian faith, other sources of "bling," or the luxurious setting of Southfork ranch in *Dallas*, most American movies, music, and television programs create fantasy worlds of extraordinary wealth. Even television shows set among the allegedly poor have their families living in relatively large houses surrounded by refrigerators, microwave ovens, dishwashers, televisions, videocassette recorders, cars, and other assorted consumer goods that are unimaginable extravagances in much of the world.

Interestingly, American television shows have been explicit in their understanding that consumption is tied to wealth, and more consumption requires ever more money. For example, Dan Malachowski at salary.com analyzed popular American television programs over time, seeking to understand how much money the fathers in those programs were said or implied to earn. He found that by 2005 fathers were seen or understood to earn twice as much money as fathers in the 1950s, even adjusted for inflation.[8] American popular culture thus presents a vision of Americans as wealthy, consumerist, and self-interested—and as becoming wealthier over time.

Like happy endings and triumphant individualism, spectacle and consumerism are logical extensions of American cultural values. Material wealth can stand in as a marker of individual success, for example, and thus it can seem that the more you have, the more successful you are. This isn't always true, of course, but it's a common perception. Wealth, opulence, and excess are symbols of an American form of individualism, and they reinforce the "me-ness" of American life.

The morality of violence. In addition to being filled with happy individuals enjoying vast wealth, American audiovisual popular culture is also remarkably violent. In fact, according to one report, the average American child sees eight thousand murders depicted on television before finishing grade school.[9] Given how many hours of television American children watch, they may see an average of ten thousand rapes, assaults, and murders each year.[10]

The popularity of police procedural television programs like *Law and Order* and *CSI*, for example, ensures that popular American television programming, especially the programming popular around the world, is awash in violence. Shows like *CSI* take as much advantage of computer graphics in presenting violence as films do. Through computer animation, audiences see bullets penetrate skin, shatter bones, and slice through arteries, leading to arcs of blood spurting across the screen and splattering across walls. Similarly, some rap musicians have linked violence and the acquisition of wealth in their songs and videos, and in the Doors' hit "The End," lead singer Jim Morrison imagines murdering his father and raping his mother. Garth Brooks, in his country hit "Papa Loved Mama," describes a jealous man driving his eighteen-wheel truck into the motel room where his wife is cheating on him, killing both his wife and her lover. And, of course, sports like American football glamorize violent contact, making heroes of extremely large, strong men as they use force to subdue their opponents.

Importantly, American movies, music, and television programs do not necessarily show violence as wrong or immoral. Instead, it can have a legitimizing moral purpose. Take, for example, the inevitable plot of an action-adventure movie. Pick one—they are all quite literally the same. These plots are transparent, to use Olson's phrase: so formulaic that audiences around the world can recognize them instantly. Such films usually show individual, heroic action in defense of what are often offered as or assumed to be American values or the American way of life. (Superman's actual purpose as a superhero is to defend truth, justice, and the American way, for example.) A hero—almost always male—stands as a lone individual facing some great evil. (In some cases the hero is reluctant; in others, anxious.) Usually heroes have some special training or power—for example, they may be Special Forces veterans or, depending on the subgenre, superheroes of one kind or another. In a few cases they are recognizably ordinary, however. The odds are usually overwhelming and the stakes are typically high: a child is being held hostage, or the safety of the world or some other grand fate hinges on the victory of the hero. Then the bloodbath begins. The hero slaughters untold numbers of the enemy and either escapes unharmed or is wounded only enough to enhance the dramatic tension. In this modern era of computer graphics, extraordinarily vivid explosions, graphic depictions of mangled flesh, and a soundtrack that drives the action at a frenzied pace accompany much of this destruction. All this violence, of course, is depicted as necessary to achieve whatever goal the hero must accomplish; anything less, and the child dies or the world explodes or evil vanquishes the innocent. We may see dozens (and more!) slaughtered, but since either they deserved it or their deaths were necessary to secure the community, the violence is appropriate and laudable. (As an aside, the Dixie Chicks' "Goodbye Earl" tells essentially the same story, only in this case with a female as the defender of the communal good.)

Important here is the use to which violence is put. When violence defends and expands community values and norms, it is laudable and worthy. Violence in defense of Americanness is thus a moral act, not an immoral one.

Gender tropes. American audiovisual culture is also deeply embedded in American cultural stereotypes of gender. In part this can be seen in the fact that most action hero individualists in American films are male. (Ellen Ripley, played by Sigourney Weaver in the *Alien* series, is a notable exception.) More broadly, the question of what roles men and women ought to play in society is a regular source of controversy in social and political life around the world. American popular culture has certainly employed issues of gender in its products; these images and themes have been and continue to be controversial both in the United States and across the rest of the globe. And, notably, they have tended to reproduce American social patterns for global audiences to emulate or fear. For better and for worse, American audiovisual culture depicts a vision of American life for the world's movie, music, and television audiences.

At least four stereotypes of women's roles in society can be identified in American audiovisual products, for example. One is the woman as sex object. In this role, women serve as little more than eye candy for the sexual enjoyment of the audience. A linked stereotype is that of woman as victim. In this role, females are dominated, often through sexual violence, into accepting the will of an authority figure—usually, although not always, a man. Another common gender stereotype in American popular culture is that of the traditional wife and mother. Explored and ultimately enshrined in such 1950s television classics as *Leave It to Beaver* and *Father Knows Best*, this image usually depicts a woman who devotes her life to her family. She is the master of the private realm of family life, working endlessly to cook, clean, care for the children, and support her husband as he interacts with the outer, public world. Admittedly, over time this role has evolved along with the American family—Carol Brady, in the 1970s TV hit *The Brady Bunch*, had to deal with a blended family, for example—but the basic pattern of the role has remained relatively unchanged. A final female stereotype is that of the "strong woman," which usually comes in one of two forms: the superwoman who balances family and career to be a success in the world at large or the victimized woman who throws off her oppressors and becomes a new, independent person.

For males, the range of gender roles tends to be more limited. As a rule, men are either strong and assertive or wimpy and effeminate—even implicitly or explicitly homosexual. Those males who are seen to have appropriately "male" values tend to be in positions of authority or athletes; in both cases, they are defined by their endless pursuit of sexual conquests. By contrast, "failed" males hold weak positions at work, are dominated and mocked by colleagues and families, or are incompetent at sexual gamesmanship. While there has been a noticeable shift toward an acceptance of gay male characters, particularly on television programs like *Modern Family* and *Transparent*, these characters almost always conform to the effeminate notion of homosexuality—and so, by extension, make the life of a nonassertive heterosexual male even more complicated by allusion to gayness. Hip-hop music is likewise noted for its regular use of expressive homophobia, and many athletes are public in their opposition to homosexuals in general and as members of their sports teams as well. Other conceptions of maleness rarely make it into American movies, music, or television programs.

The lure and challenges of sex. Sex and sexuality are also central to American popular culture. Sexuality, like violence, is enticing, engaging, and likely to hold an audience, particularly when it tests social limits on sexual expression. And, as was the case with depictions of gender, the treatment of sexuality in American movies, music, and television provides a frame on which global audiences can either be titillated or shocked by the lure, or horror, of sexual freedom.

Much sexual activity in American movies, music, and television programming focuses on the immediate gratification of individual desire, for example. In scene after scene, people are seen to meet and bed one another quickly and readily. Such couplings are rarely consequential: few people get pregnant or contract venereal diseases; people connect because they want to "hook up" and then move on. In almost all cases, these events are presented in individualist, hedonistic, self-interested terms. Movies like *The Brown Bunny* have shown established, award-winning actors engaged in explicit sex acts, and one famous episode of the popular television comedy series *Seinfeld* involved a contest to see who among the program's cast could resist masturbating for the longest period. Indeed, entire series—notably the HBO hit *Girls*—have been organized around the sexual adventures of the program's stars.

Music, too, has emphasized the fun and freedom of sexual activity. The apparent sexual energy and movements of rock and roll have been a matter of public concern at least since Ed Sullivan ordered the cameras on his 1950s-era show not to film Elvis Presley's gyrating hips during the star's first televised performance. In retrospect, such concerns seem quaint. Lyrics like those in the peppy Beach Boys hit "I Get Around," which asserts, "We've never missed yet with the girls we meet," have evolved through the Beatles' classic "Why Don't We Do It in the Road?" and beyond. Kelis, in her 2003 rap song "Milkshake," is a virtual prostitute advertising her sexual skill and superiority when she asserts, "My milkshake brings all the boys to the yard / And they're like, it's better than yours / Damn right, it's better than yours / I could teach you, but I'd have to charge." The Bloodhound Gang managed to create an entire new vocabulary of implied sex acts by describing their desire to "power drill the yippee bog / With the dude piston" and to "put the you know what in the you know where" in their rock song "Foxtrot Uniform Charlie Kilo"—the military call signs for the letters *F*, *U*, *C*, and *K*. Britney Spears offered a similarly circumspect double entendre in a 2009 hit song in which she explained, "All the boys and all the girls are begging to 'If You Seek Amy.'" The disco classic "Lady Marmalade" explicitly asks, "Voulez-vous coucher avec moi?" ("Do you want to sleep with me?"). The country classic "Help Me Make It through the Night" insists, "I don't care what's right or wrong / I won't try to understand / Let the devil take tomorrow / 'Cause tonight I need a friend."

The link between music and sexuality is nowhere more explicit than in contemporary music videos, which are among the most globally popular products of American popular culture. Song lyrics that are already aggressively sexual are regularly framed with highly erotic or sexually suggestive images and situations. From Madonna's "Like a Virgin" video, in which she rolls on the floor wearing a wedding dress and making moaning sounds while describing herself as being "like a virgin, touched for the very first time" at her lover's caress, through the Pussycat Dolls' "Don't Cha," in which scantily clad women tease a potential boyfriend with provocative dancing and questions like "Don't cha wish your girlfriend was hot like me? / Don't cha wish your girlfriend was a freak like me?" music videos have traded on sexually stimulating imagery to sell their products. Indeed, there has been something of a "race to the bottom" as once-scandalous images (Madonna kissing an African American statue depicting Jesus Christ, which brings the figure to life, for example, in "Like a Prayer") become bland. Lady Gaga has made a career of transgressing established norms—including the norms she herself sets. The next video, then, needs to capture the attention of an audience that has, quite literally, seen it all.

Issues of sex and sexuality do not stop at the depiction of heterosexual sexuality, of course. Accordingly, American popular culture also depicts other aspects of sexuality, some of which, such as homosexuality and transgendering, are controversial. The first mainstream American television program to feature a leading male character who was gay was the 1970s comedy *Soap*. Another 1970s show, *Three's Company*, revolved around the efforts of a straight male character to pass as a gay man to live with two female friends whose landlord was opposed to gender cohabitation. The popular comedy *Modern Family* features central characters who are gay. The 1970s film *Dog Day Afternoon* features Al Pacino as a bank robber motivated by the desire to raise funds for his homosexual lover's sex-change operation; twenty years later, Robin Williams and Nathan Lane played a gay couple of long standing who run a business together in a highly sympathetic portrayal of homosexuality in *The Birdcage*. More recently, the film *Moonlight* won the 2017 Academy Award for Best Picture for its searing portrayal of one gay African American's struggle to come to terms with his sexuality and his friends' and family's struggle to accept him.

Lesbianism, too, has been a common feature of American popular culture's products. The 1982 film *Personal Best*, in which Mariel Hemingway's character engages in a torrid affair with another woman, was the first significant depiction of lesbianism in a popular American movie. A similar first was broken in the 1980s sitcom *Roseanne* when Roseanne's sister kissed another woman on prime-time TV. Today such depictions have become commonplace. Ellen DeGeneres, perhaps Hollywood's most famous lesbian, has her own daily talk show. Lesbian sexuality is a central theme of the Netflix program *Orange Is the New Black*, set in a women's prison. Similarly, music videos, particularly rap and rock videos, regularly show their male stars surrounded by groups of women touching and kissing each other. If anything, contemporary American popular culture seems to celebrate lesbians—at least in the case of attractive women who appeal to men (or other women) by making sexual contact with other attractive women.

Even issues of transgendering are regular, if not common, elements of American popular culture. The shock rock star Marilyn Manson often appears on stage wearing a plastic body suit that makes him appear both nude and without genitalia. An earlier generation of rock stars, the members of the band Kiss, made themselves famous by wearing outrageous costumes and elaborate makeup. Actress Hilary Swank won an Academy Award for her portrayal in *Boys Don't Cry* of a woman who is ultimately beaten to death for hiding her gender behind male clothes and restrictive undergarments. Another Academy Award–winning film, *The Silence of the Lambs*, records the efforts of law enforcement officials to find a serial killer who, it turns out, wanted to undergo a sex-change operation but was rejected as psychologically unstable. Netflix has another breakout hit, *Transparent*, that explores the struggles of a family as its members learn that the person they knew as the father of the family is, in fact, transgender. This program has found a real-life parallel in Caitlyn Jenner, a globally prominent decathlete who won the 1976 Olympic gold medal in the decathlon as a man before declaring himself to be a woman in 2015. In American popular culture, boys will not always just be boys.

The intersection of sex and violence. At least one other aspect of sex and sexuality needs to be addressed if the link between American popular culture and global reactions to it is to be understood: its link to violence. Sex and sexuality are, of course, among the most emotionally charged aspects of human life; given the extraordinary tension that accompanies human sexuality, it is perhaps not surprising that violence is one aspect of the experience of sex. Linked to the evident marketing appeal of violence, the sex and violence dimension of American popular culture should be expected. Thus, as many of the examples of movies, music, and television programs listed above suggest, violence is a regular part of the depiction of sexuality in the products of American political culture. As noted earlier, Hilary Swank's character is beaten to death for hiding her biological sex, and Al Pacino's character is willing to rob a bank and risk killing innocent people to fund his lover's operation. In other cases, the sex-violence linkage is more purely prurient: its sole purpose is to shock and horrify the audience—for instance, with the image of a paralyzed woman being raped and murdered. Whether as an accurate expression of the pains and tensions of human emotions or as a virtually pornographic tool of exploitation and audience appeal, violence is often linked to sexuality in American popular culture.

The nuclear(ish) family. Families depicted in American popular culture tend to appear in three forms, two of which are profoundly dysfunctional and the third of which is, at best, improbable. The first form is at the root of many, if not most, situation comedies. It centers on hapless and incompetent fathers, faithful and persistent wives (if they exist in the show—many such programs feature only divorced or widowed fathers) who really hold the family together, and an array of loud-mouthed, basically disrespectful children who provide the family tensions around which the show revolves. The children, in turn, may or may not be biologically related to either or both parents. If the program admits that parents have parents themselves and includes grandparents in the program, they are a burden as often as a help—an adult version of the show's children. Every half hour, some problem is introduced, chaos ensues, and order is restored through the love the characters are eventually forced to admit they feel for one another.

A second dysfunctional family form appears on one of the most globally popular forms of American programming, the soap opera/melodrama, especially on television. Such melodramas regularly use the family as their dramatic focus; however, families in the serial universe are not mutually supportive bastions of strength to help each other through a troubled world. Instead, soap opera families are internally competitive and vicious. Brothers and fathers scheme to sleep with each other's wives and girlfriends; sisters and mothers engage in a constant barrage of gossip and criticism intended to undermine each other's self-confidence and self-worth and so enhance the gossiper's chance of sleeping with the other's husband or boyfriend. While the members of the family are often alleged to have important jobs that generate great wealth, no one ever seems to go to work; instead, the characters spend all their time attacking and manipulating each other emotionally as well as sexually. While everyone is well dressed and has expensive possessions, family is an obstacle, not a key, to happiness.

The third typical family form in American popular culture derives from the strong woman stereotype. In this convention, the mother is often important, powerful, and well off; her problems, such as they are, come from struggling to find time to balance the competing pressures of job, family, and romance. More often than not, however, the family, even if blended, is relatively harmonious, with happy children and satisfied spouses. Unlike in the 1950s, when father knew best, housework is now a shared responsibility, as is care of the kids. The result is well-adjusted children enjoying a middle-class lifestyle—or better.

Race and ethnicity. Race and ethnicity constitute yet another area of human life in which American popular culture broadcasts stereotypical, often offensive images and themes. Indeed, many of these stereotypes predate the emergence of electronic media and stand as legacies of the racist and ethnically discriminatory policies that the United States has adopted and defended throughout much of its history. Thus, in general, whites, especially white Anglo-Saxon Protestants, or WASPs, are depicted as the best-educated, most effective, most law-abiding members of society. As such, they fill most positions of authority in the political, economic, and social system. Notable exceptions to these patterns have been Catholics, Jews, and gay people: they, along with poor, usually southern whites constitute the only Caucasian groups that American films, music, and television programs consistently mock or assign cultural stereotypes to. None of this should imply that whites are only presented in heroic or positive terms; indeed, many films, television programs, and pieces of pop music make it clear that whites, typically men, are the bad guys of the piece. However, when whites are presented as evil, their evil is rarely ascribed to their cultural background—unless they are Catholic, Jewish, gay, or southern. Instead, they are responsible for their crimes—or their heroism—as individuals. It matters less what color they are than who they are as people.

The situation is not as positive or hopeful regarding the popular culture images of members of other races and ethnicities in America, however. African Americans in particular have been subject to centuries of savage, horrific portrayals in U.S. social and political life. These images persist. One image, for example, is that of the black male as criminal. Established during the era of slavery to justify the violent control of black males, as well as to frighten white women into compliance through their husbands' and fathers' threats that leaving the house made them vulnerable to attack by black men, the image of the black male as an out-of-control, sexually aggressive predator has recurred throughout American history. Indeed, the first major multireel movie, D. W. Griffith's *Birth of a Nation*, was based on *The Klansman*, a novel that depicts the horrors of black violence against innocent white women in the aftermath of the U.S. Civil War. Its heroes are members of the Ku Klux Klan, who save the women from an attack by evil blacks. (*Birth of a Nation* is still considered a classic film.) Contemporary popular culture is awash in images of violent black males, whether as sports stars, gang members, prisoners, or drug dealers. The entire genre of gangsta rap exploits and reinforces this imagery. Sympathetic portrayals of professional African American men are few and far between. (The comedian Robert Townsend mocked the limited range of roles available to African American actors in his film *Hollywood Shuffle*.)

The situation for African American women is hardly any better, with one major exception: former daytime talk show host and now media mogul Oprah Winfrey. Black women are regularly shown as un- or underemployed, usually single mothers who are inevitably lifetime welfare recipients. (Former U.S. president Ronald Reagan once famously referred to such women as "welfare queens," implying that they were living lives of comparative luxury on government handouts.) These women are also generally depicted as drug or alcohol addicted. Alternatively, particularly in rap videos and music, they are portrayed as objects of sexual desire who exist, mostly, to satisfy the sexual demands of various male partners. Only rarely does American popular culture manifest sympathetic images, such as The Cosby Show's Clair Huxtable or those associated with Oprah Winfrey, who has become one of the wealthiest people in entertainment. This pattern has continued in recent years even though, in the real world, an African American woman, Condoleezza Rice, was U.S. secretary of state during the presidency of George W. Bush—and, of course, the United States subsequently had its first African American president and first lady.

The lives of Latinos and Latinas are similarly depicted as dire in American popular culture. Early images of them were gross stereotypes of an alien "other" with which few Americans would have ever come into contact. The image of the male Mexican bandito, which was a staple of Western movies and television programs in the 1930s, 1940s, and 1950s, morphed into a 1970s cartoon character selling the snack food Fritos by singing, "Ay, ay, ay, ay, I am the Frito Bandito," while stealing various victims' snack chips. This, in turn, fed into images of Latinos as gang members, drug dealers, and drug lords in innumerable movies, television shows, and songs set in the context of the international drug trade in the 1980s and 1990s. The only other types of Latinos commonly shown were prisoners—usually arrested for gang and drug activity—and, in a few cases, police officers intent on rescuing the neighborhoods in which they had grown up from the ravages of the drug trade.

Latinas are given even less diversity in their presentation in American popular culture. The earliest images of Latinas in U.S. films centered on Carmen Miranda, an attractive woman who became a famous entertainer while wearing seductive clothing and a bowl of fruit on her head. Since then, most Latinas have been portrayed as sexual attachments of the men in their lives and thus—given the distribution of Latino characters—members or associates of gangs engaged in or managing the drug trade. They are seen to raise the men's children. On occasion a woman is shown to resist or challenge the corrupt values of the local community, but often Latinas are seen as active participants in the criminal lives of their men. Indeed, there is not a single major sympathetic portrayal of a Latina in contemporary American popular culture.

There is really only one stereotype of Asian Americans in contemporary popular culture—that of a hardworking but potentially dangerous person, whether he or she is a nerdy student, an entrepreneur, or a crime boss. This image derives from earlier cultural stereotypes about Asians in America. During World War II, for example, Asians were usually seen as devious, dangerous people who attacked the United States without warning on December 7, 1941. (Little distinction was made between Japanese and other Asians; Asians as such were usually believed to pose a threat to the United States.) This perception itself emerged from Anglo fears of Asian migration in the nineteenth and early twentieth centuries: as Asians immigrated to the western areas of the United States in the aftermath of the Civil War, usually for economic opportunities associated with the gold rush or the building of the transcontinental railroad, local Anglo-Americans passed restrictive rules against Asian employment and access to education. These were later codified by the U.S. Congress to include limitations on the numbers of Asians who could immigrate to the United States, as well as laws that barred Asians from owning property or becoming naturalized citizens. The three contemporary images of Asian Americans manifest this historical concern that Asian Americans are undermining the American way of life. In each case there is the sense that, whether student, enemy, or immigrant, Asians are so different that they will work to replace American ideals and values with their own—that they will not become fully American.

Native Americans are perhaps the only ethnic group that has seen a full-scale reversal in its characterization in American popular culture. Early in the history of electronic media, Native Americans were "savages" who brutalized settlers trying to make new lives for themselves in the American West. At best, if they cooperated with Anglos, Native Americans could serve as scouts and supporters (never leaders) of Anglo troops and wagon trains. At worst, Native American tribes were bloody raiders of innocent villages or alcoholics on reservations. All this has changed since the 1970s. It is now rare to see a negative portrayal of a Native American in American popular culture. If anything, the images of Native Americans have become stereotypically positive, as tribes are presented as environmentally sensitive, peace-loving people who acted only in self-defense against rapacious Anglos.

It is important to remember here that while each of the issues addressed above—gender, sexuality, violence, and the like—was discussed individually, they are experienced cumulatively. No film or video or song or program features only one of these controversial aspects; each inevitably contains several, if not all, of these concerns. Thus, sexual violence can be used to dominate women and pressure them into accepting traditional gender roles that bring them access to great wealth and security, particularly as protection against an alien, dangerous other—be he or she African American, Latino/a, poor, or a member of any of several other fear-inducing groups. Any or all of this can be and often is objectionable, offensive, and norm challenging both in the United States and around the world. Much of this material is further embedded in cross-marketing tie-ins, meaning that violence, sexuality, diversity, gender, and other complex social phenomena can become associated with fast-food restaurants, cell phone ringtones, clothing choices and styles, or any other commodity that can be sold through a movie, a piece of music, a performer's endorsement, or a television program. As will be seen in chapter 5, such linkage to the cultural values embedded in American popular culture provides endless ammunition and evidence for those who oppose both American values and the process of globalization.

AMERICAN CULTURE IN MOVIES, MUSIC, AND TELEVISION

This section offers a series of extended analyses of representative examples of American movies, music, and television programs that have been popular worldwide. Rather than just relying on the broad descriptions available in academic research or in scans of popular cultural products, it offers a detailed examination of the ideals, values, and themes contained within American popular culture and links them to the features of American public culture analyzed in chapter 1. Its goal is to offer a close reading of the "Americanness" of American movies, music, and television programming.

AMERICAN MOVIES

Three movies are given an extended commentary here: *Guardians of the Galaxy* (2014), a science fiction romp in which a band of literal misfits saves the galaxy; *Titanic* (1997), James Cameron's megahit, which was the most successful movie (in terms of ticket sales) of all time until another Cameron film, *Avatar* (2009), knocked it off its pedestal; and *Blade Runner* (1982), a dark, dystopian vision of a future in which the values of American public culture combine to create a nightmare version of a globalized world. Any number of films might have been analyzed here, of course, so this list should not be seen as comprehensive. Instead, what follows is intended as an exegesis of how American culture is expressed in movies, using these three films as particularly useful examples.

GUARDIANS OF THE GALAXY: E PLURIBUS UNUM

"E pluribus unum" is the motto of the United States. It translates as "out of many, one." As such, it acknowledges the ethnic and racial diversity that shapes the population of the United States but insists that this diverse citizenry molds together into a cohesive, strong nation with an "American" cultural identity. It also neatly describes the appeal of the 2014 global blockbuster *Guardians of the Galaxy*.

Guardians is based on a graphic novel series of the same name, produced by Marvel. Its story is standard-issue, big-budget action-adventure: an (American) hero, Peter Quill, whose father was an alien and who eventually makes his way through life as a space pirate calling himself "Star Lord," joins with a band of other outcasts to fight Ronan, leader of the Kree, who are bent on destroying the galaxy. (The actual reason why this might be the case is, of course, utterly irrelevant to the story.) They have a series of explosive, vivid adventures before winning and saving the galaxy from its impending doom.

Whatever the creative merits of the film, it was a global hit. It earned over $333 million in the United States alone, with a further $440 million in ticket sales generated overseas. It has generated an additional $129 million in DVD purchases just in the United States.[11] A global audience found the film appealing and engaging.

At least part of the reason for the film's success lies in its core message. As noted above, the story brings a group of misfits together to save the universe. The word "misfits" is a bit misleading, however. *Guardians of the Galaxy* may well bring together the most mismatched group of "heroes" ever combined on film. Peter Quill is an American but has an alien father. He makes an alliance with a genetically engineered, sentient raccoon named Rocket, a living tree creature known as Groot (who only says "groot" throughout the film), an absurdly muscled, heavily scarred victim of Kree violence called Drax, and Gamora, the only female member of the group, who is a former ally of Ronan and the film's other villain, Thanos. Gamora is green and has been genetically engineered as a weapon, characteristics that emphasize her "alienness" and separateness from "normal" communities.

Despite their profound differences, this motley group manages to learn to cooperate both for their own self-interest and to serve the greater cause of preserving the galaxy from destruction. They use their various and diverse skills across their cultural—indeed, species—boundaries and defeat foe after foe as the ultimate confrontation with Ronan nears. In so doing, they emphasize that profound diversity is a blessing, not a curse: they are all stronger together than they would be either alone or with their own "kind." They are truly made one from their many.

Yet they retain their individuality as well. Peter "Star Lord" Quill is irreverent, funny, and extraordinarily self-confident: the prototypical American. Rocket, the genetically engineered raccoon, recognizes his unique place in the universe and is both angry about his identity and committed to it. Drax has a complex backstory involving the murder of his family; Gamora shifts identities from ally of evil to agent of good. Groot, meanwhile, is Groot: one of a kind. Coming together, then, does not mean surrendering one's individual identity. In protecting each other, the characters are also protecting themselves. Out of many, one.

Of course, the film was not popular only because of its characters. It was also heavy on spectacle the way only big-budget Hollywood blockbusters can be. *Guardians* has high production values. Its sets and computer graphics are crisp and dynamic. Its explosions are massive—

and explosions, of course, require no cultural translation. They are transparently accessible. Its $232 million production budget is evident in every frame.[12]

Guardians of the Galaxy can also be seen as a stereotypically American movie in its profound reliance on violence as both a plot device and a tool wielded by heroes. Ronan and Thanos are not just "bad guys." They deploy world- and universe-killing violence simply because they can. Space stations explode; untold numbers of people die; violence is pandemic. Our heroes, too, deploy violence as a regular tool, albeit allegedly to serve the common good. Because of all this violence, in fact, one source has declared that *Guardians of the Galaxy* has more on-screen deaths than any other film in history: some 83,871 deaths happen in the film, most of them when Ronan's assault destroys a fleet of vessels seeking to defend the planet Xandar.[13] It does, however, manage a happy ending despite this vast body count: while Groot is killed in Ronan's final crash into Xandar, we see a shoot from Groot's tree begin to dance as the film ends.

Guardians of the Galaxy is, in the end, a big-budget Hollywood spectacle in which profoundly different individuals combine their forces in a way that both makes them stronger and empowers them as individuals. This band uses epic violence to defend against apocalyptic violence while its members retain their sense of humor and optimism. As such, it is the American motto realized in space: *e pluribus unum.*

TITANIC: CLASS AND THE AMERICAN DREAM

Titanic's success was stunning. Many people rushed back into the theater to watch the film a second and third consecutive time despite the movie's extraordinary length. It set numerous box office records on its way to smashing the all-time high-water mark at $2.1 billion in ticket sales alone—over $600 million in the United States and more than $1.5 billion globally.[14]

This success is seemingly out of proportion to the story. Essentially a love story framed in the foreshadowing context of the *Titanic*'s doomed ocean voyage, the movie follows the trials of Jack (played by Leonardo DiCaprio) and Rose (played by Kate Winslet) as they meet, fall in love, and struggle to survive while the *Titanic* sinks. Jack is a down-and-out working-class youth trying to return to America; he only boards the ill-fated ship because he has won a third-class ticket in a last-second poker game. Rose, by contrast, is the daughter of a formerly elite Philadelphia family that has fallen on hard times; she is to marry an American millionaire to restore the family fortune. Where Jack is lucky to be on the *Titanic* at all, Rose is berthed in the lap of luxury in first-class accommodations.

Despondent over her pending forced marriage, Rose decides to commit suicide by jumping off the *Titanic*. Jack, who has snuck onto the first-class deck, saves her by threatening to join her in her plunge. The two quickly establish a relationship as the poor but talented Jack sketches Rose, reads her poetry, and otherwise acts like a perfect romantic hero. By contrast, Rose's fiancé is a petty, disinterested, possessive man with little integrity or merit to recommend him. He is of no interest for anything other than his immense wealth—which he himself did not earn. When Jack's relationship with Rose is discovered, conflict ensues: as the *Titanic* sinks, Jack is imprisoned and nearly drowns before Rose saves him, returning his earlier favor, and Rose and Jack spend the last hour of the movie slowly moving toward the back of the sinking ship—the place where they had met just a few days before. They barely survive the *Titanic*'s final plunge beneath the waves and share a last good-bye before Jack freezes to death in the frigid waters of the North Atlantic. Rose is rescued, but when tempted to resume her former life by joining her fiancé—who has survived by claiming a small child as his own and using this excuse to join one of the few lifeboats *Titanic* manages to launch before it sinks—she hides. She tells a questioner that her name is Rose Dawson—giving Jack's last name, not her own. Love has survived tragedy.

Whatever the merits of this story—and it is told effectively, with good acting and stunning special effects—it is hardly unique or innovative. Accordingly, something else must account for its popularity. As will be seen, much of the film's success derives from the ways the values of American public culture emerge in the movie. They provide a transparent foundation on which others can build their interpretations of the film's significance in their own lives.

At least part of the movie's appeal lies in the everyman-versus-privilege story, for example. Despite being a poor, working-class kid, Jack is romantic, loving, engaging, poetic, artistically talented, self-sacrificing, heroic, and, above all, happy. Jack is self-made, self-confident, and successful in the most important ways: he risks his own life to save Rose, jeopardizes his personal safety to maintain a relationship with her despite threats and humiliations, tries to save several passengers (including children) as the *Titanic* sinks, and insists to his last breath that Rose must live, no matter what. By contrast, despite his supposedly superior parentage, Rose's fiancé, Cal, is shown to be deceitful, manipulative, and unconcerned about Rose or the young child he claims is his in order to escape in a lifeboat. (He hands the child off the second he takes his seat.) He orders his butler to kill Jack. Whereas Jack is a skilled artist, Cal has no interest in art or other social finery. Having money, clearly, is not the same thing as having class.

Not only is having money not the same as having class, but it also undermines the development of human character. Cal is not the only character whose life of privilege has served to promote personal selfishness. Rose's mother is horrified by the thought of a life without wealth and essentially prostitutes Rose to Cal to ensure the family fortune. She slaps Rose when she finds out about her relationship with Jack. Similarly, most of the first-class passengers treat Jack badly when he is invited to a dinner party. By contrast, the one first-class passenger who treats Jack with dignity and mocks the values of the supposed upper class has middle- or working-class origins. The character Molly Brown, based on a real woman later called the Unsinkable Molly Brown for her actions as the *Titanic* sank, treats Jack with dignity and shows real courage in pushing her boat mates to return to the sinking ship to try to rescue dying passengers. Meanwhile, her supposedly superior upper-class lifeboat mates are paralyzed by fear.

Rose finds a different reception when she joins Jack on the lower decks. She is immediately embraced and immersed in a web of dancing, friendship, and shared food and drink. The working class seems authentic, sincere, honest, and decent. By extension, then, there is no need for Jack or the members of *Titanic*'s audience to envy others' wealth. Such jealousy might, of course, encourage the audience to favor strong welfare policies or high taxes—after all, if the rich are idle and vain while the workers are decent and caring, why should the rich get to keep their money? In *Titanic*'s telling, however, the rich deserve pity more than envy. Wealth is better avoided.

As discussed in chapter 1, the sense that class is not the key to happiness or even a guarantee of good behavior is central to American public culture. Jack lives by his wits, uncorrupted by the luxuries of wealth. He may be working-class, but he has a heart of gold. He will clearly be successful and happy wherever he might go. Cal, of course, will never be happy, and indeed the film notes as it closes that Cal kills himself during the Great Depression. A central theme in the film is thus that class—the control of wealth—is unimportant. Indeed, class provides no constraints on either behavior or opportunity: since Jack can win Rose's heart, the barriers of class mean nothing.

Jack's story also emphasizes the moral importance of the individual in human life. Jack is a plucky, optimistic individualist. He gains admission to the ship through his own wits and talents, figures out how to stop Rose's suicide attempt, charms his way onto the first-class deck, and is even invited to a formal dinner (he attends wearing a borrowed tuxedo, which, since this is a love story, fits perfectly and looks dashing). He has only his talents and his intelligence. With them, however, he establishes a rapport with most of the first-class passengers and gets invited back again and again, despite the disapproval of Rose's family and fiancé. Ultimately, Jack and Rose only survive the *Titanic*'s final plunge beneath the sea because Jack reminds Rose to never quit and always struggle against the ship as it pulls her into the deep. This same pluck lets her survive and call for help as everyone else around her freezes to death. Likewise, Molly Brown's spunky character, formed outside the halls of privilege and sloth, makes her heroic. Individuals, not social backgrounds, matter.

Titanic's popularity rests at least in part on the values and variables of American public culture. The irrelevance of class, the importance of individualism, the lure of capitalism, and the distribution of talent across society are all foundations of American civic culture. In reflecting them, *Titanic*'s story reached out to the world. The world responded.

BLADE RUNNER: THE EMPTINESS OF CONSUMER CAPITALISM

Ridley Scott's 1982 film *Blade Runner* offers a strikingly different vision of American life and civic values than either *Titanic* or *Guardians of the Galaxy*. Never as popular as the other two films described in this section—*Blade Runner* only garnered $33 million in the U.S. market when it was released—the film has gone on to become a cult classic in its dystopian vision of a globalized future.[15] Yet its imagined dystopia derives every bit as much from the content of American public culture as the other two films discussed above. It simply offers a negative vision of the way American attitudes and preferences might play out over time. As such, it provides useful insight into why some people might react negatively to the values presented in American popular culture.

In the world of *Blade Runner*, society has been transformed into a disconnected mass of polyglot consumers with no evident purpose or goal other than consumption. The film is set in a future Los Angeles where it always rains, a setting that serves as a powerful symbol of the general alienation that characterizes the mood of the film, as humans have managed to change even the environment from its natural state.

Blade Runner hinges on the actions of a police officer, Deckard (Harrison Ford), who works in a special unit designed to track down and kill androids (called replicants) who return to Earth. In this future, humans have begun to colonize other worlds. Androids perform much of the dirty work of colonization, be it working in hostile environments, fulfilling the needs (including sexual needs) of human workers, or serving as soldiers in various wars. Most of the time this is a good deal for humans: machines take on much of the hard, dangerous work of colonization and combat.

The replicants are sentient, however. They are aware of the moral implications of the things they do. They are also aware of their own mortality: they have an internal clock that limits their lives to only a few years. *Blade Runner* tells the story of a group of replicants who return to Earth to confront their maker—the Tyrell Corporation and its genius owner, Dr. Tyrell—to force him to adjust their life clocks and extend their lives. Deckard works to find and kill them—a task he ultimately completes only because one of the replicants, Roy, chooses not to kill Deckard when he has the chance. Instead, in an affirmation of the value of life, Roy saves Deckard and then dies.

Blade Runner is striking in its lack of any direct examination of the politics and social life that ground its vision. It makes no reference, even obliquely, to a governing authority. Instead, viewers must tease out the film's lessons about a possible dystopic human future—which is its ultimate political point.

Of special importance in this vision is the dominance of the global/galactic megacorporations. Tyrell Corporation is clearly one of the megacorporations that run society. Its power is symbolized by its towering obelisk of a building that rises, along with those of other megacorporations, above the crowds and rain that now dominate a culturally and environmentally corrupted Los Angeles. Yet this dominance seems so well entrenched that no one finds it remarkable.

Deckard and his fellow agents seem to work largely at the will of the Tyrell Corporation. Their agency exists only to solve problems caused by Tyrell, and they kill replicants on crowded streets with little consideration for the safety of innocent civilians. Indeed, even Deckard never challenges the logic of his work: a problem exists that must be solved, and even when Deckard falls in love with a replicant and works to save her life, he never considers that laws might be changed to make Tyrell accountable for the problems it causes. No discussion ever occurs about the need to limit Tyrell's power either.

The social isolation of membership in a mass population is another important dimension of the vision of the future *Blade Runner* offers. The streets literally teem with people. Individuality is lost in the rain and decay of lower-level Los Angeles. One can buy artificial replacement body parts for only a few credits. No one appears to be going anywhere in particular or doing anything important. The endlessly circling electronic billboards that advertise cola and other products offer what action there is on the street. There is no other purpose in life beyond shopping.

An additional example of the anonymity of the masses is the language of the street. Most people speak an amalgamation of German, English, Japanese, and Spanish. The face and garb of the model on the floating billboard is clearly Asian, probably Japanese, and the mix of people on the streets constitutes a true melting pot. Styles, trends, languages, and ethnicities are all commodities to be exchanged and merged in a giant marketplace. Notably, most people pass each other without consideration or concern. Everyone is self-involved to the exclusion of any sense of community or the common good.

The anonymity and isolation of *Blade Runner*'s streets highlight the irony that, while it is possible to buy other forms of artificial life (eyes, pets, and the like), artificial humans, the replicants, are banned from Earth. Only humanoid replicants are bad. Everything else is acceptable, regardless of its artificiality.

Blade Runner thus offers a vision of the dark side of American public culture. Individualism inspires isolation, not participation. People are anonymous, not engaged. There is no exceptionalist crusade to make things better and spread truth and justice, because there is no group, organization, or government with any kind of social conscience with which to work if one desires to make the world a better place. At the root of all this empty existence is the dominance of consumer capitalism. When freedom becomes the freedom to shop for whatever one might like (including life itself), life holds no meaning or value. When liberty becomes nothing more than the freedom to choose from a series of options on the shelves of street vendors, it is an empty concept.

AMERICAN TELEVISION

This section examines three programs: *Star Trek*, *CSI*, and *Breaking Bad*. *Star Trek* offered perhaps the single clearest example of an idealized vision of American culture leading to universal happiness. *CSI* shows its global audience a technology- and violence-heavy take on American "justice," at least as filtered through the lens of a crime procedural melodrama. And *Breaking Bad* presents as searing an indictment of capitalism and the cruelties of American individualism as perhaps ever broadcast on American television screens.

THE UNIVERSE OF *STAR TREK* AND THE UNIVERSE ACCORDING TO *STAR TREK*

Star Trek, originally broadcast on NBC from 1966 to 1969, was a ratings failure in its original run. It has since grown into a global phenomenon. Its episodes have been rebroadcast for decades, its fans have developed a global subculture, and its creators have spun off thirteen movies and four television series from the original series. Combined, the films have generated over $1 billion in sales in the U.S. market alone; the eleventh film, a reboot of the old series with an altered timeline and changed sequence of events, sold nearly $128 million in tickets overseas the year it was released.[16]

Star Trek's creator, Gene Roddenberry, described the show as *Wagon Train* to the stars. *Wagon Train* was a 1950s-era television series chronicling pioneers crossing the American West. Its stories fleshed out the histories and continuing adventures of the people seeking a new life on the frontier. Similarly, *Star Trek* used its episodes to explore both the mysteries of meeting new species and encountering new phenomena in space while also addressing the interpersonal tensions among the crew of the "space wagon," the starship USS *Enterprise*, as they push the boundaries of the human experience.

There are countless reasons for the long-term popularity of *Star Trek*. Many of its stories are now classics of science fiction, and characters like Captain James Kirk, Vulcan science officer Mr. Spock, and Dr. Leonard McCoy have become cultural icons. Another reason, one particularly illustrative for a cultural analysis of the series, lies in its vision of a globalized, ethically driven, rights-respecting, democratic future—an idealized American culture made manifest on a galactic scale. For example, *Star Trek* takes place in a well-developed political-social context: the Federation. The Federation—formally titled the Federation of Planets—is organized along classic federal principles: each member planet has broad discretion to enact its politics as it pleases; however, the central authority does hold certain powers through which it can establish and enforce peaceful relations and protect the safety of its members from both internal and external threats. Kirk, Spock, and McCoy serve the Federation as members of Starfleet, the Federation's military arm.

The parallels with American federalism extend beyond the name and existence of a central governing body. In addition to electing representatives to the Federation's governing body, planetary members elect a president and a Federation council. These leaders make policy that is then ratified (or not) by the Federation's elected officers. These officials operate in the context of the rule of law and are bound by their oaths to respect the rights of all people to self-determination. In fact, the expectation that officials must follow the rule of law is a core element of many plots of the series' television episodes and feature films. In many ways, then, the Federation manifests the ideals of American democracy in actual practice. The world of *Star Trek* expresses the ideals at the core of American public culture.

Star Trek also imagines a human future that mirrors the spread of Europeans across the American continent. When human beings invent warp technology, which allows them to travel faster than the speed of light, they set out—like the Puritans coming to America—to bring their way of life to the galaxy at large. After a slow process of exploration, interaction with other species, and wars, humans sponsor the creation of the Federation. This coalition of species and cultures shares relatively common values and political practices, and its members work together to promote and defend their ideals against internal threats, like officials and others who would use their power for their own good, as well as external threats, like political and military competitors such as the Romulans and the Klingons. In its political, military, social, and economic dimensions, the Federation is a shining symbol of the capacity of technology, integration, and procedure to bring nearly universal benefits to all who embrace the Federation's vision.

At the core of this ethical expansionism is a concept the show's fans developed only after the original series went off the air: infinite diversity in infinite combinations, or IDIC. Acceptance of IDIC enables the many cultures of the *Star Trek* universe to respect each other's cultural practices and values while working together in a collective, healthy way. Many *Star Trek* plots deal with struggles to accept others and explain when it can be appropriate to intervene in diverse cultures.

The *Star Trek* vision of a global—indeed galactic—democratic future is profoundly optimistic, mirroring the claims of contemporary globalists. People are not displaced by technology; they are empowered by it. Disruptions to a former way of life do not cause pain; they are liberating. There are no fundamental tensions among cultures and communities; instead, virtually all problems that arise at the intersection of cultures can be resolved successfully. Life in the Federation is not simply rich; it is rewarding. Technology and politics work to free people from pain, want, and repression.

This vision of the relationship between globalization and democracy is as pure an example of American public culture made real as ever presented in popular culture. Tolerance promotes order, growth, opportunity, and education; democracy and a respect for rights ensure freedom; and individuals pursuing dreams leads to social harmony. The world of *Star Trek* is that of an idealized America projected onto a galactic stage.

CSI: VIOLENCE, TECHNOLOGY, AND AMERICAN "JUSTICE"

CSI—short for "crime scene investigation"—is one of the most popular programs in global television history. The original series, simply named *CSI*, was set in Las Vegas and ran on CBS from 2000 to 2015. Heavily franchised, the original series spawned many spin-offs, including *CSI:*

Miami, *CSI: New York*, and *CSI: Cyber*. The original series was rated as the most popular television series in the world five times between 2005 and 2012. Its companion show, *CSI: Miami*, earned the same recognition during the same period. (The only non-*CSI* show to be named most popular global TV show in this era was the medical procedural *House*.)[17]

The basic plot line of any *CSI* episode can be summarized quickly. Some crime is committed. The CSI team is sent to investigate. Its members use their investigative skills—and an impressive array of technologies—to identify the perpetrator. The perpetrator is (usually) caught because of the hard work of the CSI investigator. Justice, after various twists and turns, is served.

At least part of *CSI's* appeal lies in its similarity to a big-budget action adventure film. The show is shot with very high production values, excellent computer-generated images, and relatively simple story lines that almost anyone anywhere can understand. Its episodes are filled with pulsating music and video montages that express meaning and advance the plot with limited need for words—which, since they are usually in English, might not always be understood by a global audience. *CSI* is a televised blockbuster, just like *Guardians of the Galaxy*.

Moreover, like *Guardians*, *CSI* is awash in violence. The crimes investigated are typically violent ones, often depicted in explicit detail both in the story setup and in the investigators' computer re-creations. Bullets penetrate skin; bones crack; gore flies, often from multiple perspectives in endless playback. None of this requires either a sophisticated understanding of American law or American English to understand. The violence is both lure and reward: it brings you into the story and keeps you paying attention throughout the program's duration.

CSI is also notable for its high-tech appeal. The CSI investigators always have access to whatever piece of equipment they might need whenever they might need it. Much like a science fiction movie, *CSI* imagines a future in which technology can solve almost any problem quickly and definitively. This isn't true, of course: most real-world investigators don't have access to every machine they might need even if their departments have one in the first place. Moreover, most forensic tests are not as conclusive as *CSI* shows them to be. But never mind: some magic test that is both available and accessible can usually find the perpetrator.

If, by chance, technology cannot solve the problem of the night, *CSI* teaches that hard work by dedicated individuals can. Many episodes of *CSI* feature a plot line in which some barrier or other stands between the investigator and the truth. This might be anything from a savvy perpetrator too smart to confess, to an administrator reluctant to authorize an expensive test for just one case, to the simple backlog of cases clogging America's courts and police departments. The law itself can be a burden as well since U.S. criminal procedure constrains police and at least attempts to protect suspects from abusive prosecutions. Whatever the reason, however, *CSI* regularly shows its investigators cutting deals and leveraging relationships with agents in other departments to advance their case in the system. Individual effort and creativity are the keys to success.

This emphasis on individual work and achievement also exposes *CSI*'s dark side. At times CSI investigators actively defy legal standards to close a case and get to the truth. They are—or can be—justice vigilantes: they regularly violate the law in the name of the law. Thus, rather than seeing themselves as part of a legal system, accountable to society, CSI investigators all too often seem to act as the law itself. Nothing matters more than their individual success—including the rights of the accused and the integrity of the legal system.

Whatever the mistakes of its agents, *CSI*, like most big-budget Hollywood films, can also be counted on to offer a happy ending—at least most of the time. Whether through technological superiority, careful manipulation or abuse of the law, the hubris of the perpetrator, or the hard work of the investigator, bad guys usually get caught in *CSI*'s universe. The innocent, by contrast, go free. Justice—at least as imagined by *CSI*'s writers—is the result.

BREAKING BAD: EVERYTHING IS FOR SALE

Breaking Bad ran for five seasons, from 2008 to 2013, on AMC, a cable television channel in the United States. Lauded as one of the best television programs ever made, the series chronicles the life of a high school chemistry teacher with a genius IQ who, on learning that he has a severe case of lung cancer that his insurance company will not cover, turns to a life of crime to pay for his treatment and establish his family's financial security after his death. A hit in the United States,

Breaking Bad became a global phenomenon as it was streamed online around the world.

In many ways, *Breaking Bad* offers a classic, Horatio Alger–informed take on hard work and the American dream. Its "hero," Walter White, is an incredibly skilled chemist: at one point he had been involved in a technology start-up company that made his cofounders millionaires. White, however, left the company before it struck it rich and turned to teaching high school chemistry to earn his living. He supplemented that work with a part-time job at a local car wash. When he finds out about his diagnosis and prognosis, White sets about using his skills to ensure his family's future (and perhaps his own survival) by using his chemistry skills to build what amounts to a new start-up company providing chemical products to a large clientele. In so doing, White faces many of the same challenges other start-up entrepreneurs face as they build their businesses: competition, the need to grow while protecting quality, financing operations and investing proceeds, and even dealing with personnel issues—managing people is always hard. White endures these hardships, makes alliances with helpful companies and colleagues, and builds a highly successful business that can, in fact, pay his medical bills and protect his family's future finances.

But, of course, Walter White's business is making methamphetamine, a powerful and addictive stimulant that is illegal to manufacture, distribute, and use in the United States—certainly when produced by nonregistered, private manufacturers. The problems White encounters as a start-up entrepreneur are thus amplified by the simple fact that he is the head of a criminal enterprise. White's competitors aren't the kinds of organizations that sue to protect patents and leverage their political connections to undermine a rival chain's chances to expand. They are (all too often) violent drug gangs—in the case of *Breaking Bad*, violent drug gangs importing methamphetamine from Mexico into White's hometown of Albuquerque. Therefore, his personnel problems include the risk of his employees being killed, or abusing the product they make, or failing to follow White's precise recipe for quality product. His finance and logistical problems involve acquiring sufficient materials to expand his operation while hiding both the intent of the purchase of the raw materials and the profits from the sale of his very successful drug-making operation.

Through it all, White succeeds. He outwits and outfights both drug lords and the corrupt corporate conspirators he partners with to mask his material purchases, to distribute his product, and to hide his profits (at one point, in an ironic twist, he buys the car wash at which he used to work and uses it to launder his drug earnings). He saves employees from error and protects the quality of his methamphetamine. He is an American success story—but his story cannot be told in public.

Along the way, Walter White, the underpaid and undervalued chemistry teacher, morphs into Heisenberg, the name White gives himself as ruler of his drug empire. Werner Heisenberg was a twentieth-century physicist perhaps best known for developing the Heisenberg uncertainty principle, the precept that when examining an atom, one can either know where an electron is at any given moment or the direction it is heading, but it is impossible to define both variables at once. Put very simply, the principle teaches that some things are random and cannot be controlled.

No matter how hard White/Heisenberg tries to control his affairs, then, no matter how hard he works to protect his family and promote his business, his efforts always fall a bit short. His health fails; his wife finds out about his criminal operation and leaves him; he gets his best friend (who happens to be a DEA agent) killed. He also becomes increasingly inured to the violence of the world in which he works: acts that would have shocked Walter White as he first moved into drug making (the death of a drug dealer, for example) don't bother Heisenberg—Heisenberg uses a bomb to destroy a rival by blowing up a retirement home. White has succeeded, but his success has very nearly cost him his soul.

Of course, *Breaking Bad* is an American program, so despite the dark meditation it offers on the impotence of the individual in the face of reality and the amorality of American capitalism, the series manages to end on a somewhat happy note. Having evaded capture by hiding out in New Hampshire for some time, White returns to New Mexico to rescue his longtime partner/collaborator, his former student Jesse Pinkman, who has been captured by a rival gang seeking to replace the Heisenberg operation with its own. White is wounded in the ensuing gun battle and dies just before he might have been arrested by the police. As he dies, Badfinger's 1971 hit "Baby Blue" carries him to his rest. (The song saw a 3,000 percent increase in sales downloads in the week following *Breaking Bad*'s finale.[18]) The moral is plain: he lived on his own terms and died on them as well.

AMERICAN MUSIC

It is not as simple to offer an extended analysis of the way American public culture manifests itself in popular music as it is in the case of American films and television. Individual pieces of music are usually quite short (to fit the time available on commercial radio), so the medium rewards brevity and simplicity rather than complexity. In addition, most songs, even when collected into albums, are rarely linked thematically in the way that television programs and films are. Consequently, individual pieces of music usually lack the substance to provide a solid foundation for analysis.

Rather than focus on a representative song or group of songs, the analysis offered here describes the evolution of the three forms of American music that have become the most important in global trade: country, rock, and hip-hop. While brief, each history highlights the roots of one of these forms and describes its genesis in the United States. Many performers not born in the United States have become famous and rich by performing in these genres, and of course there are many forms of music other than country, rock, and hip-hop. However, these three emerged in the United States and spread across the globe. They are American forms wherever and by whomever they may be performed.

THE CULTURE OF COUNTRY

Country music emerged first among the three types of musical forms addressed in this section. Country established its modern form in the 1920s and was the first music extensively broadcast on radio: WSM-Nashville began broadcasting the *Grand Ole Opry*, a weekly variety show featuring a combination of established and up-and-coming acts, in 1925. Its weekly broadcasts drew vast audiences across rural America, particularly in the South. The show's popularity led Victor Records in Bristol, Tennessee, to sign Little Jimmie Roberts and the Carter Family to recording contracts in 1927.[19] Country music was born.

Country is an amalgam of bluegrass, folk, Appalachian mountain, and Western cowboy music. While bluegrass and Appalachian mountain music are themselves derived from Celtic folk music, by the 1920s, Celtic forms had been transformed into a distinctively American sound. In terms of instruments, for example, country emphasized the twang of steel guitars and the distinctive tone of the Appalachian violin, often referred to as a fiddle. Acoustic sounds dominated in a world in which most people learned to play without electricity in their homes or communities. Multiple traditions of music combined with acoustic instruments to create a distinctive country sound.

Country music is also distinguished by its subject matter. Country has long prided itself on reflecting the lives of real people, particularly working-class, rural Americans. Country's songs have often chronicled the struggles of individuals as they try to make it in dead-end jobs, in difficult marriages, or through addiction to drugs or alcohol. Additionally, country regularly sings the virtues of hard work, traditional love, the glory of a loving family, and unabashed patriotism. The real America, country seems to say, is the one in which people struggle but take responsibility for their personal fates. Americans fight for their honor and dignity as ends in their own right.

These stories of individual struggle and sacrifice are mirrored by populist resentment of elites and others whom country artists define as undeserving of the benefits they enjoy. In keeping with *Titanic's* depiction of the upper class, country music usually insists that elites are wimps, sycophants, and otherwise "unmanly," to adopt a gendered phrase that captures what country music asserts. Big-city folks don't really love America, country songs opine, and poor people in urban areas just wait in welfare lines for handouts rather than hitching up their pants and getting to work the way that rural people do. The real, authentic America is presented as a country America.

The country music industry became centered in Nashville, Tennessee, by the 1950s. Aspiring artists wanted to get to Nashville to show their talents, and Nashville housed the recording studios for the major labels producing country music. More importantly, the Nashville recording studios developed "the system," a way of doing business that still operates today. In the system, labels hire songwriters full-time. The songwriters take the core themes and sounds of country music and shape them into three-and-a-half-minute hits. Country performers can then review these songs and choose the ones they want to record. Big stars can place holds on songs they like, reserving the right to record them in the future so that competitors cannot do so in the meantime. This system has made it possible for country stars to remain popular for decades. Country music flourished as songwriters fashioned new material that established stars could sell through the Nashville marketing machine.

The Nashville music machine has helped country music achieve global prominence despite the tight linkage of American culture and American country music. Country star Garth Brooks is one of the best-selling artists of all time, for example, and he is in fact the most successful solo performer in the history of recorded music.[20] The industry draws performers from many foreign nations, including Australia and Canada, and country-themed clubs exist in places like London and Paris. Cover bands perform classic hits to delighted audiences across the world. Country has grown from humble roots to global prominence, all the while asserting its message about the authentic America.

IT'S ROCK AND ROLL

If country is the music of rural Americans, rock and roll is the music of America's suburban youth—especially middle-class whites. As a musical form, rock and roll is closely associated with the generation that rapidly expanded in the 1950s and 1960s and brought rock music along on the journey: the baby boomers, Americans born between 1946 and 1964. Rock and roll exploded onto the global music scene in the same period. The world has never been the same.

Like country, rock is an amalgam of other forms—including country. However, whereas country emerged from a combination of predominantly white forms of music, rock is an extension of music types popular among both whites and African Americans. In addition to white styles of music like country and folk, rock grew out of the blues music popular among African Americans and concentrated in big cities up and down the length of the Mississippi River, like New Orleans, Memphis, St. Louis, and, off on a branch, Chicago. African American musicians took the chord progressions popular in blues music and sped them up. They also took blues subjects—love, desire, yearning, and other emotions—and matched them to a driving beat. The music was built on electric guitars and drums rather than steel guitars and fiddles.

African American artists may have created rock and roll, but they did not popularize it. Most radio stations and recording companies, particularly those owned by whites, refused to record or play African American groups, usually because white audiences did not want to listen to black performers. The first generally recognized "rock and roll" hit song, "Rock around the Clock," was recorded by Bill Haley & His Comets in 1954. (Haley and his band were white.) Later, artists like Elvis Presley and Jerry Lee Lewis played important roles in introducing black music to white audiences. By the mid-1950s, rock and roll was a booming enterprise, making millions of dollars as a fast-growing teen audience enjoyed it.

Rock and roll was as much about lyrics as instruments and chord progressions. At its heart were energy, excitement, and rebellion. Rock musicians tapped into their fans' adolescent dreams and anxieties to offer brief but compelling stories of teen love (and love gone wrong), the hope for a better tomorrow, and the simple need to get up and dance. It was music of individual freedom and expression. Both the music and the culture that surrounded it seemed to reflect the needs and desires of the large generation of teenagers that rock and roll both appealed to and seemed to define as a generation.

Rock and roll had its critics, of course. It still does. At their core these critiques grew out of the same concerns long ago expressed by the Frankfurt School and mass society theory advocates. Put simply, the fact that millions of young people were attracted to rock music was taken as proof that rock and roll had (and has) a special, dangerous hold on young people. This fear was grounded in the coincidence that rock became popular at the same time the baby boomers filled America's schools and universities: rock, after all, expresses rebellion, energy, and individualism—as do teenagers. The causality seemed self-evident: as baby boomers rebelled against their parents' authority and society's rules, leading to the social changes of the 1960s, many parents and community leaders became convinced that rock and roll music played a role in fueling their rebellion. The notion that the reverse was true—that rock was popular because it expressed the angst that teenagers feel whether they listen to rock and roll or not—was generally not considered. Instead, parents and communities sought to limit sales of rock music and to control its performance—a phenomenon discussed in chapter 3. Its popularity became proof of its danger.

Whatever parents at the time desired, rock expanded across the world. The 1960s saw the so-called British Invasion, as British groups like the Beatles (still the best-selling group of all time despite having broken up in 1970) and the Rolling Stones mixed African American musical traditions like the blues with established rock styles to create what is today termed "classic rock." They helped spawn new generations of rock artists who explored rock with jazz overtones (Pink Floyd and the Grateful Dead, for example), operatic inflections (The Who and Pink Floyd again), and metal (Led Zeppelin and AC/DC). Rock became a global music phenomenon, with artists emerging from all corners of the globe, innovating new derivations like punk, grunge, and indie rock.

The core of rock's global success was its transparency. The yearnings, questions, and dreams of adolescence are universal. So, too, is the rebellion against authority that accompanies the establishment of one's individual identity. Rock and roll emerged as a compelling template based on which young people around the world could express their hopes and their fears. A musical form that grew in the unique cultural environment of the United States became global as a result. It is at the center of contemporary globalization.

DON'T STOP HIP-HOP

Hip-hop and its associated musical form, rap, is a relatively recent addition to music history. It was born in New York City as a fusion of African American, Jamaican, West African, and other forms. Crucially, it emerged in polyglot neighborhoods filled with immigrants and native-born Americans whose musical styles found new expression in the rhythms and lyrics of hip-hop. The first generally recognized hip-hop hit was the Sugarhill Gang's "Rapper's Delight" in 1979.

Fundamentally, hip-hop is an electronic musical form. Its genesis lay in the clubs of New York in which the DJs (pronounced "deejays"), the people who played the records that club patrons danced to, became stars because of the creative ways they mixed songs. They also drew note for developing the technique of scratching, which entails rapidly spinning a record backward and forward under the turntable's needle to create a distinctive sound. Hip-hop performances did not actually require the musician to play instruments. Instead, the music was often already recorded: the talent was in spinning the music and keeping the crowd excited.

DJs were usually accompanied by MCs (pronounced "emcees"), who introduced the songs, urged people to dance, and otherwise kept the party moving. In time, the role of the MC changed from just introducing songs to making up accompanying rhymes, stories, and lyrics. DJs, too, began to exploit electronic technologies to sample parts of songs and remix them with new beats. MCs could then make up new lyrics for these remixed songs.

As a style, hip-hop emphasizes heavy beats and interesting, creative rhymes. While hip-hop acts may have accompanying bands to provide the music for their songs, this is not essential. Instead, budding hip-hop stars need only a stereo on which to blast the rhythms they rhyme along with—or a good sense of rhythm that they can express using their hands or their voice. The simplicity of the instruments needed to create hip-hop music made it readily accessible to relatively poor, mostly urban teens. It also made it easy to come up with free-form compositions that could integrate the different styles of music wafting around big-city streets. Hip-hop quickly became the music of urban, usually African American, youth.

Hip-hop and rap expanded rapidly across the United States in the 1990s. Stars like Tupac Shakur and Public Enemy put out albums that became nationwide hits. Youth across America responded to the innovative rhythms and rhymes of hip-hop. This included white youth, who would in time become the largest consumers of hip-hop simply because they tended to be middle-class and as such generally had more discretionary income to spend on music.

Young people also reacted to the lyrics. Emerging as it did from the streets of major U.S. cities, hip-hop offered a trenchant critique of life in modern America. If country celebrated traditional values and patriotism and rock and roll energized the ambitions of a generation to change the world, hip-hop expressed the anger and frustration of a long-repressed community that had many grievances in what it described as a racist America. For example, Public Enemy's 1990 album *Fear of a Black Planet* continued the band's narrative journey, accounting for and describing the ways racism in America worked to repress African Americans. Hip-hop also reflected a raw form of street sexuality in which suggestive language was common. Other performers offered explicit accounts of their sexual desires and fantasies.

As happened when rock music exploded on the American landscape, a backlash followed hip-hop's emergence. Ironically, this reaction often manifested the racism that many hip-hop artists asserted was central to American life. Hip-hop, after all, was a disproportionately African American musical form, and its lyrics often complained about police violence against the African American community, along with poverty, drug dealing, and other features of life in the urban inner city that are usually seen as unattractive, dangerous, and scary. Not only were such issues inherently troubling, but the fact that African Americans, a group long viewed as outsiders by white Americans, were addressing these problems also frightened many people. The obvious conclusion, at least to so many unknowing adherents of mass society theory and the Frankfurt School, was that hip-hop was dangerous. It could corrupt the young. It could hurt children. Meanwhile, of course, no meaningful effort was made to address the problems hip-hop complained about. Instead, the black "other" had to be controlled.

It is going too far to insist that all resistance to hip-hop was racist, however. It is one thing to complain about police corruption and quite another to fantasize about killing cops and running a criminal organization—themes common in a style of hip-hop called gangsta rap. Many critics of hip-hop have also complained that hip-hop acts regularly demean women by reducing them to nothing but sex objects, particularly in music videos. In addition, an actual war broke out between purveyors of East Coast rap and their West Coast competitors. This war led to the shooting of Christopher Wallace, also known as Notorious B.I.G. or Biggie Smalls, and is alleged to have led to the death of early rap star Tupac Shakur in a drive-by shooting. Gangsta rappers took an obvious pleasure in presenting angry, defiant, and criminal personas to the public. Mainstream society may well have been racist, but the forms in which hip-hop presented itself, at least in some cases, played off that racism while reinforcing it at the same time.

Regardless of attempts to limit it, hip-hop spread rapidly both within and outside the United States. Hip-hop acts crossed genders, races, and finally international borders. There are thriving hip-hop industries in countries ranging from Japan to India to Turkey. Meanwhile, U.S. acts have achieved global prominence. Hip-hop formed in the unique cultural mix of major U.S. cities in the 1970s, but it did not stay there. As with country and rock before it, its themes, styles, and appeal transcended nationalities to become a worldwide phenomenon. The American form became a global one, with American artists and corporations at its center.

CONCLUSION

American popular culture, particularly as manifested in movies, music, and television programs, has a relatively specific content. American television shows, movies, and music inevitably emerge from the core variables of American civic culture. While the individual values evident in American public culture may be mixed in different proportions in different works and may even be used to paint a negative portrait of those values in some cases, these values substantially shape the message and meaning of television programs, music, and films. The products of American popular culture are further embedded in formulas and narrative conventions. These factors combine to define the Americanness of American popular culture as its products go out to the world.

NOTES

1. Ernest Gellner, "From Kinship to Ethnicity," in *Encounters with Nationalism* (Cambridge, MA: Blackwell, 1994), 39.

2. Allen McBride and Robert K. Toburen, "Deep Structures: Polpop Culture on Primetime Television," *Journal of Popular Culture* 29, no. 4 (1996): 181–200. All subsequent references to this research are from this source.

3. Conrad Phillip Kottak, *Prime-Time Society: An Anthropological Analysis of Television and Culture* (Belmont, CA: Wadsworth, 1990). All subsequent references are from this source.

4. Timothy Havens, "The Biggest Show in the World: Race and the Global Popularity of *The Cosby Show*," in *The Television Studies Reader*, ed. Robert C. Allen and Annette Hill (New York: Routledge, 2004), 442–56.

5. Scott R. Olson, "Hollywood Planet: Global Media and the Competitive Advantage of Narrative Transparency," in *The Television Studies Reader*, ed. Robert C. Allen and Annette Hill (New York: Routledge, 2004), 114.

6. Havens, "The Biggest Show," 451–52.

7. Daradirek Ekachai, Mary Hinchliff-Pelias, and Rosechongporn Komolsevin, "Where Are Those Tall Buildings: The Impact of U.S. Media on Thais' Perceptions of Americans," in *Images of the U.S. around the World: A Multicultural Perspective*, ed. Yahya R. Kamalipour (Albany: State University of New York Press, 1999), 265–78.

8. Dan Malachowski, "TV Dads: Real-Life Salaries Nearly $200,000," Salary.com, http://www.salary.com/tv-dads-real-life-salaries-nearly-200-000 (accessed March 1, 2012).

9. "Television and Health," Internet Resources to Accompany the Sourcebook for Teaching Science, California State University, Northridge, http://

www.csun.edu/science/health/docs/tv&health.html#influence   (accessed March 1, 2012).

10. Senator Orrin J. Hatch, Chair, Senate Judiciary Committee, Executive Summary, *Children, Violence, and the Media: A Report for Parents and Policy-makers* (Washington, D.C.: U.S. Government Printing Office, 1999), http://www.indiana.edu/~cspc/ressenate.htm (accessed March 1, 2012).

11. "Guardians of the Galaxy (2014)," The Numbers, http://www.the-numbers.com/movie/Guardians-of-the-Galaxy#tab=summary (accessed May 5, 2017).

12. Christian Sylt, "Disney Reveals Guardians of the Galaxy Was over Budget at $232 Million," Forbes.com, January 27, 2015, https://www.forbes.com/sites/csylt/2015/01/27/disney-reveals-guardians-of-the-galaxy-was-over-budget-at-232-million/#20df3e0a37c2 (accessed May 6, 2017).

13. Anita Busch, "'Guardians of the Galaxy' Slays Another Record: Hollywood's Biggest Onscreen Body Count," Deadline, October 4, 2016, https://deadline.com/2016/10/guardians-of-the-galaxy-on-screen-body-count-leads-list-deadliest-films-1201830495 (accessed May 6, 2017).

14. "All Time Box Office," Box Office Mojo, http://www.boxofficemojo.com/alltime/world (accessed May 6, 2017).

15. "Blade Runner," Box Office Mojo, http://www.boxofficemojo.com/movies/?id=bladerunner.htm (accessed May 10, 2017).

16. "Star Trek," Box Office Mojo, http://www.boxofficemojo.com/franchises/chart/?view=main&id=startrek.htm&p=.htm (accessed May 10, 2017).

17. "Most-Watched TV Show in the World Is 'CSI: Crime Scene Investigation,'" *Huffington Post*, June 14, 2012, http://www.huffingtonpost.com/2012/06/14/most-watched-tv-show-in-the-world-csi_n_1597968.html (accessed May 6, 2017).

18. Michael Gallucci, "Badfinger's 'Baby Blue' Super-Popular Thanks to 'Breaking Bad' Finale," Ultimate Classic Rock, September 30, 2013, http://ultimateclassicrock.com/badfinger-baby-blue-breaking-bad-finale (accessed May 6, 2017).

19. "Birthplace of Country Music: A Local Legacy," America's Story from America's Library, http://www.americaslibrary.gov/es/tn/es_tn_bristol_1.html (accessed May 10, 2017).

20. "Top Artists (Albums)," Recording Industry Association of America, https://www.riaa.com/gold-platinum/?tab_active=top_tallies&ttt=TAA#search_section (accessed May 10, 2017).

CHAPTER 3

THE GLOBAL SCOPE OF AMERICAN MOVIES, MUSIC, AND TELEVISION

This chapter focuses on the global spread of American movies, music, and television programs. It analyzes how the audiovisual (AV) popular culture industry developed as it has and assesses the global dominance of American AV culture. It also examines the types of American AV culture that play a particularly important role in contemporary globalization. As is discussed in detail in chapter 5, these pervasive, message-rich AV media play a very significant role in globalization today.

Before exploring this issue in detail, however, it is important to note here that a countercase can be made that, because of the hybrid way in which a great deal of AV entertainment is produced today, "American" movies, music, and television aren't that American at all. As a practical matter, much filmed programming (whether movies or television programs) seen worldwide today is made in a truly global marketplace. Independent producers seek studio financing from wherever they can find it. They seek to lower production costs by searching for international actors, venues, and markets for their films, and the behind-the-scenes talent that supports film, television, or music production might have offices all over the world and personnel who meet only digitally, not physically. In such circumstances, it is not necessarily the case that a movie or television show will be purely American.

To offer an empirical example of this conundrum, consider the *Pirates of the Caribbean* franchise. *Pirates of the Caribbean* has become one of the most globally successful movie series of all time, occupying three of the top fifty slots for highest-grossing films in history.[1] (Multiple offerings of other franchises like *The Lord of the Rings*, *Harry Potter*, and *Star Wars* fill many of the other slots in the top fifty.) The *Pirates* franchise is based on a ride at the Disney theme parks—and Disney, as discussed below, is one of the most important globalizers of American popular culture. Accordingly, *Pirates* might be seen as an American product, infused by the Disney ethos from which it was born.

Yet, as filmed, the *Pirates* movies have no particularly American content. They star Americans like Johnny Depp but also British citizens like Keira Knightley. They are set in colonial times (at least in the U.S. sense of the word "colonial"), but none of their themes or story lines seem to obviously express an American sensibility. Hence it is possible to consider the *Pirates* movies not as American but as international—carefully calibrated to meet the demands and desires of a global audience while void of meaningful, culture-specific content.

Accordingly, assessing what is or is not an "American" popular culture product is a judgment call. Here, several criteria are used: the nature of the financing, the locale, the nationalities of the central characters or performers, and the type of artifact (e.g., big-budget blockbuster, rock performance, and so on). It is therefore possible for pop culture products to be international in performance or financing but American in form and content. Indeed, such hybridity is, today, the norm rather than the exception. (As an aside, and to return to the earlier example, by this rubric the *Pirates of the Caribbean* films are not considered "American" movies in this book.)

THE MOVIE, MUSIC, AND TELEVISION
MACHINE IN THE GLOBAL ERA

Most popular AV culture produced today is made or otherwise controlled by a select group of popular culture–producing corporate giants. Moreover, while not all AV popular culture is controlled by American-based corporations, as will be seen later in this chapter, the early U.S. dominance in the creation of movies, music, and television programming has served to create conditions in which much of the global trade in popular culture is done in genres created in the United States under labels traditionally associated with American companies and performers.

Two concepts have been crucial to this concentration of power and control: synergy and convergence. The term *synergy* describes the vertical and horizontal integration of entertainment companies and the products they market. For example, when the same company that produces a performer's album also owns a venue like a radio station on which to play and thus market the album, synergy is said to exist. Synergy is enhanced when the company can also place the song in a popular television program it produces or make it the theme song for a movie it has financed. Multiple marketing outlets reach different audiences to hopefully increase sales. This serves to concentrate profit in the controlling company and lets the company spread the risk of creating a movie, an album, or a television program across an array of businesses: a movie might not make money in the theaters, for example, but it may sell and rent well enough in the post-theater market that, if the same company that produces the movie also controls the companies that produce and rent the videos, it can earn a profit.

Janet Wasko explored the way synergy drives contemporary popular culture in "The Magical Market World of Disney." In rolling out the 1997 animated film *Hercules*, Disney created a vast array of tie-ins, cross-promotions, and marketing opportunities to advertise and monetize the film beyond the movie theaters in which it was shown. Before the film premiered, Disney placed trailers advertising it in theaters at Christmas and on videocassette copies of *Toy Story* and *The Hunchback of Notre Dame*. In February, before the film's summer release, Disney sponsored a twenty-city, five-month tour of U.S. shopping malls at which a variety of attractions promoted *Hercules*'s coming premiere. Atlanta, Georgia, mayor Bill Campbell read a proclamation from the governor declaring a statewide "Hercules Day." Disney also created an ice show, *Hercules on Ice*, to promote the film. It played in twenty-eight cities, netting 310 performances over five years.

Meanwhile, *Hercules* also provided Disney's marketers with the opportunity to market toys, tie-ins, and other *Hercules*-themed items. Wasko reports that nearly one hundred manufacturers produced officially licensed *Hercules* merchandise, encompassing six to seven thousand products. Book shoppers could choose among fifteen different *Hercules* publications and then stop in at McDonald's (a film sponsor) for a *Hercules* plate. *Hercules* music was easy to find, and Disney created a themed website to support the movie as well. Disney also leveraged its ownership of the ABC television network to show a *Hercules* introduction/marketing special as the movie opening neared. As Wasko quotes a Disney executive, "It's a unique attribute of the Disney company, the ability to create synergy between divisions, whether it's interactive games, Buena Vista television, or the Disney Channel. We all work together and we do it on a year-round basis and we do it aggressively. The success of those ongoing roles makes everything in the company work better. We actually have people in every division that are responsible for the synergy relationships of the company and every division has that. We take it very seriously. Disney CEO Michael Eisner takes it very seriously."[2] The movie was almost incidental to this marketing onslaught.

The term *convergence*, or *consolidation*, refers to the long process by which synergy in the entertainment industry was created, describing how the many companies and individuals who used to make popular culture have been reduced in number to the few corporations that control the trade today. Essentially, companies merged so that each could control enough products and have enough marketing and distribution opportunities to spread the risk of financing any individual project across many enterprises. If one expensive movie bombed at the box office, a large company might survive because other films, music, and television shows it produced could generate enough income to keep it alive. By contrast, if a film produced by a small company flopped, the company could easily fail. In the long run, then, only large corporations had the economic power to survive market competition, leaving the popular culture industry in the hands of only a few major producers.

Today, the bulk of audiovisual popular cultural products are financed, created, and marketed by a relatively small number of global corporations. While it is not possible to pin down every player in the global popular culture market, key players include Comcast, 21st Century Fox, Sony, Charter Communications, CBS/Viacom, and the Walt Disney Company. They control an array of film, television, and music production companies and labels, as well as other entertainment venues like theme parks, cruise lines, and websites. This control allows them to dominate the global production of popular culture.

Sony, for example, the giant Japanese corporation, is one of the largest movie studios in the world. Its holdings as of August 2014 included Columbia Tristar Motion Picture Group, itself composed of Columbia Pictures, Sony Pictures Classics, and Screen Gems. It owned Tristar Pictures as well. Its music holdings included Columbia and Epic Records, Legacy Recordings, Star Time International, RCA Records (Arista Records, Battery Records Black Seal, J Records, Jive Records, LaFace Records, Polo Grounds, and RCA Records), and Sony Music Nashville (Arista Nashville, BNA Records, Columbia Nashville, and RCA Nashville)—among many others. Sony also owned Sony Pictures Television and an array of global television networks. Sony, of course, is also the producer of the PlayStation video game system as part of its vast holdings in Sony Electronics and Sony Computer Entertainment America. It is a major force in the contemporary popular culture industry.[3]

Another major player in the global pop culture industry is likely unfamiliar to most but controls a substantial amount of television programming around the world: Charter Communications. Charter achieved this stature in 2016 when it purchased the media giant Time Warner, inheriting that company's vast global television holdings.[4] Via Time Warner, Charter Communications now owns a host of entertainment companies, such as HBO and Turner Broadcasting System, which itself controls television networks like CNN, TNT, and the Cartoon Network. Its film industry holdings include the movie production studios Warner Bros., New Line Cinema, and DC Entertainment. It can advertise programming in an array of publications ranging from *Time, Sports Illustrated,* and *This Old House* to niche magazines like *VW Camper & Bus* and many others. It might also promote or distribute its products through online platforms like NASCAR.com, PGA.com, or any of its other diverse array of Internet holdings.[5]

One of the most famous entertainment conglomerates is the Walt Disney Company. Built from a few cartoon characters first drawn in the early twentieth century, Disney has grown into a central corporate power in the global production of popular culture—especially that intended for use by children. Its film production holdings include Walt Disney Pictures, Touchstone Pictures, Marvel Entertainment, Lucasfilm, and Pixar. In music it owns Hollywood Records and Walt Disney Records. Disney is a major player in the television industry, owning partially or outright the ABC network, the Disney Channel (which has a global presence), SOAPnet, and the international sports powerhouse ESPN. Finally, it has a substantial Internet presence through its ownership of websites like the Baby Einstein store, Club Penguin, ESPN Zone, and the Disney Store. Disney even owns its own cruise line. Perhaps most important of all, it owns destination theme parks in California, Florida, France, Japan, and China.[6] It has a television channel in Russia.[7]

CBS and Viacom are technically separate companies that nonetheless deserve to be considered together. They were, in fact, once part of the Viacom network, and National Amusements, an umbrella organization that owns several movie theater chains, has a controlling interest in both companies. Taken together, CBS/Viacom own a significant number of companies that produce popular culture. Viacom, for example, focuses on the film and cable television industries. It owns the film production and distribution studios Paramount Pictures and Paramount Home Entertainment, as well as Paramount Vantage, MTV Films, and Nickelodeon Movies. In television, it owns or has a significant interest in thirty networks or cable/satellite channels, including MTV, Nickelodeon, CMT, VH1, and Comedy Central. It also owns the digital production house SouthParkStudios.com.[8]

Notably, the company also controls the *Star Trek* franchise, which spans thirteen feature films, five television series, and innumerable books, magazines, and collectable paraphernalia. In 2012, one source estimated that its combined revenues have exceeded $100 billion since *Star Trek*'s inception in the 1960s.[9] Its earnings can only have risen in the years since.

CBS, meanwhile, focuses on broadcast television operations as well as print publishing. The CBS network encompasses twenty-nine television stations and more than a hundred radio stations. CBS owns the CBS Television Network, including components such as CBS News, CBS Sports, and CBS Films. It also owns the Showtime networks and has a major presence in the print industry, owning Simon & Schuster's adult and children's publishing houses.[10]

21st Century Fox was spun off from Rupert Murdoch's News Corporation in June 2013. It controls the entertainment empire previously associated with News Corporation, most significantly the Fox label. 21st Century Fox owns twelve film production studios, including 20th Century Fox, Fox Animation/Blue Sky Studios, and Fox Searchlight Pictures. In television, it owns the Fox Broadcasting Company, Fox Sports, and twenty-nine broadcast television stations. It also owns an array of cable networks, including the Fox News Channel, Fox Kids Network, Fox Sports, FX, and the National Geographic Channel. Its Fox International channel holdings have three hundred channels across four continents broadcasting in forty-four languages; STAR India counts thirty channels broadcasting in seven languages.[11]

Comcast, like Charter Communications, is a relative newcomer to the status of global producer of popular culture. In 2011, Comcast completed the purchase of a 51 percent stake in NBC Universal, which it bought from the global megacorporation General Electric (GE). (GE divested itself of its holdings in NBC Universal in 2013.) Consequently, Comcast owns ten NBC-affiliated local news stations and sixteen Spanish-language Telemundo-affiliated stations. Comcast owned forty-two cable television channels as well, including Bravo, CNBC, MSNBC, Syfy, and the Weather Channel. It owned the NBC television network, NBC Universal Domestic Television Distribution, and NBCUniversal International Television Distribution. It owned Universal Pictures and Focus Features and had majority control of Universal Parks and Resorts and Universal Pictures. It even owned sports franchises like the Philadelphia Flyers.[12]

Not all AV popular culture is produced by these firms, of course. However, as suggested by the partial listing of the various companies that each of these corporations owns, a remarkable array of global AV popular culture is produced by a remarkably small circle of companies. These companies carry movie, music, and television styles largely created and promoted by Americans to the world.

THE DEVELOPMENT OF THE MODERN AMERICAN MOVIE, MUSIC, AND TELEVISION INDUSTRIES

This section traces the historical, economic, social, and political forces that led to the global rise of the American AV pop culture industry. It explores both why U.S. corporations had an advantage in the global competition for audiences and how the music, television, and film industries developed into their contemporary forms.

As this section will show, however, recent technological changes in the ways that AV products are made and distributed globally have worked to both expand and challenge American dominance in these pop culture forms. The digitization of AV products, both in their creation and their transmission to an increasingly Internet-connected, wirelessly linked world has provided American movies, music, and television products with access to global markets that no producer could have imagined at the height of the Cold War. The ease with which such products can be reproduced and retransmitted has also profoundly undermined producers' ability to generate profits from these media. The digital revolution, which hit music first and hardest, has the potential to restructure the ways AV popular culture is made and experienced. American producers may be better positioned than most other movie, music, and television program makers to adapt to this changed environment—but the pace and scope of the digital revolution may overwhelm any efforts to maintain historical modes of production, distribution, and profit.

WHY AMERICA? EXPLAINING THE RISE OF "AMERICAN" POPULAR CULTURE

Perhaps the first question that needs to be answered in any assessment of one group or community's dominance in a particular field is, why? Why was it possible for this group and not another to rise to such a position? After all, while American corporations and American forms of entertainment dominate the global AV pop culture industry today, it did not have to be this way. The first movie ever made that was recognizably a movie in the modern sense of the word was filmed in France, for example; had things worked out differently, Paris, not Hollywood, might well be the center of the world's film business today. Similarly, the first television broadcast was in London, and the first recordings of speech and music were made in Europe. At least in terms of origin, then, there was no logical or inevitable reason that the AV popular culture industry would be concentrated in the United States, especially in Hollywood, California.

The path that American popular culture took to global preeminence began in what might be termed the "American exception." The exception in question had to do with the relative lack of government regulation of the early tools of mass communication: first the movable-type printing press and then later technologies like radio and television. As discussed in detail below, American mass communication developed largely free of state regulation and control. This freedom—at least in comparison with the legal and political context in which the mass communication industries in Europe and similar regions grew—allowed American producers of popular culture to respond to market opportunities and demands largely without state constraints. American producers thus had much more flexibility to create content as they pleased for the markets they focused on.

WHY NOT EUROPE?

Given that Europeans invented the movable-type printing press well before Britain and Spain established permanent colonies in the New World of the Americas, and given that those countries (with France) held colonial control over much of the Americas for centuries, it would be reasonable to imagine that European countries would dominate the mass communication and popular culture industries. After all, they developed their systems first, and their colonial systems afforded them the opportunity to implant their ideas and their practices in the communities they governed. Yet this has not turned out to be the case.

To a large extent, the answer to the question of Europe's failure to establish its popular culture products as globally preeminent can be found in the fact that European states and other official institutions (like the Catholic Church) regulated and attempted to control their mass communication industries as tightly as possible. They, like later critics of mass communication, worried that unfettered access to newspapers, books, Bibles in languages other than Latin, and other artifacts of "popular" culture would undermine the political and social order of the day. Therefore, they imposed significant religious, political, and economic controls on printed materials almost as soon as printing was invented. Put simply, religious and political authorities of the time were afraid that the new media of print would be used to undermine the power of the state or the authority of church officials who claimed to interpret God's will. They would not allow their religious and political authority to be challenged in print. State authorities therefore passed and enforced laws defining what could and could not be printed, and they penalized violators with imprisonment and even death.

Printing freedom was further limited when Europe's printers formed guilds that controlled the industry and limited access to printing by establishing a system of extended apprenticeships. This had the effect of protecting the economic power of the few printers who were in the guild: if people wanted something printed, they had to go to one of the businesses that could operate legally and had to pay the price asked for the work done. While black markets for illegally produced items (e.g., vernacular Bibles, political texts) existed, meeting demand was dangerous. Printing therefore expanded slowly in most of Europe. Literacy and markets for the printed word grew slowly as well.[13]

Later, when the audiovisual industries like radio and television developed, most European states adapted the controls they had placed on print media to the new, electronic context. Governments imposed regulations on their AV industries with the intent of controlling citizens' access to information—especially information governments did not want them to have. Thus, governments used their power to regulate their airwaves to create state-sponsored radio and television broadcasters that offered programs the state deemed appropriate and acceptable. Additionally, many governments provided subsidies to their native film industries—exerting varying degrees of state control of the content of the films the state subsidized. Consequently, the AV industries in those countries developed in cooperation with, and sometimes under the direct control of, the political leadership of their respective nations.

The tight regulation of the AV industries across Europe (and elsewhere, for that matter, as audiovisual technology spread globally) effectively turned those industries into tools of state policy. Political leaders limited the freedom of mass communication industries to create and market products, preferring to insulate their citizens from ideas, attitudes, values, and behaviors that society's leaders deemed dangerous—

especially if elites considered those ideas dangerous to themselves. In other words, movies, music, and television programs became another means by which political and economic elites could manage society as they saw fit—by controlling the information their citizens got and the entertainments they enjoyed. The AV industries, in other words, were political: they served to promote specific political values. They were not, accordingly, market driven and opportunistic: the producers of state-sanctioned AV products did not have a significant opportunity to explore or experiment with popular culture products that might be enjoyed on a global scale.

THE AMERICAN EXCEPTION

In the United States, the printing and other mass communication industries developed very differently than they did in Europe. Occasional early efforts to regulate what was printed in the United States, as well as to limit access to printing technology through apprenticeship systems and taxes on paper, proved relatively ineffective. The United States' large geographic area and relatively weak central government meant that the state was unable to check the spread of mass communications in the face of a literate population seeking both religious and commercial publications. Consequently, printing spread rapidly throughout the American colonies. Literate, market-driven Americans sought Bibles, entertainment, and the opportunity to advertise their goods and services to the growing population that was quickly spreading across a large territory. Printing provided an ideal means to spread both the word of God and the world of consumer goods to the American people. Mass communication thus emerged as a means of both personal salvation and personal enterprise.

The twin forces of profit and proselytization would push the American mass communication industry to expand rapidly and to innovate to meet the needs of a diverse market. From 1790 to 1835, for example, the number of American newspapers grew from 106 to 1,258 (more than 1,100 percent), even though the U.S. population grew only 400 percent in the same period. The number of newspaper subscriptions per 100 households grew from 18 or 19 in the 1780s to over 50 in the 1820s. (Great Britain, for comparison, was much more heavily populated than the United States in this period but had only 369 newspapers in the entire country in 1835—only 17 of which were produced daily.[14]) In the United States, mass communication became an agent of both God and mammon, as individuals and entrepreneurs explored ways to use it for both their commercial and their ecclesiastical ends. It was not a tool of state power, at least not directly.

What was true for the printing industry was true for the AV industries that followed: telegraph, telephone, radio, recording, film, and television. In general, not only was there less regulation of American industries as compared to European ones, but the American economic and political environment supported the creative adaptation of AV technologies as they developed. For both legal and economic reasons, American mass communication industries were relatively free to develop and market whatever goods and services they thought would satisfy audience appetites. American producers could create whatever they thought would sell much more easily than European producers could. While American popular culture did not develop completely free of state sanctions, as discussed later in this chapter, it was at greater liberty to develop than was the case in most of the rest of the world. The mass communication industries in the United States therefore became individualistic, capitalist, and entrepreneurial. American popular culture production companies were, accordingly, well positioned to enter the international market as it developed in the nineteenth and twentieth centuries.[15]

At least one other factor in the rise to global preeminence of the audiovisual American popular culture industries deserves attention here: the interaction of the relative wealth of the American market for popular culture and the existence of a globally diverse audience for American movies and music within the United States itself. (Television had not yet been invented in the period under discussion.) The music and movie industries, as discussed below in some detail, rose in the late 1800s and early 1900s. This timeframe corresponded with a period of mass immigration to the United States. Millions of people from around the world came to the United States to pursue economic and other freedoms. At the same time, the United States saw a sustained period of economic growth (barring occasional but very severe recessions). Thus, the period combined great and increasing wealth with a remarkably diverse audience that both wanted to be entertained and could afford to spend discretionary income on "newfangled" products like recorded music and nickel movies.

As a practical matter, then, American popular culture producers had a strong economic incentive to do two things that would give them a substantial advantage in emerging as global providers of audiovisual entertainment. First, they had an incentive to make lots of movies and music. The market was large and insatiable. Market demand, then, pushed the AV industries to make lots of entertainments to fill this market. Second, the industries had to learn how to make music and movies that could appeal to what amounted to a global audience within the United States itself. As millions of immigrants moved to America, film and music makers had to learn to concoct stories that were appealing across a broad—indeed a global—audience just to satisfy the domestic American market. This era of mass immigration meant that no product capable of exploiting the market fully could be culturally opaque. Rather, as Scott Robert Olson has explained, such products had to be culturally transparent: they had to appeal across cultural boundaries.[16] They had to make cultural sense to large and diverse audiences just to be profitable in the United States alone. In time, this fact would inform the spread of U.S. popular culture outside the nation's borders: American products would be globally attractive even before they entered foreign markets. This interaction of the size of the American market, its cultural diversity, and the political and economic ability American producers enjoyed to make appealing products worked to promote American pop culture makers as the dominant force in the global market.

A BRIEF HISTORY OF THE MOVIE INDUSTRY

The first of the three great AV industries to be invented and eventually come under American dominance was the movie industry. While France was the first locus of the nascent movie industry, in time Hollywood emerged as the center of the film universe. Hollywood in turn helped spread American popular culture—indeed, American culture—around the world.

In the early days of filmmaking, individual entrepreneurs, not giant global corporations, dominated the industry. Tinkerers and inventors made short reel films of horses galloping or people running and jumping or other live-action events that would then be shown in nickelodeons at theaters and carnivals around the world. The first recognizable film, in the sense of being a story told over several minutes' duration, was Georges Méliès's *A Trip to the Moon*. It was made in France in 1902.

France's head start as the home of the film industry did not last long, however. The Edison Company quickly overwhelmed it. Inventor Thomas Edison's enterprise, already an international giant due to its founder's inventive prowess, combined the efficiency of mass production with the marketing advantage of a national and international corporation to turn movies into profit-making endeavors. The hundreds of short silent movies it produced became profitable and were watched by large audiences.[17]

Edison's film operations were in part responsible for another transition in the American film industry: its relocation to Southern California. Early in the 1900s, Edison leveraged his corporate power to create the Motion Picture Patent Company, a cartel that dominated filmmaking in New York and New Jersey. It used Edison's control of numerous film-related patents to determine who could access the film and other equipment needed to create a movie. Independent producers were largely excluded by Edison's monopoly.[18]

In response, numerous producers left the New York area and relocated to Southern California. Land there was relatively inexpensive, and the region's abundant sunshine opened moviemaking to outdoor landscapes as well as indoor sets. In addition, the courts in California did not always enforce Edison's patents and monopoly as aggressively as courts in New York and New Jersey did. The first California-based film studios opened in the early 1910s, and by the 1920s the international movie industry was concentrated in Hollywood.[19] A few companies, such as Universal, Metro Goldwyn Mayer (MGM), First National, and Fox controlled most of the industry. The bulk of the world's successful writers, directors, producers, and distributors made their living in Hollywood. Stars were signed to exclusive contracts to guarantee the studios profits on films showed at theaters they often owned. This combination allowed the studios to generate enormous profits, produce elaborate extravaganzas that no other nation's film companies could duplicate, and take control of the international movie industry. Indeed, by the end of World War I, American films were shown as much as 80 percent of the time on screens in other countries—particularly those that had not established quotas to protect their domestic film industries. By the 1930s, Hollywood earned 35 percent of its income from the overseas distribution of its films, two-thirds of which came from Europe.[20] During this same period, a commentator for the British newspaper *Daily Express* bemoaned that British movie audiences "talk America, think America, and dream America. We have several million people, mostly women, who to all intent and purpose are temporary American citizens."[21] As early as the 1930s, then, American films were internationally pervasive.

Hollywood maintained its global dominance of the film industry despite a major shock to its funding model in 1948. That year, the U.S. Supreme Court decided that the production companies' ownership of theaters constituted an unconstitutional restraint on trade—a monopoly. *United States v. Paramount Pictures*, known as the Paramount case, led to a significant change in the way movies were produced and distributed: divorcement. Under the terms of the ruling, Hollywood production studios had to sell—divorce—their theater chains. This change stripped the production studios of a major source of revenue: ticket sales. In response, the major studios reduced the number and quality of the films they produced, preferring to focus on a smaller number of likely blockbusters. This, in turn, allowed smaller, independent producers to emerge to fill the parts of the market the major producers had abandoned. In time, the major and minor producers developed a series of financial relationships, including one that remains common today: the distribution deal. The major companies could contribute some money, but not all, to independent companies that took responsibility for making specific movies. The major company then marketed and distributed movies it did not actually make. Profits, if any, were shared according to the terms negotiated in the contract.[22] Subsequently, most of these quasi-independent producers remained in Hollywood, where writers, directors, special-effects persons, lighting and stage designers, and other specialists required to make movies were, and still are, largely centered. They simply worked as independent contractors rather than as employees of the major production studios.

One consequence of the rise of the independent film producers and production companies was the introduction of a degree of economic vulnerability into making and distributing movies. Independent companies were, as a rule, much smaller than the major studios they replaced. Independent producers were thus much more vulnerable to the success or failure of individual movies. A big hit could make an independent a major player in the movie industry, while a flop could destroy it. Moreover, a hit could provide a company with the resources to buy another, weaker competitor, while a flop could make it vulnerable to a takeover. Many small producers collapsed and were swallowed up because of this vulnerability. A few major producers therefore came to dominate the industry.

In recent years, three technological developments in the distribution of movies have changed the economic model on which American movie industry dominance was built, in the process threatening the United States' role as the globally dominant film producer. These are videotapes, digital video discs (DVDs), and the Internet. The industry learned how to adapt to the first two and remain profitable. However, the Internet has posed new and ongoing challenges to the film industry, which it is just beginning to address. (All discussion of the effects of the new digital era on the movie industry will be included in an analysis later in this chapter of how the television and music industries have been affected as well.) Consequently, while the industry is dominated by a small number of producers today, this may change as the web alters the ways movies are financed and distributed.

Videotapes emerged in the 1980s and offered home consumers a smaller, cheaper, less sophisticated version of the taping equipment available to broadcasters and film producers. With videotape and a videocassette recorder (VCR), people could copy material from their television sets. This included broadcasts of previously released movies. Alternatively, consumers could watch tapes of films that they rented or purchased from distributors. In either case, videotape posed a significant challenge to the film industry, which had made most of its money on ticket sales in theaters since the industry emerged in the early 1900s. Now, with VCRs, people did not have to go to the theater. The movies eventually came to them. Ticket sales dropped, and numerous production houses struggled.

In time, the film industry adapted to the VCR and its electronic successor, the DVD. Some production companies signed contracts with video-rental firms to share profits and offer filmed content exclusively in one store or the other for some period, while others bought video distribution companies to add that stream of revenue to their portfolios. Movie companies began to market and sell videotapes, and later DVDs, of their products to the mass audience. In addition, a whole new industry of direct-to-video movies emerged, as filmmakers exchanged high-quality and expensive production values for the fast profits available from a cheap movie produced quickly and marketed to home viewers without expensive promotion campaigns. Companies that successfully negotiated the challenges and opportunities of the video era emerged stronger and bigger; other companies failed.

The economic twists and turns of the film industry have in large measure worked to create the modern film industry as it stands today. Major corporations have bought numerous other companies and entered into distribution deals with many others. While who owns what is subject to constant change, the basic long-term effect of the economic history of the film industry has been to leave it with only a few dominant producers that share the market with an array of minor, independent houses. Each new economic challenge changed which company was dominant in each era, but the overall trend reinforced the relative dominance of American producers and American forms of global popular culture.

In addition to these economic forces, certain social pressures have shaped the modern film industry. These emerge from the same sentiment that has engendered critiques of the tools of mass communication since their advent: many people resent and resist what they perceive as the power of movies to mold a society's culture. From the earliest days of film, many people have strongly opposed popular movies by arguing that they are culturally corruptive—dangerous to the moral order. For example, in 1909 *American* magazine worried that "four million people attend moving pictures theaters [sic], it is said, every day. . . . Almost 190 miles of film are unrolled on the screens of America's canned drama theaters every day in the year. Here is an industry to be controlled, an influence to be reckoned with." Likewise, in April 1916, *Outlook* insisted, "The version of life presented to him [the audience] in the majority of moving pictures is false in fact, sickly in sentiment, and utterly foreign to the Anglo-Saxon ideals of our nation." In April 1929, *Commonweal* complained, "And if the speech recorded in the dialogue [of talking pictures] is vulgar or ugly, its potentialities for lowering the speech standard of the country are almost incalculable. The fact that it is likely to be heard by the less discriminating portion of the public operates to increase its evil effects; for among the regular attendants at moving picture theaters there are to be found large groups from among our foreign-born population, to whom it is really vitally important that they hear only the best speech."[23] As popular forms of entertainment and communication, movies have faced criticism since they were first invented for failing to uphold high standards of conduct and values.

In an effort to forestall externally imposed censorship, in 1930 the major film producers created a production code under the leadership of former U.S. postmaster general Will Hays. It remained in force until 1968, when it was replaced with the ratings system in effect in the United States today. The Motion Picture Production Code effectively governed the behavioral and moral content of movies. For example, it controlled depictions of sexuality and violence in film, setting up a self-enforced censorship board for the industry. Likewise, the code mandated that characters with "good" values had to be victorious over those who were "bad." Consequently, the code pushed the studios to adopt acceptable formulas that they repeated again and again. In turn, the formulas proved to be box office gold. The "American" movie was born.[24]

Another round of social pressure hit the movies in the late 1940s and early 1950s. This was the result of McCarthyism and the Red Scare. During the Cold War, Hollywood found itself on public trial to prove its "Americanness." Actors, directors, writers, and others were called to testify before Congress—particularly before the evocatively named House Un-American Activities Committee—about whether they were, ever had been, or knew members of the Communist Party. Those who refused to testify or were identified as party members found themselves blacklisted and denied the opportunity to earn a living. Others, like Screen Actors Guild president Ronald Reagan, became politically active: Reagan joined the conservative wing of the Republican Party after testifying to Congress against many of his fellow actors and Hollywood professionals. (Reagan parlayed this experience into an active role in Senator Barry Goldwater's campaign for president in 1964, his own election as governor of California in 1966, and his election and reelection as president of the United States in 1980 and 1984.) Hollywood got the message: its films espoused anticommunism throughout the 1950s.

In 1968, amid changing social standards about issues like sexuality, the proper roles of women and minorities in society, and other contentious matters, the motion picture industry perceived it was likely to face another bout of pressure to regulate its products. In response, the Motion Picture Association of America created a ratings system for movies. This was intended to allow filmmakers to experiment with complicated adult themes while providing parents and community members with sufficient information to make informed choices about which films they and their children went to see. In effect, G and PG movies would tell safe, traditional "American" stories, while R-rated films might touch on topics and stories not otherwise allowed under the terms of the production code.[25] In time, a PG-13 rating was added for movies too violent or sexual for a simple PG label; likewise, an NC-17 rating was established for those films whose content was considered too mature for children to attend at all. (PG-13 films are not supposed to admit children younger than thirteen without parental or guardian permission; NC-17 films are not supposed to admit anyone under eighteen.) Notably, this effort at self-regulation has been only moderately successful: as the need to develop the PG-13 and NC-17 ratings suggests, filmmakers have continued to stretch the limits of what is socially acceptable in the movies.

The production code, the reaction to the Red Scare in the 1950s, and the imposition of voluntary ratings in the 1960s were particularly important to creating and sustaining the "American" movie. In large measure, the conventions and genres established in response to the code have survived to today. The pressures of these events worked to sustain the "American" movie well beyond the time it was an exclusively American phenomenon. Thus, even as foreign companies bought "American" production companies, they purchased the expertise and experience of filmmakers shaped by making American movies for a global audience. In turn, the early U.S. dominance of the industry let it establish many of the conventions and genres in which movies are presented worldwide. It also meant that the labels on many, if not most, of the films distributed around the world are associated with the United States, not other countries. Therefore, while movies may star non-U.S. actors, receive financing from outside the United States, or otherwise be global in production, they are often recognizably American.

So just how dominant are American movies on the global market? The most obvious measure of this is box office sales—that is, how much money films make, both in the United States and overseas. By this measure, American movies are globally dominant. As of the end of 2016, most of the top-grossing films of all time, worldwide, were made by

American or American-based studios, starred Americans, had themes and values recognizably in line with American public culture, or were set in a definably American locale. The list includes the all-time top-grossing film *Avatar*, with worldwide ticket sales exceeding $2 billion, as well as *Titanic*, two *Jurassic Park* movies, *Star Wars* (two of its seven parts), *The Lion King*, and *Captain America*. Moreover, as table 3.1 makes clear, not only were the films American, but in most cases they generated more sales overseas than they did in the United States itself. Twenty-seven of the highest-earning movies of all time can be seen to be "American" as described in chapter 1.

The "biggest earners" definition of global dominance is problematic for several reasons, however. First is the matter of inflation. As a practical matter, ticket prices have gone up over time. More recent movies may well generate a lot more sales in dollar terms but sell far fewer tickets than older movies did. This is even more likely given the premium price people pay today to attend 3-D and IMAX films—types of movies that did not exist until very recently. Sales may thus present a skewed measure of a film's popularity.

Moreover, in recent years, Hollywood and other major film producers have turned to franchise films as a core component of their annual offerings. Producers have preferred to reproduce known money makers rather than experiment with new films or characters. This has led to a profusion of big-budget action films that carry the same characters through various scenarios over and over again. The *Transformers*, *X-Men*, and *The Avengers* franchises all stand as useful examples of this phenomenon. Accordingly, the "highest-earning" movies are increasingly repetitive: the same film, or very nearly so, in different guises. Earning a lot of money may not be an appropriate measure of global presence in this environment.[26]

An examination of ticket sales rather than box office earnings offers a similar but usefully different insight into the prominence of American movies. *Avatar*, for example, is fifteenth on the list of tickets sold, at more than 97 million. *Gone with the Wind*, a 1939 classic set in Atlanta, Georgia, during the Civil War, is the most popular movie ever, at over 200 million tickets sold. The original *Star Wars* comes in at number two, with 178 million tickets sold, followed by *The Sound of Music* (not American but based on an American Broadway musical), *E.T.*, and *Titanic*. Notably, while only twenty-seven of the fifty highest-grossing

Table 3.1. All-Time Top Box Office Films, U.S. and International

Rank	Title	Domestic Box Office	International Box Office	Worldwide Box Office	Percentage (International)
1	Avatar (2009)	$760,507,625	$2,023,411,357	$2,783,918,982	72.7
2	Titanic (1997)	$658,672,302	$1,548,943,366	$2,207,615,668	70.1
3	Star Wars: Episode VII—The Force Awakens (2015)	$936,662,225	$1,122,000,000	$2,058,662,225	54.5
4	Jurassic World (2015)	$652,198,010	$1,019,442,583	$1,671,640,593	61.0
5	The Avengers (2012)	$623,279,547	$896,200,000	$1,519,479,547	59.0
6	Furious 7 (2015)	$351,032,910	$1,165,715,774	$1,516,748,684	76.9
7	Avengers: Age of Ultron (2015)	$459,005,868	$945,700,000	$1,404,705,868	67.3
8	Harry Potter and the Deathly Hallows: Part II (2011)	$381,011,219	$960,500,000	$1,341,511,219	71.6
9	Frozen (2013)	$400,738,009	$873,496,971	$1,274,234,980	68.6
10	Iron Man 3 (2013)	$408,992,272	$806,400,000	$1,215,392,272	66.3
11	Minions (2015)	$336,045,770	$831,199,596	$1,167,245,366	71.2
12	Captain America: Civil War (2016)	$408,084,349	$743,600,000	$1,151,684,349	64.6
13	The Lord of the Rings: The Return of the King (2003)	$377,845,905	$763,562,762	$1,141,408,667	66.9

(continued)

Table 3.1. *(Continued)*

Rank	Title	Domestic Box Office	International Box Office	Worldwide Box Office	Percentage (International)
14	Transformers: Dark of the Moon (2011)	$352,390,543	$771,400,000	$1,123,790,543	68.6
15	Skyfall (2012)	$304,360,277	$806,166,704	$1,110,526,981	72.6
16	Transformers: Age of Extinction (2014)	$245,439,076	$858,600,000	$1,104,039,076	77.8
17	The Dark Knight Rises (2012)	$448,139,099	$636,300,000	$1,084,439,099	58.7
18	Toy Story 3 (2010)	$415,004,880	$654,813,349	$1,069,818,229	61.2
19	Pirates of the Caribbean: Dead Man's Chest (2006)	$423,315,812	$642,900,000	$1,066,215,812	60.3
20	Pirates of the Caribbean: On Stranger Tides (2011)	$241,063,875	$804,600,000	$1,045,663,875	77.0
21	Jurassic Park (1993)	$395,708,305	$643,104,279	$1,038,812,584	61.9
22	Star Wars: Episode I—The Phantom Menace (1999)	$474,544,677	$552,500,000	$1,027,044,677	53.8
23	Rogue One: A Star Wars Story (2016)	$521,017,843	$505,714,843	$1,026,732,686	49.2
24	Alice in Wonderland (2010)	$334,191,110	$691,300,000	$1,025,491,110	67.4
25	Finding Dory (2016)	$486,295,561	$536,321,815	$1,022,617,376	52.4
26	Zootopia (2016)	$341,268,248	$678,654,735	$1,019,922,983	66.5

27	*The Hobbit: An Unexpected Journey (2012)*	$303,003,568	$714,000,000	$1,017,003,568	70.2
28	*The Dark Knight (2008)*	$533,345,358	$469,546,000	$1,002,891,358	46.8
29	*The Lion King (1994)*	$422,780,140	$564,700,000	$987,480,140	57.2
30	*Despicable Me 2 (2013)*	$368,065,385	$607,151,450	$975,216,835	62.3
31	*Harry Potter and the Sorcerer's Stone (2001)*	$317,575,550	$657,179,821	$974,755,371	67.4
32	*The Jungle Book (2016)*	$364,001,123	$599,900,000	$963,901,123	62.2
33	*Pirates of the Caribbean: At World's End (2007)*	$309,420,425	$654,000,000	$963,420,425	67.9
34	*The Hobbit: The Desolation of Smaug (2013)*	$258,366,855	$702,000,000	$960,366,855	73.1
35	*Harry Potter and the Deathly Hallows: Part I (2010)*	$295,983,305	$664,300,000	$960,283,305	69.2
36	*The Hobbit: The Battle of the Five Armies (2014)*	$255,119,788	$700,000,000	$955,119,788	73.3
37	*Harry Potter and the Order of the Phoenix (2007)*	$292,004,738	$650,939,197	$942,943,935	69.0
38	*Shrek 2 (2004)*	$441,226,247	$495,781,885	$937,008,132	52.9
39	*Finding Nemo (2003)*	$380,529,370	$555,900,000	$936,429,370	59.4
40	*Harry Potter and the Half-Blood Prince (2009)*	$301,959,197	$633,124,489	$935,083,686	67.7

(continued)

Table 3.1. *(Continued)*

Rank	Title	Domestic Box Office	International Box Office	Worldwide Box Office	Percentage (International)
41	The Lord of the Rings: The Two Towers (2002)	$342,548,984	$592,154,195	$934,703,179	63.4
42	Harry Potter and the Goblet of Fire (2005)	$290,013,036	$606,898,042	$896,911,078	67.7
43	Spider-Man 3 (2007)	$336,530,303	$554,345,000	$890,875,303	62.2
44	The Lord of the Rings: The Fellowship of the Ring (2001)	$315,544,750	$571,672,603	$887,217,353	64.4
45	Ice Age: Continental Drift (2012)	$161,321,843	$718,443,294	$879,765,137	81.7
46	Spectre (2015)	$200,074,175	$679,546,748	$879,620,923	77.3
47	Harry Potter and the Chamber of Secrets (2002)	$261,987,880	$616,991,754	$878,979,634	70.2
48	The Secret Life of Pets (2016)	$368,384,330	$507,573,978	$875,958,308	57.9
49	Batman v Superman: Dawn of Justice (2016)	$330,360,194	$537,800,000	$868,160,194	61.9
50	The Hunger Games: Catching Fire (2013)	$424,668,047	$440,200,000	$864,868,047	50.9

Source: "Worldwide Grosses," Box Office Mojo, http://boxofficemojo.com/alltime/world (accessed May 8, 2017).

Table 3.2. All-Time Ticket Sales

Rank	Title	Estimated Tickets	Unadjusted Gross	Year
1	Gone with the Wind	202,044,600	$198,676,459	1939
2	Star Wars	178,119,600	$460,998,007	1977
3	The Sound of Music	142,415,400	$158,671,368	1965
4	E.T.: The Extra-Terrestrial	141,854,300	$435,110,554	1982
5	Titanic	135,474,500	$658,672,302	1997
6	The Ten Commandments	131,000,000	$65,500,000	1956
7	Jaws	128,078,800	$260,000,000	1975
8	Doctor Zhivago	124,135,500	$111,721,910	1965
9	The Exorcist	110,599,200	$232,906,145	1973
10	Snow White and the Seven Dwarfs	109,000,000	$184,925,486	1937
11	Star Wars: The Force Awakens	108,115,100	$936,662,225	2015
12	101 Dalmatians	99,917,300	$144,880,014	1961
13	The Empire Strikes Back	98,180,600	$290,475,067	1980
14	Ben-Hur	98,000,000	$74,000,000	1959
15	Avatar	97,255,300	$760,507,625	2009

(continued)

Table 3.2. *(Continued)*

Rank	Title	Estimated Tickets	Unadjusted Gross	Year
16	Return of the Jedi	94,059,400	$309,306,177	1983
17	Jurassic Park	91,922,000	$402,453,882	1993
18	Star Wars: Episode I— The Phantom Menace	90,312,100	$474,544,677	1999
19	The Lion King	89,146,400	$422,783,777	1994
20	The Sting	89,142,900	$156,000,000	1973
21	Raiders of the Lost Ark	88,526,800	$248,159,971	1981
22	The Graduate	85,576,800	$104,945,305	1967
23	Fantasia	83,043,500	$76,408,097	1941
24	Jurassic World	79,049,200	$652,270,625	2015
25	The Godfather	78,922,600	$134,966,411	1972
26	Forrest Gump	78,614,600	$330,252,182	1994
27	Mary Poppins	78,181,800	$102,272,727	1964
28	Grease	76,969,200	$188,755,690	1978
29	Marvel's The Avengers	76,881,200	$623,357,910	2012

30	Thunderball	74,800,000	$63,595,658	1965
31	The Dark Knight	74,463,500	$534,858,444	2008
32	The Jungle Book	73,679,900	$141,843,612	1967
33	Sleeping Beauty	72,676,100	$51,600,000	1959
34	Ghostbusters	71,173,700	$242,212,467	1984
35	Shrek 2	71,050,900	$441,226,247	2004
36	Butch Cassidy and the Sundance Kid	70,557,900	$102,308,889	1969
37	Love Story	69,998,100	$106,397,186	1970
38	Spider-Man	69,484,700	$403,706,375	2002
39	Independence Day	69,268,900	$306,169,268	1996
40	Home Alone	67,734,200	$285,761,243	1990
41	Pinocchio	67,403,300	$84,254,167	1940
42	Cleopatra	67,183,500	$57,777,778	1963
43	Beverly Hills Cop	67,150,000	$234,760,478	1984
44	Goldfinger	66,300,000	$51,081,062	1964

(continued)

Table 3.2.   (Continued)

Rank	Title	Estimated Tickets	Unadjusted Gross	Year
45	Airport	66,111,300	$100,489,151	1970
46	American Graffiti	65,714,300	$115,000,000	1973
47	The Robe	65,454,500	$36,000,000	1953
48	Pirates of the Caribbean: Dead Man's Chest	64,628,400	$423,315,812	2006
49	Around the World in 80 Days	64,615,400	$42,000,000	1956
50	Bambi	63,712,400	$102,247,150	1942

Source: "Domestic Grosses," Box Office Mojo, http://www.boxofficemojo.com/alltime/adjusted.htm?adjust_yr=1 (accessed May 8, 2017).

movies were identifiably American, more American films populate the "tickets sold" list. Some thirty-four American films appear in this tabulation, even ignoring options like *101 Dalmatians* and *Fantasia* (Disney animation classics) as shown in table 3.2.

As might be expected, given the percentage of tickets purchased worldwide, American films dominate a surprising array of nations' moviegoing. One 2011 study, for example, found that of thirty-one countries examined, twenty-four bought more than 50 percent of their tickets for American movies. This included countries like Mexico, the United Kingdom, Germany, Russia, Brazil, Italy, Canada, Australia, the Philippines, South Africa, Taiwan, Singapore, and Venezuela. (The exceptions were India, China, France [barely], Japan, South Korea, Turkey, and Egypt.) It further found that of the twenty highest-grossing films of that year, all were at least partially produced by Hollywood studios; thirteen were entirely produced in Hollywood.[27]

The year 2011 offers a snapshot of a long-standing reality. American films took 85 percent of European film revenues in the early 1990s, for example, grossing $1.7 billion of total film receipts of $2 billion. This dominance occurred despite the fact that France alone produced an average of 150 movies per year during the same period—suggesting that American movies were vastly more popular than their local counterparts. Indeed, by the early 1990s, almost 60 percent of French spending on movies was for attendance at American films. For example, when the American megahit *Jurassic Park* opened, it occupied one-quarter of all movie screens in France. Likewise, in Germany, American movies grew from a one-third market share to two-thirds between 1972 and 1991. By the end of this time frame, American movies controlled more than 80 percent of the European market collectively. In return, European movies accounted for less than 2 percent of American ticket sales.[28] Thus, even in competition with European films in the European market, American movies expanded in popularity throughout the post–World War II era.

More recently, in 2007 American films made almost twice as much money in Russia as Russian-produced films did: 8.3 billion rubles ($325 million) as opposed to 4.5 billion rubles for Russian films. By 2010, the difference was even starker, with American films taking five times as much of the Russian market as Russian films did. Similar growth has occurred in China, despite Beijing's allowing only twenty foreign films into the country each year: in 2010, American films grossed $1.5 billion in sales.[29] Notably, China was projected to pass the United States in absolute number of movie screens by November 2016, offering just that many more opportunities for American movies to reach Chinese viewers.

Another way to consider the global popularity of American films is to explore which movies are most pirated (i.e., downloaded illegally). (The problem of piracy will be addressed later in this chapter and in chapter 5 as well.) The website NME.com reports that for 2016, the most pirated movies were *Deadpool, Batman v Superman, Captain America: Civil War, Star Wars: Episode VII—The Force Awakens, X-Men: Apocalypse, Warcraft, Independence Day: Resurgence, Suicide Squad, Finding Dory,* and *The Revenant.* Other than *Warcraft,* these are essentially "American" movies as described earlier.

However one examines it, then, American movies have a dominant global presence on the world's movie screens. As this chapter will show, this dominance is reflected on global television screens as well, since a large portion of global television programming consists of rebroadcasts of American films. Hollywood built American film dominance around the world.

A BRIEF HISTORY OF THE MUSIC INDUSTRY

Like the movie industry, the recording industry has faced a series of technological, financial, and social pressures that have led to its contemporary form. However, the history of the American recording industry cannot be understood only in terms of recorded music sales. The modern music industry is the result of both sales of recorded music and the emergence of radio as a form of communication, particularly once radio lost control of mass-market entertainments to television. It is therefore necessary to understand how the modern recording industry developed, in terms of both recordings themselves and how radio served as a venue to advertise and promote recorded music. In addition, music videos played on television would eventually become a means by which music was marketed around the world and so deserve attention in this section as well.

The recording industry is the product of Thomas Edison's invention of a "talking machine" in 1877. (Edison's patenting of this machine brought him the funds to move into the film industry a few years later.) This device used wax cylinders as the recording medium. Speakers or musicians shouted or played into an acoustic horn that scratched marks into the cylinder that could later be sensed by a needle and amplified through another acoustic horn into sounds loud enough to hear. Quality, unsurprisingly, was poor.[30]

Record players were marketed to consumers beginning in the 1890s. These early machines included the capacity for owners to record their own music or speech. Given the low quality of these recordings, however, a market quickly developed for prerecorded discs on which highly skilled performers overcame the limitations of the media and created impressive recordings. This preference was reinforced when, in the years prior to World War I, recording discs (as opposed to cylinders) were invented. While these could not be recorded on, they provided sound quality superior to that possible with cylinders. By 1919, almost two hundred companies were selling 2 million records per year; in 1921, total record sales surged past 100 million.[31]

The phenomenon of recorded music as mass entertainment very nearly collapsed just as quickly as it arose. The causes of this near-collapse were, first, the Great Depression and, second, the emergence of radio as a source of entertainment. Once the Great Depression hit in 1929, people had very little money to spend on entertainment niceties like recorded music. Record sales dropped dramatically. There were only 6 million record sales in 1932, for example, more than 94 million units below the peak sales of 1921. Indeed, the only bright spot for the recording industry during this period lay in the emergence of a new technology: the jukebox. By 1939, there were 225,000 jukeboxes playing 13 million records. By 1942 that number had nearly doubled.[32]

Radio's contribution to the near-demise of the recorded music industry was also powerful. Recorded music played little, if any, role in the early days of radio. Instead, live performances, usually of comedy shows, soap operas, or mysteries/dramas, dominated early radio broadcasts. These live performances were broadcast over one of the true entrepreneurial innovations of the early AV industry: networks. A radio network is a contractual affiliation between a series of stations and a production company to present the production company's programming. Radio networks shared programming produced by a central production company such as the Columbia Broadcasting System (CBS), the National Broadcasting Company (NBC), or the American Broadcasting Company (ABC). Individual stations within a given network were usually owned independently, but they received much of their programming from a common production company. Thus, independently owned stations did not have to create hours of programming to fill their airtime; rather, they broadcast programs produced by another company.

Economic pressures drove the creation of radio networks. Radio stations are expensive to purchase and run. Owners must buy the station, get a license, maintain the equipment, hire staff, and develop and present programming. They had to incur these substantial costs even before programming aired. If a station had to create its own program all by itself, this would add to its relative operating costs. However, if several stations shared production expenses, the relative cost of creating programming would go down. Each station's chances of making a profit would therefore go up. By 1945 some 95 percent of radio stations in the United States, even independently owned ones, were affiliated with a broadcast network.[33]

In addition to sharing programming costs through networks, early American radio executives developed another innovative scheme to finance their operations: paid advertising. Unlike movie theaters, where patrons pay an entry fee to see a film, radio is broadcast for free on public airwaves. It can be picked up by anyone with a receiver. The early radio pioneers decided that they could make money from radio by having advertisers pay for the programs. The public would listen free of charge. (Today's satellite and cable services challenge this financial model, as addressed later in this chapter, but over-the-air broadcast television and radio still work on this model.) The purpose of the radio program, then, was to deliver an audience to an advertiser. The greater the number of listeners, the higher the fee the stations could charge for advertising time. Profit was generated from advertisers rather than from ticket buyers.

In the earliest days of commercial radio, local radio stations gave producers airtime for advertisements as compensation for the right to broadcast the program the producer created. If the radio station anticipated selling fifteen minutes of advertising in each hour, for example, it might have to cede five minutes of that fifteen-minute block to the producer. The producer, rather than the local station, earned the profit from the five minutes of advertising it booked. The local station earned revenues from the remaining ten. The local station thus forewent some of its potential revenue (from the five minutes of advertising time it ceded to the network) to avoid the substantial costs associated with creating radio programming.

Between the 1920s and the 1950s, radio drew vast, unprecedented audiences across the United States, almost all of it for live programming. Record sales languished. This changed, however, when television (discussed later in this chapter) took over the general in-home entertainment market in the United States after the end of World War II. As radio lost market share to television, radio stations began to target niche markets otherwise not served by television programming. Many began to specialize in broadcasting specific music genres, such as jazz, classical, or country. The most important of these markets was rock and roll. Arriving at the same time as a large generation of teenagers known as the baby boomers, rock music linked radio to teen markets in immensely profitable ways. The industry took advantage of a new technology—the 45-rpm record, which was smaller and more durable than the older 78s—to aggressively market rock music to the baby boom generation. From 1955 to 1957, for example, record sales increased from $277 million to $460 million. This was followed by the shift of rock music to LPs—long-play albums on which performers could explore musical complexities in rock and other genres and take advantage of the higher fidelity, stereo sound, and audio quality available on FM radio bands. The industry again saw increasing sales. For example, the Beatles' album *Sgt. Pepper's Lonely Hearts Club Band* (1967) sold 7 million LP copies, an unheard-of number for rock music prior to that time.[34] In a stunning reversal from its days as the nemesis of recorded music, radio had become the primary tool for marketing records to American audiences.

As with movies, the music heard on these networks was the product of large global corporations. Major producers, usually centered in cities like Los Angeles, Detroit, and Nashville, took responsibility for identifying new talent and marketing it to the broad U.S. market. Alternatively, when independent producers created and marketed new sounds like hip-hop or rock and roll, established labels either purchased the upstart labels or started their own record companies to compete for listeners' entertainment dollars in the emerging market. In other words, these companies used their skills at recognizing and marketing talented acts both within the United States and across the world. They carried American music to a global audience.

Like the film industry, the recording industry has faced an array of social pressures that have shaped its character. As music evolved in the early twentieth century, for example, it developed the fast rhythms of Dixieland and the innovative harmonies of jazz. In response, people began dancing differently. No longer did they use the formal patterns and prescribed movements of ballroom dancing. In their place arose free-form dancing, often at a fast pace and mimicking, in various degrees of specificity, sexual contact. Persons of conventional morality were shocked, seeing in this new explicit music and dancing the corruption of Western civilization. Accordingly, they pressured music companies and radio stations to censor or otherwise control the suggestiveness of "new" music. In one particularly humorous example, the Cole Porter song "Let's Put Out the Lights and Go to Bed" was renamed "Let's Put Out the Lights and Go to Sleep" before being aired on radio.[35] More ominously, Billie Holiday's "Love for Sale" was banned altogether for its allusions to prostitution.

Music producers and distributors have also faced regulatory pressure from the U.S. government. Radio (and, as will be discussed, broadcast television) is regulated by the federal government through the auspices of the Federal Communications Commission (FCC). The FCC has this power because the U.S. government licenses the use of specific frequencies to radio station owners. Unlike what happens when someone wants to open either a movie studio or a movie theater, a radio station owner/operator gets a license from the federal government to broadcast on a specific radio band. Only the licensed radio station is permitted to broadcast on that frequency in what is known as a "market." The license regulates how powerful the radio station may be, thereby limiting its effective range and allowing the same frequency to be used in neighboring markets. In exchange for the exclusive right to use a specific frequency, which the federal government enforces by seeking out and penalizing anyone broadcasting without a license, station owners must agree to a series of limitations on their freedom to do business. While these limits have varied over time, they have included rules about the number of stations one individual or company can own and a requirement that a certain amount of the station's programming must serve the public interest through functions like news broadcasts or emergency broadcasts in times of war or other crises.

Regulations governing the moral content of a station's broadcasts have also shaped the industry's evolution. The federal government has generally insisted that, on penalty of losing their license or facing serious fines, broadcasters must uphold high moral standards in their programming. Offensive language and controversial speech were thus effectively banned for much of the history of radio. By extension, these limits also worked to limit how scandalous most music might become, since music companies relied on radio to market their records. Because of FCC restrictions, corporations regularly edited the music they distributed for play on the radio, bleeping out or otherwise obscuring offensive words and language.

The rock and roll explosion in the 1950s and the subsequent music movements of the 1960s offered a strong challenge to the limitations embedded in FCC rules—especially once producers discovered that music about drugs, sex, and rock and roll sold well. More and more performers offered adult, challenging, and even offensive music, ranging from 1970s hits like Blue Oyster Cult's "Don't Fear the Reaper," a song commending the virtues of suicide, to Madonna's 1980s classic "Like a Virgin," which most decidedly does not applaud the virtues of virginity. (The possible examples that might be offered here are innumerable.) Such challenges to conventional morality only increased as the music industry fragmented and differentiated into new genres like hip-hop, dance, and Latin music. To avoid FCC regulation, music companies regularly released two versions of songs: one for radio and one for the home consumer. A significant gap therefore often emerged between what one might hear in cleaned-up or obscured versions of songs on the radio and what was actually on a given album.

Tipper Gore, wife of then U.S. senator (D-Tennessee) and later U.S. vice president Al Gore, discovered this gap between radio and home versions while listening to one of her children's albums in 1985. Shocked by the explicitness of what she heard in the home version in contrast with what she had heard on the radio, Gore worked with numerous allies to form the Parents' Music Resource Center (PMRC). The PMRC asked Congress to find that offensive music was pornographic and should be restricted, at least in sales to children. Like generations of concerned people before them, the PMRC claimed that violent, sexually explicit music contributed to the decline of the American family and to the moral decay of society in general. To support their contention, in 1985 they issued a list they called the "Filthy Fifteen," which included songs like Sheena Easton's "Sugar Walls" and Twisted Sister's "We're Not Gonna Take It," which the PMRC claimed were harmful due to their explicit references to sex and violence.[36]

Rather than face congressional regulation, the major record companies adopted a voluntary labeling system in which they placed stickers on albums that contained offensive material. The idea was to forestall the imposition of government-mandated rules by providing parents with important information they could use to exercise informed control over what their children listened to. Subsequently, the giant discount retail chain Walmart announced it would not carry any albums deemed offensive; this led many major producers to create two versions of their products—one for Walmart and one that the performer had intended to create.

Cumulatively, the technical, economic, and social forces that shaped the development of the American music industry encouraged consolidation among music houses, as they had with movie and television production studios. (The effects of the digital revolution on the recording industry will be addressed later in this chapter.) The major producers had advantages in the areas of money, technical capacity, marketing and licensing, and royalty management. These advantages allowed them to survive when many minor producers failed. The result was the dominance of American music producers and American musical forms in international musical production and distribution.

As with American movies, there are several ways to assess the pre-eminence of American music in world entertainment. A review of the top-selling albums of all time suggests the dominance of American music, for example. Even considering only certified sales as evidence of success—since there is no way to account for the untold millions or billions of illegal downloads of music in the digital era, a problem to be addressed later in this chapter—American performers are a dominant global music presence. As of April 2017, twenty-eight albums had sold at least 15 million copies each worldwide, and fifteen were the product of undeniably American acts. Michael Jackson's *Thriller* is the number one best-selling album of all time, with at least 33 million albums sold; the Eagles' *Their Greatest Hits* takes second place with 29 million sales.

Other American performers on the list include Billy Joel, Boston, Hootie and the Blowfish, Garth Brooks, and Guns N' Roses. As was the case with the top-selling groups of all time, the top-selling non-American albums were made in genres created by Americans: rock (Pink Floyd's *The Wall*, Led Zeppelin's *Led Zeppelin IV*, the Beatles' *The Beatles*) and country (Canadian Shania Twain's *Come On Over*).[37]

Similar evidence for American music prominence can be found in considering the individual artists and groups in terms of their certified global record sales. The most successful musical act of all time, for example, is not American: it is the Beatles, with 178 million album sales in their history (playing rock music, of course, but expanding the genre along the way). However, the majority of the highest-selling acts of all time are American, starting with number two, Garth Brooks, who has sold more than 148 million albums worldwide, and number three, Elvis Presley, with 136 million album sales. The rest of the list is populated with either American performers (Billy Joel, Michael Jackson, Bruce Springsteen) or performers of American genres like rock, country, and hip-hop (Led Zeppelin, AC/DC, U2).[38] Only American Barbra Streisand and Canadian Celine Dion make the top-sellers list without performing in one of those musical styles.

Not all music is produced in the United States, of course. Other nations and cultures have distinct musical forms. American preeminence is substantial, not total, and is particularly focused in the rock and country genres. Hip-hop also plays a significant role in global music, although American acts do not sell as well globally as American rock and country performers do. That said, hip-hop has been integrated into youth cultures around the world and plays a significant role in many societies. Accordingly, one should look at rock and country, and to a lesser extent hip-hop, to assess the way(s) people around the world are attracted, repelled, lured, and horrified by the appearance of contemporary globalization as expressed by the United States. (Other American musical forms, like jazz and blues, though creative and important, are not addressed here because they play small roles in the global music trade.) In other words, it is in American rock, country, and hip-hop that American music expresses U.S. values, worldviews, and desires to a global audience.

The dominance of American rock, country, and hip-hop is perhaps most evident in the direct linkage of music and television created in

1981 with the formation of the cable network MTV, or Music Television. In their endless search for venues in which to promote their products, music companies and artists hit upon the idea of filming videos to accompany the songs that were playing on the radio. These videos were, in effect, mini-movies that linked television and film directors with musical groups to create visually exciting accompaniments to songs that might otherwise be marketed only on radio stations. The videos served as televised advertisements for the songs and albums. The genius of MTV—owned by media giant Viacom—is that having watched the videos, which are commercials for songs, artists, and albums (and which music companies paid MTV to show in the first place), viewers would then watch formal, traditional commercials for which the network would be paid just like every other network. This was a moneymaking breakthrough: everything, whether advertisement or video, brought MTV a fee for airtime. (The 2001 documentary *The Merchants of Cool*, produced by PBS's *Frontline* documentary series, offers a fascinating inquiry into MTV's outsized role in shaping youth popular culture.)

An idea this profitable was sure to spread, and spread it did. Just ten years after its creation, MTV was available in 201 million households in seventy-seven countries ranging from Australia to Brazil to Hong Kong. MTV Europe grew from 3 million households in 1988 to 14 million in 1991 and then 37 million in 1992.[39] By 1995, almost every country in the world (barring most of Africa and a few countries in South America, along with a scattering of nations elsewhere) had MTV or copycat music television networks.[40] MTV has now spread across the globe.[41] (Copycat networks featuring country music, hip-hop, and electronic dance music have also proliferated worldwide.) While the network adapted its playlist to local tastes and preferences, it concurrently provided a platform linking American music to global television audiences.[42]

Radio's market reach to domestic U.S. country, rock and roll, and hip-hop fans in combination with the global megacorporations that came to oversee and market these styles around the world made American music globally pervasive. MTV then sealed the deal and linked television to music in a global phenomenon. Whether for American acts or music created in forms native to the United States, there is a vast global audience for American music today.

A BRIEF HISTORY OF THE TELEVISION INDUSTRY

As was the case with both the film and music industries, technological, fiscal, and social developments have shaped television's contemporary role in global entertainment. These forces have also encouraged the growth of major corporations as controlling agents of popular television programming. Notably, as the last of the AV media to be invented, television entered a world in which American pop culture programming was already globally dominant. Accordingly, American television programming did not have to invent a global presence. The concentration of talent in Hollywood, combined with the storytelling prowess of producers capable of satisfying the large, diverse, and wealthy U.S. market, created conditions in which the American television industry would grow to have the same global influence as the American film and music industries. It built on the economic, cultural, and production advantages created by the movie and music industries to grow into a worldwide phenomenon.

Television grew as an entertainment medium only when the technology necessary to send pictures in radio waves and to receive and interpret those signals and convert them into visual images was invented in the 1930s. The first broadcasts began in 1939; by 1940, there were twenty-three television stations broadcasting to approximately ten thousand television sets around the world (mostly in New York and London). These broadcasts were quite primitive, and the development of television was put on hold during World War II. The postwar economic boom in the United States, however, led to the dramatic expansion of the American middle class. This new, large population demanded new forms of entertainment. Television fit the bill, and the number of television sets in the United States grew over 700 percent just between 1951 and 1953.[43]

Like radio in its earliest days, television programming in its infancy usually saw performers present live on stage. In many cases, radio hits simply transferred to television; in others, radio formats crossed over but with different actors. Accordingly, early television sets showed soap operas, quiz shows, talk shows, and variety performance shows. New programming was offered every week; almost all of it was broadcast live.

These early broadcasts were usually local. It only became possible to offer coast-to-coast programming in 1957. Before then, if producers wanted to distribute a program across the nation, they had to film it off a television screen and then distribute the resulting kinescopes to other stations for presentation. The kinescopic copy was inevitably quite poor. Only the invention of videotape in 1956 made it possible to distribute quality programming across the nation: videotape could capture action as it was being performed and then could easily be edited into a final product without first being shown on a television screen. The resulting quality was much higher than that of the kinescope. This made it much easier to create shared programming across networks of television stations.[44]

As television expanded, it adopted not just the genres but also the basic business practices of radio. These included the use of networks to produce and distribute programming and reliance on advertisers to pay for programming. Individual television stations were usually owned and operated independently, but they received at least half of their programming from central production companies like CBS, NBC, and ABC (among others). In other cases, programming was directly produced by advertisers and provided to stations outside the network system.[45] In either case, it was provided to consumers free of charge in exchange for the network's receiving the right to sell advertising on the local station or for the advertiser's having its name and product embedded in the show.

Over time, the costs of producing television programs grew as casts, plots, sets, and special effects became more complex. Only the networks had access to the array of marketers, advertising executives, promoters, developers, directors, actors, writers, and other components of the television production process to make the production of television programming economically viable. Accordingly, only they had the practical ability to continue producing television programs. Networks largely replaced advertisers as developers and distributors of programming in the 1960s.[46]

Three major networks, ABC, CBS, and NBC, dominated the television industry between 1957, when true coast-to-coast network broadcasts began, and the 1970s. These networks offered pretaped programs to their affiliated stations, although news and sporting events were usually, although not always, shown live. (Famously, for example, the U.S. hockey team's defeat of the Soviet hockey team at the 1980 Olympic Games—the so-called "Miracle on Ice"—was shown on tape several hours after it had ended, not live.) In the 1980s, Fox Television was founded, creating a fourth major broadcast network. Independent stations existed, usually in local areas, and the Public Broadcasting System (PBS) was created by congressional mandate to provide programming independent of the need to sell commercial time. The commercial broadcast networks were dominant, however, and would remain so as long as television signals were received at home over the airwaves.

Starting in the 1970s, however, cable and satellite technologies developed through which nonnetwork entrepreneurs could make money by collecting the broadcast signals of the networks (and other stations) and sending them packaged together directly into individual homes. Consumers paid a fee to the cable and satellite companies, which in turn paid fees to the networks and other producers for the right to package network and other signals for transmission through cable lines or satellite signals. Cable and satellite companies generated the bulk of their revenues from subscriber fees; however, they also demanded advertising time on broadcasters' programs. Cable and satellite companies began competing with the networks for advertising dollars even as they collected subscriber fees. Network broadcast television networks were forced to compete for revenues in ways they never had before.

From the 1990s on, the rise of cable and satellite companies and the multiplication of niche channels that ensued with the increased transmission capacity of these new technologies drew viewers away from traditional broadcast networks and toward cable and satellite programming. Movie, sports, news, and other specialty channels garnered increasing shares of the viewing audience. In many cases, these niche channels provided superior service to the traditional broadcasters. At the start of the 1990–1991 Gulf War, for example, CNN was the only network with reporters still in Baghdad, and by the end of the war, it was America's most-watched news network. Similarly, ESPN, a cable network founded in 1979, quickly took a leading position in providing sports programming to viewers. By 2000, viewership of the traditional networks had declined precipitously, and the distinction between "broadcast" and "other" television had substantially blurred.

Yet, while the networks' share of the overall television market declined, the reach of American programming grew throughout this period. The new networks that emerged to fill the bandwidth available on cable and satellite channels began to produce substantial amounts of programming. HBO, USA, TNT, and other networks began to create and broadcast their own shows. In turn, these networks licensed their programs to cable and satellite companies for rebroadcast around the world. For example, Phnom Penh Cable TV (PPCTV), the major cable provider for the capital city of Cambodia, offers an array of channels including FOX Action Movies, CNN International, Nat Geo Wild, Discovery, Cartoon World, Animal Planet, Syfy, Nickelodeon, and Crime and Investigation Network.[47] One of its offerings, History HD, was showing *Milwaukee Blacksmith*, *Mountain Men*, *Swamp People*, *Appalachian Outlaws*, and *Pawn Stars* on April 6, 2017, alone.[48]

The rise of alternatives to broadcast television like satellite, cable, and the Internet combined with technological developments like the remote control and the VCR/DVR to change the ways television programs were produced. As the number of channels proliferated, the margin of profit per channel grew quite thin. As was the case with the movie and music industries, only the major producers had sufficient resources and talents for marketing and synergy to increase their chances of profiting from any individual channel or program. Networks stopped producing their own programming, except for news and sports programming, and instead grew to rely on external producers to create the content the network, cable, and satellite channels later broadcast. This process concentrated the production of television programming in the major studios in and around Hollywood, California.

Just as they shaped the movie and music industries before it, social, political, and economic forces have shaped the contemporary television industry. TV has found itself under repeated attack as a force for social evil and moral chaos. As early as 1949, for example, the *Saturday Review* worried, like so many critics before it,

> Here, in concept at least, was the most magnificent of all forms of communication. Here was the supreme triumph of invention, the dream of the ages—something that could bring directly into the home a moving image fused with sound—reproducing action, language, and thought without the loss of measurable time. Here was the magic eye that could bring the wonders of entertainment, information and education into the living room. Here was a tool for the making of a more enlightened democracy than the world had ever seen. Yet out of the wizardry of the television tube has come such an assault against the human mind, such a mobilized attack on the imagination, such an invasion against good

taste as no other communications medium has known, not excepting the motion picture or radio itself.

Similarly, just five years later, in 1954, the *New Republic* opined, "Seeing constant brutality, viciousness and unsocial acts results in hardness, intense selfishness, even in mercilessness, proportionate to the amount of exposure and its play on the native temperament of the child. Some cease to show resentment to insults, to indignities, and even cruelty toward helpless old people, to women and other children."[49]

Notably, these attacks occurred even though the FCC regulated television broadcasts like it did radio transmissions. Regular television is broadcast on radio frequencies, and the U.S. government imposes on television the same conditions of public ownership of the airwaves, monopoly licensing in exchange for protection of markets, and other restrictions as it does on radio. Indeed, as was the case for radio, the FCC announced decency standards for television programming like those embedded in the production code for movies: sexual conduct was to be avoided; individuals were to behave with decency and dignity or, if they did not, were to be the "bad guys" of the story; bad language was not to be used. These restrictions were enforced even when they were inherently absurd, as was the case when the top-rated *I Love Lucy* showed star Lucille Ball's bedroom in one episode (a shocking event at the time). The program was forced to show the room as containing only twin beds placed several feet apart—even though Ball was pregnant in real life, her pregnancy was written into the show, and her real-life husband, Desi Arnaz, was her on-screen husband and the program's costar as well. Popular shows of the era, like *Father Knows Best* and *Leave It to Beaver*, likewise reinforced conventional morality as delimited in FCC regulations.

Social changes in the 1950s and 1960s challenged the conventional morality of the time. The desire to broadcast rock performances placed intense pressure on television executives to stretch the boundaries of social acceptability. For example, *American Bandstand* presented popular musicians and bands live on stage as teenagers danced, often provocatively by the standards of the time. Variety show host Ed Sullivan allowed rock and roll superstar Elvis Presley to appear on his show, though he only televised Presley's performance from the waist up since Presley's gyrating hips were deemed too sexually suggestive for the television audience. Over time, a distinction emerged between programming aimed at adults, generally broadcast after 9 p.m. Eastern time, and children's programming, shown earlier in the day. Later programs could be more sexually explicit and adult themed, although outright nudity was still banned. Language limitations were loosened at the same time, leading one comedian, George Carlin, to offer a routine called "The Seven Dirty Words You Can't Say on TV," lifted directly from the FCC's banned-words list.

There have been occasional efforts to turn toward stricter FCC enforcement of morals regulations on broadcast television and radio. One such effort resulted from an incident at the Super Bowl on February 1, 2004: during the halftime show, pop singer Justin Timberlake removed a patch covering pop singer Janet Jackson's right breast. This event, which was quite mild compared with much of the programming available even on broadcast television in the later evening, much less on cable or satellite networks, nonetheless caused a substantial outcry from many people across the United States. In response, however, the FCC launched an investigation of the incident and fined CBS $550,000 for the violation. The FCC then turned its attention to radio broadcasts: several network programs, including numerous ones by nationally prominent radio star Howard Stern, were noted for their apparent obscenity and fined.[50] (The FCC fine on CBS was overturned in court in 2011.)[51]

More recently there has been a loosening of standards for frank depictions of sexuality and violence. Shows like *CSI* and *Breaking Bad*, like *The Sopranos* before them, are noteworthy for their depictions of drugs and violence in U.S. society. Hits like *Orange Is the New Black*, *Transparent*, and *Girls* have done the same for the expression of sexuality. The FX blockbuster *The Americans* manages to push limits in both areas. Indeed, some critics have referred to this television era as a golden age, given the remarkable amount of high-quality programming that stretches historical boundaries of acceptability and normal practice.[52]

The various economic, social, political, and technological forces that have shaped the development of the television industry have combined to both concentrate television-making power in the hands of a few megacorporations and to position American products as dominant in the world market. The television industry combined the business model of radio with the talents of Hollywood's filmmakers to establish

its central position in global television. Thus, American television programs dominate the global market. For example, less than ten years
after the fall of the Soviet Union, seventy-five cents of every dollar
spent internationally on purchasing television programming went to
U.S. companies, mostly to the studios that dominate the production
of television programming. In fact, these studios generated at least 25
percent of their revenues from international programming.[53]

Much of this imported programming has been feature films intended for broadcast on television. One study of European television,
for example, showed that 80 percent of program imports were feature
films; of these, 53 percent were American. The percentage of American
movies shown on European television screens grew from 46 percent to
53 percent between 1988 and 1991. In Norway, 100 percent of films
shown on the commercial television station TV Norge during the same
three years were American; Sweden's TV3 broadcast American movies
81 percent of the time over the same period. Commercial television stations in France and Italy likewise broadcast American movies at least
73 percent of the time in the same period. Meanwhile, the percentage of
domestic movies shown on these same stations in that period declined
approximately 10 percent.[54]

Television series have been another area in which American programs have been successfully marketed globally. In Europe, only the
United Kingdom produces most of its own programming; in general, 83
percent of television series shown in Europe are from elsewhere—particularly the United States and Australia. From 1988 to 1991, American
programming was popular even in non-English-speaking European
countries. Commercial television stations in West Germany showed
imported television series 99 percent of the time during this period,
for example. Between 1988 and 1991, imports of American television
series grew from 36 percent to 56 percent of total programming across
Europe, while domestically produced European series declined from
37 percent to 16 percent.[55] Similarly, in the mid-1980s, the global TV
satellite service Sky Channel filled two-thirds of its broadcast time with
American situation comedies and rebroadcasts of American movies. In
1987, Lorimar Studios licensed the nighttime soap opera *Knots Landing*
for broadcast in France for $50,000 an episode.[56]

More recently, U.S. dominance on European television screens can
be seen in the degree to which American programming and service pro-

viders control the delivery of television services to viewers. At the end of 2013, for example, U.S. market share in Europe had grown to 66.4 percent of cinema, television, on-demand services, recorded music, and video games—up from 57.7 percent in 2009. One study in 2014 found that a sampling of European channels each showed at least 52 percent American programming, and 59.5 percent of video-on-demand broadcasts were American.[57]

A survey of the most popular television programs across the world suggests just how broad and deep American influence is. In 2015, *Modern Family* and *How I Met Your Mother* were the most popular shows in South Africa. *Scandal* and *Dragons* occupied the same positions in South Korea. *The Big Bang Theory* and *Quantico* pleased Australians; *Homeland* came in second to national programming in both Sweden and the United Kingdom. Germans were attracted to the crime procedurals *CSI* and *NCIS*. Romanians watched *CSI: New York* along with *Lie to Me*. Their neighbors in Hungary preferred *The Mentalist* and *CSI: Miami*. The United States' neighbors, Canada and Mexico, both of whom produce significant amounts of television programming on their own, favored *The Big Bang Theory* and *Quantico* (Canada) and *Spongebob Square Pants* and *Malcolm in the Middle* (Mexico). Brazilians liked *The Blacklist* and *Under the Dome*; their Argentinian neighbors preferred *The Simpsons* and *ER*.[58]

As was the case with movies and music, American television programming drew on the core economic conditions of the United States, its vast and diverse audience, and its comparative political freedom to develop products that could be marketed successfully around the world. It drew on the skills and talents already present in Hollywood to offer both rebroadcasts of American movies and newly produced filmed entertainments to a global audience. It thus became another piece of the U.S. global empire of AV popular culture.

THE DIGITAL AGE

The two decades since the fall of the Soviet Union in 1991 have brought new opportunities for American AV cultural products to spread worldwide. The collapse of the regimes of Eastern Europe removed the last effective barriers to the spread of American popular culture into those once Communist nations. (The world's other great Communist nation,

China, survives, of course, and imposes several restrictions on the infusion of American popular culture in contemporary China, as discussed in chapter 5.) The end of the Cold War once and for all broke the Soviet Union's ability to control or significantly shape the cultural messages its citizens could receive. American popular culture products rushed in to fill the void.

Moreover, advances in digital technology made the production and dissemination of movies, television, and especially music remarkably easy over these same twenty years. Both movie studios and movie theaters are resource intensive, for example, requiring trained staffs and formal buildings with appropriate equipment to create and market films. Television and radio stations and production studios are likewise expensive to buy and maintain and only make economic sense to operate if enough people in their local communities have the money to buy TV and radio sets and the goods being advertised on them: conditions not met in large parts of the world. The advent of mobile phone service and wireless broadcasting has largely obviated these expensive opportunity costs, however. It is simply no longer necessary to have enough money to buy and operate a television or radio set (or both) to access American programming. Now all you need is a cell phone, a tablet, or a laptop and Internet access of one form or another. Similarly, production costs for some programming have dropped dramatically as high-quality handheld cameras and production facilities have spread globally. Access to American products is, in many countries, no more than a mouse click or app download away. At least for those people living in reasonably open societies with Internet access, American movies, music, and television are increasingly available on demand.

Ironically, even as this digital era has expanded global access to American movies, music, and television, it has also created powerful challenges to the economic basis on which the creation of such programming has existed for nearly a century. The problem, at least from the point of view of those seeking to make money from the global distribution of films, music, and television, is that once these products are digitized, as they must be to be distributed today, they can be transmitted via any digital media—including media the producer does not control and cannot charge money for. For example, a DVD, in the end, is just a tool to carry around encoded digital information conveniently and comparatively safely. If someone can copy, or rip, the contents of a

DVD or otherwise gain access to a digital copy of a movie, it is relatively easy to commit what the industry calls piracy: storing the entertainment in a computer and then distributing it across an increasingly fast Internet to an increasingly connected world. Crucially, at least from movie producers' point of view, once the film is available on the Internet, the producer's ability to control who sees it by forcing viewers to buy a ticket or a DVD is pretty much lost. DVDs might be shared among friends today, of course, and illegal theaters might show a DVD to a large paying audience, but the fact that one person or group must be in physical possession of the DVD to show the film puts a practical limit on how many people can see a film without paying for the privilege. Such limitations are meaningless on the Internet. One copy of a movie can be downloaded and perhaps viewed by millions of people all at the same time—for free. The Internet has therefore posed a major challenge to filmmakers as they try to make money in the movie business.

This financial problem has grown exponentially with the seemingly endless number and variety of devices on which filmed or recorded content can be viewed. While it is at least possible to find out about and raid the site of an illegal theater showing bootleg copies of a major motion picture, the development of laptop computers with wireless connections and the spread of devices like the iPod and smartphones have put digital content into the hands of hundreds of millions, if not billions, of people. Whereas only about 700 million people had cell phones in 2000, by 2014 that number had grown to the point that there were approximately as many cell phones in use in the world as there were people: approximately 7.2 billion. Admittedly, not all of these devices are smartphones capable of viewing digital material, and the experience of watching a movie on an iPhone, Android device, or iPad screen might not equal that of viewing it in a theater, but the iPad and similar Android-based devices travel with the user, are discreet, and can only be expected to grow in use globally. In the fourth quarter of 2016, for example, Apple sold 78.3 million iPhone 7 devices in an already heavily saturated market filled with perfectly fine mobile phones—despite the phone's high price and reported lack of innovative features. This was over 2 million units more than the company had been expected to sell.[59] As a practical matter, the universality of mobile phones, tablets, and laptops makes enforcement of copyright and other laws restricting the right to view digital content essentially impossible to enforce. (Chapter 5 addresses these concerns as well.)

The challenge to the profitability of American movies, music, and television offered by the digitization of AV pop culture hit the recorded music industry first and hardest because music files are relatively small and thus easy to download from the Internet. Whereas once consumers went to a music store and purchased a record, a cassette tape, or a CD, much music is captured online today. While many albums are still sold this way, electronic downloads have become increasingly common.[60] There were more than 1 billion legal music downloads in 2008, an increase of 27 percent from 2007.[61]

MP3s and other digital recordings are easy to export around the globe, whether they are downloaded to private digital music players or to another person's computer. This has made them particularly vulnerable to piracy. Music sharing sites like Napster and Kazaa offered large numbers of people the opportunity to download music from the Internet for free and to upload their music for others to take. The Recording Industry Association of America (RIAA) estimates that some 30 billion songs were illegally downloaded between 2004 and 2009.[62] Meanwhile, legal music purchases have declined more than 50 percent since 1999—the year Napster was created—from $14.6 billion to $7.0 billion in 2013. The RIAA further reports that only 37 percent of music acquired in the United States was paid for, while American consumers used BitTorrent to download almost 97 million pieces of music in just the first half of 2012. BitTorrent clients in an additional nine countries downloaded another 176.5 million songs.[63]

The digital era has had similar effects on the film and television industries. Among other things, it has led to a dramatic reduction in sales of programs to the home entertainment market. DVD sales—still the major studios' primary means of earning money in the at-home entertainment market—were down from $6.9 billion in 2014 to $6.1 billion in 2015. This 12 percent decline in revenue in 2015 came on top of a 10.9 percent drop from the year before. Subscription services—like Netflix (to be discussed)—are offering film production companies some support, but they are not as lucrative as DVD sales.[64]

This shift to digital from "hard" delivery systems is unlikely to change any time soon. In a survey of likely purchases, people in the key advertiser demographic of twenty-five to thirty-four years old indicated that the first expense they would cut back on in an economic downturn was movie tickets; the last thing they would cut was their broadband Internet connection. And while the experience of watching a film on an iPod might not come close to watching a movie in the theater or even on a high-quality television, consumers are increasingly choosing to access American popular culture on the screens they have in their hands rather than via television sets, stereos, or movie screens.

In response to these pressures, the American audiovisual popular culture industry has created several means by which it hopes to turn potential pirates into paying customers. Apple's iTunes service, for example, offers a convenient way to purchase, download, and manage one's music, movie, and television purchases or rentals across multiple devices. In 2013, it passed the 25 billion mark in songs downloaded; more than 15,000 songs were purchased every minute through iTunes that year for a total of over 21 million a day.[65] Similarly, iTunes customers downloaded $1 million worth of the big action-adventure hit movie *Iron Man* in the first week it became available online.[66]

Music subscription services like Spotify also have emerged to try to reach consumers who might not want to purchase music but wish to customize the music they listen to throughout the day. Spotify enters into agreements with music publishers and artists to pay them royalties based on how often their songs are streamed by clients who either see advertisements or pay a fee to access the service. It has nearly 50 million paid subscribers, while nearly as many use the advertising version of the service. These clients have access to 30 million songs they can stream throughout the day.[67] The number of music streaming subscribers from all services is expected to exceed 200 million by 2019.[68]

Netflix and similar services, like Hulu and Amazon Video, are trying to do for the television and movie industries what iTunes and Spotify have done for the music world: turn potential pirates into paying customers. Netflix, for example, started as a mail-order service in which people selected films and television programs they wished to watch and then received them by mail, only receiving whatever program was next in their queue when they returned the product they were using. While that option still exists for Netflix's customers, increasing numbers of users are taking advantage of wirelessly connected phones, tablets, laptops, and televisions to exploit Netflix's streaming service. Users pay Netflix a flat fee for access to a digital database that lets the service stream programs directly on their devices. This has proved a very popular service: by May 2011, of example, Netflix was responsible for 30 percent of prime-time web traffic as users chose to download their nightly entertainment—both movies and television programs—directly from Netflix's servers rather than wait for it to be delivered as a DVD or see the movie in a theater.[69]

Netflix has been growing for the last several years, both in the United States and internationally. At the end of 2016, it had 47.91 million subscribers in the United States, with an additional 41.19 subscribers across the world. This was a dramatic change from just two years before, when it already had 37.7 million U.S. subscribers, but only 16.78 million elsewhere. This growth does appear to be shifting the economic foundation of the film industry: as DVD sales decline, an increasing part of the studios' revenue is coming from the fees Netflix and the other services pay for the right to stream their products.[70] It remains to be seen, however, if the revenues generated by streaming fees are sufficient to offset losses in the DVD market, which threaten to undermine the financial foundation of the film and television production industries. It is simply not clear that the industry has really figured out how to generate sustainable revenues in the digital era. Moreover, as Internet download speeds increase, online film and television piracy may well increase to the levels common in the music industry.

Pressures such as these led content makers in the film, music, and television industries to promote two pieces of legislation in the U.S. Congress in the fall of 2011. The Stop Online Piracy Act (SOPA) was introduced in the House of Representatives, while a similar bill, the Protect Intellectual Property Act (PIPA), was offered in the Senate. These bills were ostensibly aimed at cutting off third-party sites that hosted illegally downloaded content or served as link points for accessing illegal downloads. Under the proposed legislation, U.S. authorities would be empowered to shut down any web service that provided access to illegal downloads of copyrighted music, movies, or television programs. Persons running such websites would be subject to arrest, fines, and up to five years in prison for their role in hosting and disseminating pirated content.

While the benefits of these proposed laws to major film, television, and music producers should be obvious—entertainment companies would find an ally in the U.S. government in their war to stop illegal downloads of their products—the legislation faced substantial opposition from what might be termed the "e-world." Companies like Google and Facebook worried that they and their officers would be held liable if a user posted illegally downloaded content to servers the Internet giants operated. They feared that if you or I found a copy of the newest episode of a favorite television program online on a BitTorrent site and then reposted it on YouTube, Google employees might go to jail, and Google might face enormous fines—for actions that Google itself did not undertake. They and many other Internet companies and activists supported an online petition campaign to stop SOPA and PIPA in their tracks.

Ultimately, SOPA and PIPA were shelved in the aftermath of an Internet campaign against them and after President Barack Obama indicated he would veto SOPA if it came to his desk. The issues of piracy and control of downloaded content that drove the creation of SOPA and PIPA have not gone away, however. As a practical matter, the AV industries are likely on the cusp of another significant change driven by the nature of their economics. Smaller producers, whether in the United States or elsewhere, will likely have a harder time surviving the loss of ticket and DVD sales. This is true, ironically, at the exact same time that the spread of laptops, smartphones, and other handheld electronic devices makes it easier for more people worldwide to view the movies made by the American pop culture machine.

In the end, even as MP3s, digital technology, music-sharing websites, and services like Netflix have hurt corporate profits, they have enhanced the spread of American popular culture worldwide. Untold billions of downloads have occurred both legally and illegally in the decade since music sharing became common. While access to the Internet varies widely across the globe, almost anyone who can access it can download American AV popular culture—and with it American values, attitudes, behavioral norms, and culture. And while there is little doubt that the companies involved in the production and distribution of global AV entertainment will change as some negotiate the challenges of the Internet era while others fail, American producers, because of their size and the global transparency of the products they create, are uniquely poised to exploit the global commercial opportunities of the new period.

CONCLUSION

Because of the business, technological, and social factors noted throughout this chapter, the production of mass popular culture has always been centered in the United States, even as Americans have reached out to the rest of the world for ideas, money, and markets. In addition, much, if not most, of the music, films, and television programming generated by the major popular culture corporations carries an American label regardless of the nation of origin of the company that owns it. American movies, music, and television programming have become the dominant forms of AV entertainment worldwide.

NOTES

1. "All Time Box Office," Box Office Mojo, http://www.boxofficemojo.com/alltime/world (accessed May 7, 2017).

2. Janet Wasko, "The Magical Market World of Disney," *Monthly Review* (April 2001): 58.

3. "Who Owns What: Sony Corporation," CJR, http://archives.cjr.org/resources/?c=sony (accessed August 22, 2017).

4. Anne Steele and John D. McKinnon, "Charter Communications Completes Acquisition of Time Warner Cable," *Wall Street Journal*, updated May 18, 2016, https://www.wsj.com/articles/charter-communications-completes-55-billion-acquisition-of-time-warner-cable-1463581387 (accessed May 8, 2017).

5. "Who Owns What: Time Warner Company," CJR, http://archives.cjr.org/resources/?c=timewarner (accessed May 8, 2017).

6. "Who Owns What: The Walt Disney Company," CJR, http://archives.cjr.org/resources/?c=disney (accessed May 8, 2017).

7. "Disney Channel Russia | A Children's Channel," wTVPC, http://wtvpc.com/streaming-tv/disney-channel-russia-kids-tv-streams (accessed May 8, 2017).

8. "Who Owns What: Viacom, Inc.," CJR, http://archives.cjr.org/resources/?c=viacom (accessed May 8, 2017).

9. Matt Russell, "A Short History of *Star Trek*," Trekkies, http://www.trekdoc.com/database/fanfeed/43.htm (accessed March 1, 2012).

10. "Who Owns What: CBS," CJR, http://archives.cjr.org/resources/?c=cbs (accessed May 8, 2017).

11. "Who Owns What: 21st Century Fox," CJR, http://archives.cjr.org/resources/?c=21st_century_fox (accessed May 8, 2017).

12. "Who Owns What: Comcast," CJR, http://archives.cjr.org/resources/?c=comcast (accessed May 8, 2017).

13. Paul Starr, *The Creation of the Media: Political Origins of Modern Communications* (New York: Basic Books, 2004), 23–46.

14. Starr, *Creation*, 47–86.

15. Starr, *Creation*, 267–402; see also Robert C. Toll, *The Entertainment Machine: American Show Business in the Twentieth Century* (New York: Oxford University Press, 1982).

16. Scott R. Olson, "Hollywood Planet: Global Media and the Competitive Advantage of Narrative Transparency," in *The Television Studies Reader*, ed. Robert C. Allen and Annette Hill (New York: Routledge, 2004), 111–29.

17. Toll, *Entertainment Machine*, 19–30; see also Starr, *Creation*, 295–326.

18. Matthew Lasar, "Thomas Edison's Plot to Hijack the Movie Industry," *Ars Technica*, September 2, 2010, https://arstechnica.com/tech-policy/2010/09/thomas-edisons-plot-to-destroy-the-movies (accessed May 8, 2017).

19. "Motion Picture Patents Company," Wikipedia, https://en.wikipedia.org/wiki/Motion_Picture_Patents_Company (accessed May 8, 2017). I am grateful to David Silverman for alerting me to an error in a prior edition that has now been corrected.

20. Richard Maltby, *Hollywood Cinema*, 2nd ed. (Malden, MA: Blackwell, 2003), 126.

21. Maltby, *Hollywood Cinema*, 29–30.

22. Maltby, *Hollywood Cinema*, 128–76.

23. All these quotes are from Stanley J. Baran and Dennis K. Davis, *Mass Communication Theory: Foundations, Ferment, and Future* (Belmont, CA: Wadsworth, 1995), 42.

24. Maltby, *Hollywood Cinema*, 60–63, 593–97; Starr, *Creation*, 318; Richard Maltby, *Harmless Entertainment: Hollywood and the Ideology of Consensus* (Metuchen, NJ: Scarecrow Press, 1983), 97–102; Robert Sklar, *Film: An International History of the Medium* (New York: Abrams, 1993), 96–125.

25. Maltby, *Hollywood Cinema*, 177–79.

26. "The 2016 Summer Movie Season Was a Bust Because Hollywood's Go-To Formulas Stopped Working," *Vox*, updated September 5, 2016, https://www.vox.com/platform/amp/2016/9/5/12734258/2016-worst-summer-movie-season (accessed May 8, 2017).

27. "World Domination by Box Office Cinema Admissions," Green Ash, http://greenash.net.au/thoughts/2011/07/world-domination-by-box-office-cinema-admissions (accessed July 13, 2017).

28. Benjamin R. Barber, *Jihad vs. McWorld: How Globalism and Tribalism Are Reshaping the World* (New York: Ballantine Books, 1996), 92–93.

29. "Bigger Abroad," *Economist*, February 17, 2011, http://www.economist.com/node/18178291 (accessed September 16, 2011).

30. Toll, *Entertainment Machine*, 46–47.

31. Toll, *Entertainment Machine*, 48.

32. Toll, *Entertainment Machine*, 48–59.

33. Starr, *Creation*, 381.

34. Toll, *Entertainment Machine*, 70–74.

35. Starr, *Creation*, 368.

36. Darrick Lee, "Parental Advisory Warning Labels Steeped in Controversy," *Hush Your Mouth!* (Spring/Summer 2003), http://www.hushyour mouth.com/parental--advisory--labels.htm (accessed March 1, 2012).

37. "Top 100 Albums," Recording Industry Association of America, https:// www.riaa.com/gold-platinum/?tab_active=top_tallies&ttt=T1A#search_sec tion (accessed May 8, 2017).

38. "Top Selling Artists," Recording Industry Association of America, https://www.riaa.com/gold-platinum/?tab_active=top_tallies&ttt=TAA#search _section (accessed May 8, 2017).

39. Corinna Sturmer, "MTV's Europe: An Imaginary Continent," in *Channels of Resistance: Global Television and Local Empowerment*, ed. Tony Dowmunt (London: BFI Publishing, 1993), 51–52.

40. Barber, *Jihad vs. McWorld*, 105–7.

41. "Our Brands: Global Reach," Viacom, http://www.viacom.com/our brands/globalreach/Pages/default.aspx (accessed November 23, 2011).

42. Jack Banks, "MTV and the Globalization of Popular Culture," *International Communication Gazette* 59, no. 1 (1997): 43–60.

43. Toll, *Entertainment Machine*, 60–61.

44. Toll, *Entertainment Machine*, 61–65.

45. Toll, *Entertainment Machine*, 66.

46. Toll, *Entertainment Machine*, 66–67.

47. "List of Channels on Phnom Penh Cable Television (PPCTV)," TV Channel Lists, https://www.tvchannellists.com/List_of_channels_on_Phnom_ Penh_Cable_Television_(PPCTV) (accessed April 6, 2017).

48. "TV Schedule," PPCTV, http://www.ppctv.com.kh/tvguide/tvschedule .xhtml?main=1 (accessed April 6, 2017).

49. Both quotes are from Baran and Davis, *Mass Communication Theory*, 42–43.

50. Corey Deitz, "FCC Fines Howard Stern, Two or More Clear Channels Stations, Revises Bono Ruling," About.com: Radio, March 19, 2004, http://ra dio.about.com/cs/latestradionews/a/aa031904a.htm (accessed March 1, 2012).

51. "Court Tosses Out CBS's Superbowl Indecency Fine," *PBS NewsHour*, http://www.pbs.org/newshour/updates/media-july-dec08-fcc_07-21 (accessed November 26, 2011).

52. Hope Reese, "Why Is the Golden Age of TV So Dark?," *Atlantic*, July 11, 2013, https://www.theatlantic.com/entertainment/archive/2013/07/why-is-the-golden-age-of-tv-so-dark/277696 (accessed May 8, 2017).

53. Kerry Seagrave, *American Television Abroad: Hollywood's Attempt to Dominate World Television* (Jefferson, NC: McFarland, 1998), 1.

54. Julian Petley and Gabriella Romano, "After the Deluge: Public Service Television in Western Europe," in *Channels of Resistance: Global Television and Local Empowerment*, ed. Tony Dowmunt (London: BFI Publishing, 1993), 31.

55. Petley and Romano, "After the Deluge," 31–32.

56. Colin Hoskins and Stuart McFayden, "The U.S. Competitive Advantage in the Global Television Market: Is It Sustainable in the New Broadcasting Environment?," *Canadian Journal of Communication* 16, no. 2 (1991), http://www.cjc-online.ca/index.php/journal/article/viewArticle/602/508 (accessed November 23, 2011).

57. "There's NOTHING on TV in Europe—American Video DOMINATES," *Register*, July 21, 2014, https://www.theregister.co.uk/2014/07/21/us_video_even_more_dominant_as_european_initiatives_fail (accessed May 8, 2017).

58. Josef Adalian, "The Most Popular U.S. TV Shows in 18 Countries around the World," *Vulture*, December 2015, http://www.vulture.com/2015/12/most-popular-us-tv-shows-around-the-world.html (accessed May 8, 2017).

59. Sarah Perez, "iPhone 7 Sales Helped Apple Reclaim the Top Spot in the Global Smartphone Market," *TechCrunch*, February 1, 2017, https://techcrunch.com/2017/02/01/iphone-7-sales-helped-apple-reclaim-the-top-spot-in-the-global-smartphone-market (accessed May 8, 2017).

60. The Weeknd, "An Explosion in Global Music Consumption Supported by Multiple Platforms," IFPI, http://www.ifpi.org/facts-and-stats.php (accessed (May 8, 2017).

61. Ben Sisario, "Music Sales Fell in 2008, but Climbed on the Web," *New York Times*, January 1, 2009, http://www.nytimes.com/2009/01/01/arts/music/01indu.html (accessed March 1, 2012).

62. "News," Recording Industry Association of America, http://www.riaa.com/faq.php (accessed December 5, 2011).

63. Edoardo Bonacina, "No Need to Pay? The Impact of Piracy on the Music Industry," *Drayton Tribune*, http://www.draytontribune.com/no-need-to-pay-the-impact-of-piracy-on-the-music-industry (accessed May 8, 2017).

64. Andrew Wallenstein, "Why 2015 Home Entertainment Figures Should Worry Studios," *Variety*, January 6, 2016, https://variety.com/2016/digital/news/home-entertainment-spending-2015-studios-1201673329 (accessed May 8, 2017).

65. Alex Pham, "iTunes Crosses 25 Billion Songs Sold, Now Sells 21 Million Songs a Day," *Billboard*, February 6, 2013, http://www.billboard.com biz/articles/news/1538108/itunes-crosses-25-billion-songs-sold-now-sells -21-million-songs-a-day (accessed May 8, 2017).

66. Brooks Barnes, "For a Thrifty Audience, Buying DVDs Is So 2004," *New York Times*, November 23, 2008, http://www.nytimes.com/2008/11/23/ business/23steal.html (accessed March 1, 2012).

67. Craig Smith, "57 Amazing Spotify Statistics and Facts (March 2017)," DMR, updated March 18, 2017, http://expandedramblings.com/index.php/ spotify-statistics (accessed May 8, 2017).

68. "Number of Music Streaming Subscribers Worldwide from 2010 to 2020 (in millions)," Statista, https://www.statista.com/statistics/669113/ number-music-streaming-subscribers (accessed May 8, 2017).

69. Cecilia Kang, "Netflix Biggest Driver of U.S. Internet Traffic, Puts Spotlight on Broadband Pricing," *Washington Post*, May 16, 2011, http://www .washingtonpost.com/blogs/posttech/post/netflix-biggest-driver-of-us-inter net-traffic-puts-spotlight-on-broadband-pricing/2011/05/16/AFg3yg5G_blog .html (accessed December 1, 2011).

70. Wallenstein, "Why 2015 Home Entertainment Figures Should Worry Studios."

CHAPTER 4

THE AMERICAN GLOBAL CULTURAL BRAND

While American movies, music, and television programs are important parts of U.S. global pop culture, they are not the whole of it. The values, ideals, mores, attitudes, behaviors, norms, and rituals that embody life in the United States can be found embedded in a host of other artifacts. Consumer goods and other values combine with the products of the audiovisual pop culture industry to create a seemingly seamless, integrated American popular culture that can be found almost everywhere in the world.

This chapter examines some of the other features of globalized American pop culture. It offers case studies of how Coca-Cola, McDonald's, blue jeans, the National Football League (NFL), and social media giant Facebook became or are trying to become global entities. Whether the product in question is a car, a restaurant, clothing, or a sport, American brands, styles, and even identities have had a profound impact on markets, values, and attitudes across the planet. Moreover, the relatively new phenomenon of social networking adds layers of complexity and subtlety to both the marketing and the branding of pop culture artifacts. Understanding the impact of American popular culture on the process of globalization necessarily entails exploring at least some of the other ways American pop culture crosses national and cultural boundaries. This chapter offers a partial look at this multifaceted phenomenon.

FRANCHISING AMERICA

The practice of franchising has played a significant role in helping American popular culture artifacts become global phenomena. For example, four of the popular culture case studies offered in this chapter are enterprises that employ franchising to advance their businesses. Franchising, then, is an important part of spreading the American cultural brand.

A franchise is a contractual relationship between a company that controls a brand label for a good or service and a private individual or company that buys the right to use the brand's name and products but otherwise operates the business solely. The franchiser—the McDonald's corporation, for example—establishes rules and standards it expects its franchisees (those who operate the stores selling McDonald's products) to meet. The franchisee, in turn, enjoys the flexibility of owning a store on its own while benefitting from the brand identity of the franchiser.

Franchises offer several advantages that have encouraged their use. Some of these are practical, and some are matters of loyalty and brand identity. From a franchisee's point of view, for example, buying a franchise can significantly reduce the cost and complexity of starting a business. One does not need to establish contracts with local vendors to provide things like hamburger to a restaurant; instead, the franchiser may have preexisting networks of vendors the new franchisee can rely on to get the goods needed to run the business. In addition, franchisers usually have management-training programs so that new franchisees can learn how to recruit and manage their employees. The franchiser is also likely to have a complex set of rules and regulations defining workers' rights and responsibilities—a fact that means that franchisees do not have to develop rules and policies on their own. Even rules governing the layout of floor space simplify the task of opening and managing a new business. By buying a franchise, the new owner gives up some freedom to run things as he or she might wish but also simplifies running the business by relying on the skills and expertise of the franchiser.

Another major benefit of the franchise derives from the concept of economies of scale. Franchisers typically buy large volumes of goods and services from vendors. They can negotiate price reductions from these vendors that smaller purchasers (who are often local, individually owned businesses) cannot: vendors accept lower prices for bulk sales in order to get the contract for the major sale. Franchisers pass these cost reductions on to their franchisees, meaning that the franchisee can often provide a good or a service to the customer at a lower price than an independent business can. If necessary, then, franchisees can beat independent businesses on price, enhancing their market competitiveness.

Franchises also provide regularity and predictability to both franchisees and consumers. Colas from the same franchise taste pretty much the same wherever they are concocted, just as the hamburgers taste the same, just as the coffee tastes the same. Consumers can be pretty sure that they will get a predictable and safe product from any of a chain's stores, just as franchise owners can be pretty sure that competing franchises will not be opened in the area—at least not competing franchises of the same company. This uniformity may strike some people as unfortunate, since it often entails the destruction of local businesses unable to compete with the franchise's economies of scale, but given the choice, consumers seem to flock to franchise businesses instead of local ones. Predictability and regularity are powerful market forces.

Perhaps the biggest benefit to buying a franchise is not managerial at all. Instead, it is perceptual. Franchisers invest substantial amounts of money in establishing their brand identities, mostly through advertising. Franchisers spend a great deal on advertising their product's label to a broad audience. This advertising both builds brand awareness and creates a public image for the franchiser's goods and services. For example, Ford, the automobile manufacturer, once offered a campaign centered on the notion that "quality is job one," suggesting that if consumers wanted safe and reliable cars, they should buy Fords. Starbucks' advertising suggests it is not just a coffee shop but a destination for those who have discriminating taste and demand superior coffee.

McDonald's offers decent food served quickly in a way that is supposed to mimic the feeling of home. And Coca-Cola ties itself to wholesome imagery, once promising that it would "like to buy the world a Coke, and keep it company."

This brand identity making is not an accident. Franchisers establish brand identities to create and maintain markets for their products. One goes to Starbucks not simply because of the coffee; one goes to Starbucks to be seen to be someone who goes to Starbucks. Starbucks-goers form a subculture with their own rituals and norms—in this case organized around elaborate processes for ordering cups of coffee. Nike buyers "just do it." Mountain Dew drinkers "do the Dew." Meanwhile, McDonald's customers promise others, "I'm lovin' it."

Franchisers augment this subcultural identity making by physically labeling their customers and turning consumers into walking (and driving) advertisements for their products. Coffee cups can be emblazoned with the brand label, as can shopping bags. Automobiles and many brands of clothing come with labels that advertise the product's maker—and label the driver or wearer as someone who uses that company's goods and services. Some consumers respond to this labeling and identification by buying gift items emblazoned with the product's labels. Brand identity is a central feature of creating and maintaining markets for a franchiser's products.

Buying a franchise therefore means buying a brand identity and its associated market. Franchisees are largely freed of the need to convince consumers to come to their stores. Instead, they simply inform consumers of their location in order to give those who appreciate the brand's identity the chance to shop for that store's products—and to be seen to shop for those goods and services.

Such arrangements have proved useful, flexible means for corporations to spread their brands at minimal risk to their bottom lines. After all, when a company owns a store—which does happen, even in some franchised businesses—it assumes the risks associated with purchasing or leasing business space, hiring staff, marketing and building a market, and other matters. If a company-owned store fails, the company loses a substantial amount of money. By contrast, in a franchise arrangement, the franchisee accepts most of this risk. Consequently, franchisers can offer franchise opportunities in places and markets too uncertain for the company to invest in otherwise. The franchise brand can therefore spread more quickly and into otherwise unreachable markets more easily than could an unfranchised company.

Through franchising, consumers across the world have become aware of the brand identities of large numbers of American popular culture products, like clothing, fast food, vehicles, sports, and innumerable other things. Brand identity making can combine with price advantages to make American goods popular with foreign consumers. People across the globe have proven willing to pay to associate themselves with American brands of clothing, food, and other products. America itself has become, at least in part, a global franchise.

THE GROWTH OF THE AMERICAN
FRANCHISE EMPIRE

Franchising, it should be noted, is not an American business innovation. Rather, the notion of franchising began, at least in a limited way, in Europe. Beer manufacturers there established franchise arrangements with local pubs: franchised pubs would sell only beers from a specific brewery. However, franchising never became as prominent in Europe as it did in the United States. Instead, whether because the United States had an entrepreneur-friendly culture or because of its vast size, once franchising began there in the 1800s it quickly grew as a tool by which manufacturers could distribute their goods nationally—and ultimately globally.[1]

The earliest American franchises were in manufactured goods. As early as the 1850s, makers of expensive items like Isaac Singer's sewing machines or Cyrus McCormick's tractors offered these products to franchisees who then sold them out of their stores. The manufacturer did not own the store in which its goods were sold. Instead, the franchiser sold the goods to the franchisee. The franchisee then made a profit (or tried to) by marking up the price of and servicing the item and perhaps by earning incentive payments from the manufacturer if the company sold a large number of units.

Other industries followed the Singer/McCormick plan. The first automobile franchise was granted in 1898, for example, just a decade or so after the first recognizably modern car had been invented. Auto franchises allowed dealers to establish businesses at which to sell and service vehicles purchased from the manufacturer at a discount. This arrangement remains the way most new cars are sold in the United States today.

Franchises were integrated into the food and service industries in the 1880s. The first truly successful franchise of a food product was Coca-Cola, the invention of an Atlanta, Georgia, druggist named John S. Pemberton. Pemberton, who sold the formula for his concoction before his death in 1888, mixed kola root, caffeine, and coca extract into a sweet, soothing formula. The person who bought the secret formula (which remains secret to this day), Asa Candler, created a franchising deal in which the Coca-Cola Company sold premixed syrup base to franchisees. (Coca was eventually removed as an ingredient of the formula.) The franchisees then added carbonated water, bottled the soda, and marketed it in their areas of operation. In time, as discussed later in this chapter, Coca-Cola, aka Coke, would be bottled and drunk around the world—always with the same base syrup shipped from the Coca-Cola Company.

Restaurant franchises developed in the early twentieth century. For example, after Roy Allen and his partner, Frank Wright, bought the formula for a new drink called root beer from an Arizona druggist in 1919, they founded the A&W restaurant franchise in 1922. A few years later Harland Sanders invented a flavor packet that he added to the fried chicken he had learned to cook quickly at the restaurant he ran at his gas station and motel complex in Corbin, Kentucky. He began selling the flavor packets and licensing his quick-cook technology to other entrepreneurs in 1930. While that business ultimately failed, his model became the foundation for the Kentucky Fried Chicken (KFC) restaurant chain. In the same period, Howard Johnson, a pharmacist from Quincy, Massachusetts, began to sell ice cream and a small selection of other items in his store; he franchised the concept in 1935. In time both the menu and the ice cream choices expanded, and distinctive orange-roofed Howard Johnson's restaurants spread across the United States.

The emergence of the automobile as the major mode of American transportation after World War II provided the opportunity for massive expansions in franchising across the United States. Americans began traveling on wide, well-built highways in comfortable cars. They also moved to suburbs with their attendant large yards and commuter lifestyles. Travelers sought reliable, consistent places in which to eat and spend the night; car owners desired the security of knowing they could get their cars serviced at reliable, reputable chains across the United States; and consumers with money to spend pursued whatever fashion, music, or fad was hot at the moment. Franchised restaurants, hotels, automobile-service chains, and clothing stores rushed in to serve this market. Chains like McDonald's, Kentucky Fried Chicken, Holiday Inn, and Western Auto grew dramatically.

Table 4.1 summarizes the top fifty franchises by earnings that have at least one thousand locations outside the United States. Fast-food restaurants are disproportionately represented, although service industries like real estate sales, tax preparation, and janitorial services also make the list. The chain of 7-Eleven convenience stores is far and away the largest international chain; however, McDonald's remains the sales champion among global franchises. Subway has more restaurants than McDonald's overall, but McDonald's has a more than $65 billion advantage in global sales. In any case, the American way of eating is spreading around the world in ever-expanding networks of franchises.

Fast food, services, and convenience stores are of course not the only global franchises for American products, goods, and services. Ford and General Motors sell millions of cars globally, for example. (Chrysler, the third major American car manufacturer, was taken over by Italian manufacturer Fiat after the global financial crisis that started in 2008.) Ford sold more than 3 million vehicles outside North America in 2015.[2] General Motors sold as many cars in China alone in 2015 as Ford did outside North America that same year.[3] The company's Buick brand is particularly popular in China.

Other aspects of American cultural life have also expanded across the world in recent years. The megaretailer Walmart has a global presence now, and it influences both how products are created and how they are sold to people around the world. For example, Walmart has 6,200 stores in twenty-seven countries outside the United States, with 427 stores in China alone.[4] Its focus on the quality of its products is pressuring Chinese producers and vendors to increase the quality of the goods and services they provide to Chinese consumers.[5] The National Football League has scheduled four games in London in 2017. The National Basketball Association (NBA) is aggressively seeking to expand in global markets; players like the now retired Chinese-born Yao Ming provided the league with entrée into that vast nation. (Jim Yardley's 2013 *Brave Dragons: A Chinese Bas-*

Table 4.1. Global Franchises with 1,000+ Branches, U.S. and International

Rank	Company	System Sales	U.S. Locations	International Locations
1	McDonald's	$82,714,300,000	14,251	36,525
2	7-Eleven	$81,500,000,000	7,995	58,711
3	KFC	$22,600,000,000	4,248	19,952
4	Burger King	$17,303,700,000	7,166	15,003
5	Subway	$17,100,000,000	26,831	44,105
6	Ace Hardware	$14,856,000,000	4,402	4,981
7	Pizza Hut	$12,000,000,000	7,766	16,063
8	RE/MAX	$10,296,429,420	3,550	6,986
9	Wendy's	$10,065,000,000	5,722	6,479
11	Domino's	$9,900,000,000	5,200	12,530
13	Taco Bell	$9,000,000,000	6,444	6,692
14	Dunkin' Donuts	$8,300,000,000	8,431	11,750
16	Chick-Fil-A	$6,735,000,000	1,966	1,966
17	Hampton by Hilton	$6,500,000,000	1,978	2,108

18	Circle K	$6,493,481,488	5,220	6,687
19	Tim Hortons	$6,349,800,000	647	4,413
20	Holiday Inn Express	$6,250,000,000	2,106	2,425
21	Holiday Inn Hotels & Resorts	$6,075,000,000	772	1,226
24	Courtyard	$5,250,000,000	916	1,037
25	Applebee's	$5,043,000,000	1,878	2,033
26	Panera Bread	$4,836,757,000	1,955	1,972
27	Sonic Drive-In	$4,390,000,000	3,526	3,526
28	Dairy Queen	$4,300,000,000	4,511	6,762
29	Chili's	$4,147,100,000	1,567	1,580
30	Little Caesars	$4,100,000,000	4,256	5,299
31	Comfort Inn & Suites	$4,000,000,000	1,725	2,257
34	Buffalo Wild Wings	$3,635,000,000	1,135	1,163
35	Arby's	$3,540,000,000	3,214	3,341
36	Papa John's	$3,490,000,000	3,290	4,893

(continued)

Table 4.1. *(Continued)*

Rank	Company	System Sales	U.S. Locations	International Locations
38	Jack in the Box	$3,395,542,000	2,248	2,249
40	GNC	$3,345,000,000	4,456	6,763
42	H&R Block	$3,285,000,000	10,286	11,950
43	IHOP	$3,250,200,000	1,604	1,683
46	Popeyes Louisiana Kitchen	$3,060,000,000	1,970	2,539
47	Aaron's	$3,048,881,669	1,989	2,039
50	Denny's	$2,700,000,000	1,598	1,714

Source: "Franchise Times Top 200+," *Franchise Times*, http://www.franchisetimes.com/FT-Top-200 (accessed May 9, 2017).

ketball Team, an American Coach, and Two Cultures Clashing provides a fascinating look into the world of professional basketball in China.)

Not all American goods and services are marketed globally by franchises, of course. Some companies own the stores in which they sell their products globally, and other distinctively American items like blue jeans have developed a global presence separate from the original manufacturers' control. Starbucks, for example, does not offer a traditional franchise to its operators. Instead, it owns most of its stores but licenses independent businesspersons to run stores on its behalf. Such arrangements have made it possible, as of May 2017, for Starbucks to operate more than twenty-four thousand stores in seventy countries worldwide.[6]

Whether franchised or not, brands like McDonald's, Coca-Cola, Starbucks, and 7-Eleven carry an American identity and an American set of cultural values and practices to the larger world. They are as embedded in American culture as movies, music, and television programming. They offer entangling threads in which American pop culture spins into global prominence.

AMERICAN BRANDS, GLOBAL PRESENCE

This section explores the ways in which specific American brands, franchises, and cultural forms have been integrated into global life. It offers brief histories of Coca-Cola, McDonald's, blue jeans, the NFL, and Facebook as case studies of the many ways American pop culture has spread worldwide. These companies and products offer insight into brands that have been long established as global forces (Coke, McDonald's, blue jeans) and those that are seeking to expand their worldwide influence (the NFL). Their international prominence offers evidence of the power of American popular culture on a global scale.

That this section focuses on these companies and products does not mean that they stand as *the* examples of American pop culture corporate globalization. The discussion offered here of how these companies and products have risen to global prominence is intended to explore the ways in which American pop culture has gone global. It does not provide an exhaustive list of those corporations that have spread across the planet. Coca-Cola and McDonald's are only two branches of a complex tree of fast-food and beverage companies with a global scope, and American sports like baseball have had a global following for a century or more. The analyses offered here are presented as a tool to explore the ways American brands became global. While each is presented individually, they and the other forces of American pop culture globalization have a collective impact on the people who use American products and integrate them into their lives.

A Brief Global Cultural History of Coca-Cola

Coca-Cola has been called the most profitable brand in world history. Interbrand, an international consulting firm, lists the international trademarks that are understood to have generated the highest economic returns for their owners. Only those that generate more than one-third of their sales outside the United States are considered. For 2016, Interbrand estimated Coke to be the third most valuable brand in the world, behind only Apple (#1) and Google (#2). Its value, $73 billion, far outpaced the next-ranked soda giant, Pepsi, which came in twenty-third at $20.2 billion. Coca-Cola's brand was even seen to exceed that of fourth-placed Microsoft, whose software can be said to drive most global commerce.[7]

It is hard to imagine that Coca-Cola's inventor, Atlanta pharmacist John S. Pemberton, foresaw such a future for a company that emerged from a store-mixed, coca-extract-laced drink. Pemberton brewed the concoction in 1886 to increase sales at his store. He made little money from his work and even sold the rights to his drink several times over before his death in 1888. It wasn't until 1891, when Asa Candler bought back all the rights Pemberton had sold, that the growth of Coca-Cola into a global powerhouse began. (Buying the rights back from the various people to whom Pemberton had sold the formula cost Candler $2,300—perhaps the best twenty-three hundred dollars anyone has ever spent.) Candler and his brother John joined with several other local businessmen to incorporate the Coca-Cola Company in 1892. The company's distinctive, script-based logo was registered as an official trademark in 1893.[8]

Coca-Cola is a mix of a secret syrup, sugar, and carbonated water. The key to its success is its syrup, which has been manufactured on a large scale since 1894. In the company's early years, the syrup was shipped to pharmacies and other stores. There, employees called "soda jerks" mixed the soda on the spot by manipulating the flow of syrup from one spout and carbonated water from another spout to create the soda the customer would drink. (This is the way draft beer is still poured today.) In 1894, a Vicksburg, Mississippi, businessman named Joseph Biedenharn decided that he could increase his sales even more if the soda were prebottled rather than "jerked": customers could buy several sodas at a time but drink them later at home. Bottled Coca-Cola has been available ever since.

Nationwide franchising of Coca-Cola began in 1899. A group of Chattanooga, Tennessee, businessmen secured the rights to bottle Coca-Cola across the United States that year. However, they quickly discovered that they could not raise enough capital to build bottling plants around the United States to serve the national demand for the product. They identified bottling partners across the country and created zones of operation, guaranteeing each control of a specific territory. Over a thousand bottling plants were established across the United States in the next twenty years.

Coca-Cola's growth was international in these years, although not to the degree it would later enjoy. Asa Candler's oldest son took a batch of syrup with him on a trip to England in 1900, and the company received an order for five gallons of the concoction from the United Kingdom later that year. Bottling plants subsequently opened in Cuba, Panama, Puerto Rico, the Philippines, and Guam in the early years of the twentieth century and in Canada and France by 1920. In 1926, Coca-Cola established an international marketing unit, and in 1928, the company shipped one thousand cases of the soda to the Olympic Games in Amsterdam. This began a long association between the company and the world's premier sporting event. The soda was bottled in forty-four countries by the late 1930s. That number would double by the end of the 1960s.

The cultural importance of Coca-Cola was illustrated during World War II when the soda became part of the U.S. war effort. While in North Africa in 1943, the commander of U.S. forces there, General Dwight Eisenhower, sent a message to the company asking it to ship enough material to build ten bottling plants. It also requested that 3 million bottles of the soda be shipped to the front immediately, along with supplies needed to fill a quota of 6 million bottles a month.

In all, Coca-Cola shipped materials for sixty-four bottling plants around the world, including to far-flung outposts like New Guinea.

Additionally, the Coca-Cola Company made a commitment to provide five-cent bottles of Coke to all servicemen regardless of what it cost the company to produce the drink. Military personnel drank some 5 billion bottles of soda during the war—a number that does not include soda and automatic fountain dispensaries. By the end of the war, a generation of Americans, and for that matter a generation of people touched by American military operations around the world, had been introduced or otherwise exposed to Coca-Cola.

While Coca-Cola was the dominant soda brand in the United States in the postwar period, competition from its main rival, Pepsi, induced the company to make what, in retrospect, was one of the biggest marketing and branding mistakes of all time. Concerned that Pepsi's sweeter formula was stealing market share, Coca-Cola executives initiated plans to replace traditional Coca-Cola with a new formula labeled, simply enough, New Coke. The new formula had won numerous blind taste tests against both the old formula of Coca-Cola and Pepsi as well, and in 1985, company leaders decided that it was time to launch a new chapter in the product's history. "Old" Coke ceased production, and New Coke was presented as "the" Coca-Cola.

To say the new product flopped would be kind. Executives received hate mail about the new flavor even as consumer lobbying groups formed to boycott the new drink and demand the return of "real" Coke—all in the days before the Internet made such communications comparatively easy. Company claims that sales were good and the new formula was popular met with howls of derision. National news broadcasts covered the marketing disaster. When news leaked that the original Coca-Cola was to return to store shelves in July 1985, barely three months after New Coke was presented to the world as "Coke," then U.S. senator David Pryor (D-AR) announced on the floor of the Senate that the news was "a meaningful moment in American history."[9] "Old" Coke, now dubbed "Classic," was marketed alongside New Coke until New Coke was pulled from the market entirely. (It should be noted that by the end of 1985, Coca-Cola's market share had grown dramatically, leading some to conclude that the introduction of New Coke had been a cunning advertising strategy. The company has always denied this.) In January 2009, the company announced that Coca-Cola Classic would drop the "Classic" from its name. Coke would be just Coke again.

At the heart of this disaster was the failure to appreciate the iconic position Coca-Cola had come to hold in American society. Coca-Cola had worked hard to affiliate its brand with the notion of America itself. Changes to the brand meant change to the emotional connection many consumers felt not just with the soda but also with the idea of the soda's existence as a cultural touchstone. To drink Coke was to be an American, and if Coke could change, then so could America—and not in a good way. The switch to New Coke was seen as a betrayal of the brand identity that Coca-Cola had worked hard to create.

Coca-Cola faced a similar, if less intense controversy during the 2011 Christmas season. The company decided to change the color of its cans from red to white during the holidays to honor polar bears and raise awareness of the loss of Arctic habitat for the bears and other regional wildlife. The campaign caused confusion among some drinkers who thought they were buying Diet Coke, which is sold in silver cans, and got "real" Coke instead. But others were outraged that Coke had abandoned its iconic red color. Coca-Cola, it seems, had to be offered for sale only in red cans to be "real" Coca-Cola.

Notably, the popular sense that Coca-Cola had an iconic, cultural identity that ought not be violated by silly issues like marketing and flavor was in many ways itself a result of Coke's efforts to turn itself into a quintessentially American product. From its early decision to use the script-lettered Coca-Cola label (drawn by John S. Pemberton's partner and bookkeeper, Frank Robinson), the company showed remarkable creativity and success in branding its product. In 1916, for example, the company created the iconic contoured Coke bottle as a tool to ensure consumers were getting—and choosing—Coca-Cola instead of a competitor's products. (This shape was granted a trademark by the U.S. Patent Office in 1977.) In 1929, the company introduced a distinctive fountain glass to be used in pharmacies, restaurants, and other venues that served Coke products; this glass is still used in many restaurants and can be purchased for home use as well. In 1933, the company introduced the automatic fountain dispenser at the Chicago World's Fair. This device allowed consumers to pour their own sodas as the water and syrup were mixed in the dispenser rather than by a soda jerk, enabling millions more drinks to be dispensed than ever could be before.

Coke also invented Santa Claus. Or, put another way, Coca-Cola's marketers helped establish the now classic vision of Kris Kringle as a jolly fat man with a white beard dressed in red from top to bottom. Coca-Cola co-opted Santa's image to get people to drink soda in the winter and in the process created the modern image of Santa Claus. Prior to 1931, when a series of magazine ads for Coca-Cola featuring Santa Claus first hit American magazines, Father Christmas had been portrayed in an array of ways. In some cases he was seen as an elf; in others, as a tall, thin, somewhat austere man. (This image remains popular in some parts of the world.) At times he wore a clerical robe; at others, he was dressed in the furs of a Norse hunter. When cartoonist Thomas Nast drew Santa in the U.S. Civil War era, the character's clothes were tan, although in time Nast changed them to red.

Consumers became so obsessed with the images Coke produced that they scanned each year's drawings for changes. One year, when Santa appeared without a wedding ring, people wrote in wondering about Mrs. Claus. Another year readers asked why Santa's belt was on backward. An icon was thus made, courtesy of Coca-Cola.

What was true for Santa Claus was true for a stunning array of consumer collectibles as well. It is possible to collect a vast amount of Coca-Cola-labeled products, ranging from trays and bottles and bottle caps to advertising, games, smoking paraphernalia, and company gifts.[10] If it has a logo on it, it is a potential collectible; if it is older and genuine, it is likely to have substantial economic value. But of course economic value is not the only reason people collect: surrounding oneself with Coca-Cola-labeled products links one to the brand and the values it expresses. Many people collect Coca-Cola for its distinctive colors and logos rather than its potential sales value. It is a subculture.

It is also a global symbol. At least two international movies have put Coca-Cola paraphernalia at the center of their films. The 1980 cult hit *The Gods Must Be Crazy* makes the brand's distinctive glass bottle the point of dramatic tension around which the movie hinges, for example. When a Coke bottle falls from a passing airplane into the hands of a tribe of hunter-gatherers in the Kalahari Desert in southern Africa, the tribespeople find it useful for grinding food and other things until, in a fit of jealousy, one hits another over the head with the bottle. One member, Xi, decides that the gods were crazy to give them the bottle and goes on a quest to return it to its rightful owners. Along the way, viewers get a travelogue of life in the modern world as seen through the eyes of one tribesman—and his Coke bottle.

Another film, *The Cup*, an indie hit from 1999, focuses less on Coke but uses one of its iconic symbols, its distinctively colored aluminum can, as an evocative introduction to the film. The movie is set in India in a Buddhist monastery filled with young monks obsessed with the World Cup soccer tournament. It chronicles their efforts to rent a satellite dish and television so they can watch the competition despite the supposed asceticism of life in a monastery. The film opens with a scene of young monks using a Coke can as a soccer ball in their courtyard. An older monk interrupts to take the can to his master; we see that the master has used many such cans to create oil lamps in his study. Coke is quite literally everywhere—and quite literally recognizable around the world.

Along with its iconography, Coca-Cola has become a force of economic globalization. At one level, this is the result of the substantial economic impact Coca-Cola has around the world. The opening of bottling plants brings an array of other jobs and services to the communities that house them. Coca-Cola bottling facilities rely on local water and local sweeteners to mix with the base syrup, meaning that local bottlers must establish relationships with local providers for these services. Bottles, whether plastic or glass or aluminum, are usually produced locally, delivered to the plant, and used to store the soda. Trucking firms have to hire drivers to deliver the product to the many venues in which it is sold. Then, as the result of an economic principle known as the multiplier effect, the employees of the trucking company and the water provider and the sweetener company and the bottling plant and the places that sell Coke all have money to spend on new goods and services. People with money in their pockets tend to go to restaurants and movies and to buy cars and better televisions—or televisions in the first place. In turn, this financial boon causes other businesses to hire workers as restaurant servers and car sales staff and television repair people. Bringing a large business like a Coca-Cola bottling facility to a new area is expected to promote economic growth broadly throughout the community.

Yet Coke is not always perceived as a good force in global affairs. In part this is because the reality of local economic development is never as clearly beneficial as the process described above. Corrupt officials and their cronies do better than they ought to from the deals the company strikes in the local area, and many people do not experience the economic benefit expected under the logic of the multiplier effect. There are also concerns that as local suppliers of water, sweeteners, and bottles and distribution networks expand to meet the company's demands, they replace rain forests and other natural areas with sugar fields and build roads across previously undisturbed countryside, displacing endangered animals and plants in the process—not to mention disrupting and possibly devastating the lives of the people tied to more traditional and established ways of life. The diversion of large amounts of water from their natural sources to satisfy the demand for soda can likewise harm the local environment.

Many people also wonder if addicting people to sweetened, caffeinated beverages in a world of limited resources and growing obesity is really a very good idea from a public health perspective. Indeed, since sodas are American beverages, the criticism arises that American soda manufacturers are contributing to making the world's peoples obese, all while destroying the local cultures, flavors, and styles of consumption innate to other societies. For some, then, Coke is a symbol of cultural degradation rather than a tool of global economic development.

One other critique aimed at Coke pertains to its alleged role in repressing global labor movements, particularly in Colombia. Organizers of the "Killer Coke" campaign argue that Coca-Cola officials have been complicit in or actually caused the murders and/or kidnappings of numerous labor organizers at Coke bottling plants in Colombia.[11] Coca-Cola, then, is seen to be a central player in the efforts of global megacorporations to dominate the worldwide labor market by keeping costs low and profits high. The company of course denies these claims.

Regardless of one's position on the economic or moral significance of the Coca-Cola Company, it is clearly an iconic representative of American pop culture across the globe. Its products, its logos, its values, and its brand identity have found a worldwide market and a worldwide audience. It is hard to imagine going pretty much anywhere on the planet that is inhabited by people who have ever had contact with groups from the outside world without being able to buy a Coke or similar product when visiting. Indeed, it seems probable that one could visit a tribe or group that has pretty much been left alone by the outside world and find, quite by chance, someone wearing a Coca-Cola T-shirt or, à la _The Gods Must Be Crazy_, using a Coke bottle as a tool. Coca-Cola is a global symbol of American popular culture.

A BRIEF GLOBAL CULTURAL HISTORY OF MCDONALD'S

McDonald's is, like Coca-Cola, a global powerhouse. It is, of course, ubiquitous. There are McDonald's restaurants all over the world. They serve as a haven both for American tourists and for other customers. When McDonald's opened stores in Moscow and Beijing, for example, the lines of locals waiting for service stretched for blocks. Its 50,776 stores seem to be quite literally everywhere.

In addition, McDonald's stands as a powerful symbol of American cultural globalization. Its golden arches logo is as distinctive as the American flag. Its restaurants grew in concert with the American love of the automobile, a fact reflected in the presence of drive-through lanes at many of its locations. What could be more American than to not have to get out of one's car even to eat? McDonald's is thus both an indicator of globalization and evidence of the American cultural way of life.

The success of McDonald's was grounded in a simple idea: providing desirable food and drink at low cost, fast. This was by no means a new idea: Ray Kroc, the creator of McDonald's as a nationwide chain, experienced this kind of dining when he visited a group of restaurants in Los Angeles, California, to which he had sold what seemed to Kroc to be a surprisingly large number of Mixmaster automatic milkshake machines. Kroc could not understand why some of the Los Angeles restaurants needed as many as eight of these machines in a single store since each machine could make five milkshakes at a time. On visiting this mini-chain, called McDonald's, Kroc was impressed with the production-line nature of the stores' operations—and with the line of customers who waited outside the restaurants' doors from the moment they opened until the moment they closed. The stores sold hamburgers for fifteen cents; cheese was four cents extra. In 1954, at the age of fifty-two, Kroc bought into the McDonald's partnership and in 1955 began franchising its stores nationwide. The first modern McDonald's opened in Des Plaines, Illinois, on April 15, 1955. It stands as a museum today.[12]

Not only was the idea not new to Ray Kroc—it wasn't new in the United States. Chains like Burger King, Carl's Jr., In-N-Out Burger, Krystal, Steak 'n Shake, White Castle, and Burger Chef all sold hamburgers before Kroc franchised his first McDonald's.[13] There were, moreover, competitive chains selling chicken, sandwiches, and ice cream across America in those years, along with an array of more formal, sit-down, full-service restaurants catering to the ever wealthier and ever more mobile American market. However, through a combination of factors like picking good sites for stores, systematizing operations across all restaurants, and effective marketing, McDonald's caught on with American consumers quite quickly. By 1958, there were 34 McDonald's restaurants in the United States; 67 more opened the next year, for a total of 101. Sales escalated accordingly: in 1963, the company sold its one-billionth hamburger, and in 1968 it opened its one-thousandth store. In 1972, the company had $1 billion in sales, and by 1976 the company passed $3 billion in sales—and 20 billion in total hamburger sales.

McDonald's updated its product offerings regularly to attract repeat business and entice new customers into its restaurants. It added the Filet-O-Fish sandwich to its national line in 1965 after a Cincinnati, Ohio, franchisee noted that he was losing business on Fridays, when Catholics were supposed to avoid eating meat. Kroc initially rejected the idea of a fish sandwich for the restaurant, but he was persuaded when the local owner developed a sandwich on his own and proved that it sold well. Local pressures likewise inspired the Big Mac: a Pittsburgh, Pennsylvania, storeowner discovered that local steel mill workers weren't satisfied with the size of a single burger. They wanted a single hamburger that filled them like a meal. The Big Mac was the answer and was added to the McDonald's national menu in 1968. McDonald's developed the Egg McMuffin breakfast sandwich in 1973 and expanded to offer a full breakfast menu in 1977. By 1987, 25 percent of all breakfasts eaten outside the home in the United States were eaten at McDonald's. In time, products like the Happy Meal for children, Chicken McNuggets, and salads were added to the franchise's lineup. While not all these product innovations succeeded—the McLean burger, with less fat, was a notable failure—they continued to draw consumers to the restaurants.

McDonald's greatest product accomplishment may well have been the french fry. The original McDonald's restaurants in Los Angeles made fresh fries daily. They were a big hit. However, when Kroc tried to duplicate this item in his franchise, the result was failure: potato storage took up a large amount of floor space in each facility, and the potatoes had to be dried under a fan to become starchy enough to withstand washing and frying. These problems were overcome when a McDonald's potato supplier, Jack Simplot, invented a technique to cut, freeze, and prepare fries at his potato-processing facilities. The resulting precut and pre-prepared potatoes could be shipped directly to the restaurants, where they could then be fried. This process saved space in the stores and guaranteed product uniformity throughout the McDonald's chain.

Other innovations made McDonald's a destination restaurant with a strong brand identity. The chain changed mascots in 1963, replacing the "Speedee man" with a circus clown–like character, Ronald McDonald. Ronald McDonald would become the instantly recognizable face of the franchise and also the character and face of Ronald McDonald House Charities, which provides places for the parents and loved ones of children with cancer to stay during their children's treatment. Eating at McDonald's could thereafter be justified as an act of charity, not just self-indulgence.

McDonald's offered other innovations to attract customers. In 1971, it opened its first McDonald's Playland, a play area for children now in many McDonald's restaurants. It became heavily involved in movie cross-promotions, regularly providing figurines based on popular films as part of Happy Meals and thereby drawing in more children and their families. And while the company did not invent the idea of a drive-through lane for its restaurants, it added them in 1975. The drive-through would eventually account for more than half of all McDonald's sales across the franchise.

At least one other aspect of McDonald's success deserves attention: its linkage of architecture and advertising. At its beginning, McDonald's integrated its distinctive golden arches logo into the actual architecture of its early restaurants. In time, the arches were moved from the building to the restaurant's sign, with the arches linked together to form an instantly recognizable M at the beginning of "McDonald's." Interbrand ranks McDonald's as the twelfth most valuable brand in the world, worth $39.4 billion in 2015.[14]

After first establishing restaurants across the United States and Canada, McDonald's went global in the 1970s. It opened its first international store in Costa Rica and then opened stores in Germany, Holland, Australia, and Japan in the early years of the decade. It opened its five-thousandth store, in Japan, in 1978.

While expansion continued throughout the 1980s, it wasn't until the fall of the Berlin Wall and the end of the Cold War that McDonald's was able to establish itself as a ubiquitous global presence. In the early 1990s, for example, McDonald's operated in fifty-eight foreign countries with more than thirty-six hundred restaurants. It only opened its ten-thousandth store in April 1988, thirty-three years after its first franchise. Since the fall of the Berlin Wall in 1989, however, its growth has been explosive. It only took the company eight more years, until 1996, to add another ten thousand stores to its portfolio, for a total of twenty thousand in 1996. By the end of 1997, the chain was opening two thousand new restaurants a year. That is one every five hours.

International growth drove much of this increase. The chain added over seventy-four hundred new stores overseas between 1991 and 1998. It had franchises in 114 countries in that time. It entered the Middle East (Israel) in 1993 and India in 1996. It developed the McSki-thru in Lindvallen, Sweden, that same year. When a McDonald's opened in Kuwait City, Kuwait, in 1994, the line at the drive-through was seven miles long. This growth led to a shift in the sources of McDonald's revenues: in 1992, the company generated 60 percent of its sales in the United States, but by 1997 that percentage had fallen to 42.5. This global shift has, if anything, intensified in recent years: McDonald's is seeing greater sales overseas even as its domestic U.S. sales have been declining.[15]

Two stores, one in the heart of the former Soviet Union in Moscow and the other in Beijing, China, near Tiananmen Square, stand as particularly striking examples of the global growth of McDonald's. The openings of these two stores were highly symbolic and seemed to confirm political theorist Francis Fukuyama's claim that the fall of the Soviet Union meant the "end of history," the end of great global ideological struggles. American-style liberal capitalist democracy had won.[16] Indeed, the Moscow McDonald's, opened in 1990, quickly became the city's biggest attraction, serving twenty-seven thousand customers a day.[17] Some of them waited for hours to be served. The situation in Beijing was, if anything, more dramatic: opened on August 23, 1992, the Beijing McDonald's served forty thousand people on its first day.[18]

In January 2017, McDonald's extended the franchise concept to its operations in China. The company sold controlling interest in its 2,400 formerly corporate-owned stores in mainland China, along with another 240 stores in Hong Kong, to a Chinese conglomerate. This, in turn, is expected to allow the new owners to pursue the opening of Mc-Donald's restaurants in smaller Chinese markets that the McDonald's corporation might not have been willing to risk entering. If successful, this franchise arrangement will likely see the McDonald's brand expand even further throughout China.[19]

One reason McDonald's has been so successful is its adaptability. Company stores and franchisees have been careful to shape their products in ways that meet the needs and expectations of the local communities they serve. It has had its restaurants inspected as kosher for Jewish customers and as halal, the equivalent standard, for Muslims. It has changed the composition of its fry oil, once based on beef fat, to accommodate the religious requirements of India's Hindu population. (Problems achieving this standard are addressed below.) The company also adapts its menus to meet the expectations of its local consumers. It is possible to buy beer in McDonald's restaurants in Germany, for example. McDonald's in Istanbul, Turkey—like almost all other fast-food restaurants in the city—delivers.

The adaptability of McDonald's is reflected in a series of studies compiled by James Watson in *Golden Arches East: McDonald's in East Asia*. The restaurant offers espresso and cold pasta in Italy; chilled yogurt drinks in Turkey; teriyaki hamburgers in Japan, Taiwan, and Hong Kong; a grilled salmon sandwich called the McLak in Norway; and Mc-Spaghetti in the Philippines. It offers the McHuevo in Uruguay. Waiters in Rio de Janeiro serve Big Macs with champagne at candlelit restaurants. McDonald's restaurants in Caracas, Venezuela, have had hostesses seat customers, place orders, and bring customers their meals. It has thus integrated itself as a provider of local cuisines around the world.[20]

McDonald's has also shaped Asian cultures in several ways, some quite predictable, others less so. For example, the restaurants are common hangouts for young people, serving as a place where teenagers can escape the relative strictures of life at home. Consequently, the restaurants have at times been turned into leisure centers and after-school meeting places. Unsurprisingly, french fries have become a staple part of younger people's diets across Asia—fries are in fact the most globally consumed item in the McDonald's line.[21]

But such predictable changes do not fully describe the many ways in which the chain's restaurants have influenced Asian culture. Many

Asian women apparently find McDonald's a safe place to relax and avoid aggressive, often sexual harassment. Additionally, McDonald's has made birthday parties a central feature of life in parts of East Asia: in Hong Kong, for example, it was historically the practice to record dates of birth for use later in life—for instance, to check the horoscopes of prospective marriage partners—but to make little of annual birthdays. McDonald's made birthday parties a central part of its marketing, thereby placing a premium on families' knowing and celebrating—and being seen to celebrate—their children's birthdays. On another front, it was once very rare for people to eat with their hands in Japan. The spread of McDonald's and other fast-food restaurants has made this both more common and more acceptable.[22]

McDonald's has also shaped consumer culture. Even something as seemingly common as standing in a line to wait one's turn to order from a preset and limited menu is in fact a cultural adaptation. As McDonald's restaurants opened, their employees and advertising had to teach potential customers how to behave. For example, employees at the Moscow McDonald's moved up and down the line explaining that at McDonald's smiles are an expected part of the service and should not be confused with threats or mockery, which smiles were previously seen to indicate in Russia. Even cleanliness standards changed under pressure from McDonald's: the company has strict standards for hygiene in its kitchens and restrooms, and competitors were forced to change their practices as consumers grew accustomed to the McDonald's way of doing business.[23]

As was true of Coca-Cola, the global scope and significance of McDonald's has led to serious criticisms of the company as a global entity. International concerns about rising global obesity have focused on the chain's offerings; American documentarian Morgan Spurlock filmed *Supersize Me*, named for the restaurant's "supersize" drink and fries offerings, to chronicle his experiences eating only McDonald's for thirty consecutive days. His doctor forced him to quit before the thirty days were up because of the severe impact that its high-fat, high-calorie offerings were having on his health. (McDonald's subsequently eliminated its supersize menu.) Eric Schlosser offered a broader indictment of fast-food restaurants and the lifestyles that developed to accommodate them in his 2001 *Fast Food Nation: The Dark Side of the American Meal*.[24]

Lifestyle changes like those seen across East Asia provoke further worries on the part of many commentators and analysts. McDonald's has changed various consumer cultures, eating styles, and social relationships. As discussed in chapter 1, such changes inevitably engender substantial resistance, fear, uncertainty, and even anger. People worry that local cultural products will be replaced by those offered by the global corporation, even as they see local business practices and relationships changed to meet the needs of the global, transnational company. They also worry about the fact that their children spend their time in new places, making new contacts and, perhaps most worryingly, adopting new styles and cultural behaviors—like eating lots of french fries or learning English from a McDonald's menu board. Such changes can—or can be seen to—cause a wide range of cultural changes that work as a subtle form of cultural imperialism. Local cultures might be displaced in favor of a global, consumerist, effectively American one.

McDonald's has also not always lived up to its dietary commitments. On entering the Indian market, for example, the chain promised that the oil in which its fries were cooked would contain no beef fat. This promise was made to meet the dietary restrictions of Hindus, for whom cows are sacred and beef is forbidden. However, McDonald's continued to add a small amount of beef fat to its fry oil mixture to ensure the desired taste for the fries. The company was forced to change its oil formula when this practice was discovered and it lost a lawsuit. The incident left many people with concerns about whether the restaurant would live up to its other dietary promises.

Like Coca-Cola, McDonald's has faced an array of criticisms from environmentalists. McDonald's is a hamburger restaurant, after all, meaning that its growth necessitates an increase in the amount of beef available to feed its customers. This is quite separate from the chain's reliance on vast amounts of chicken, potatoes, and other crops to produce its food. Beef production is particularly troubling to many environmentalists because it takes a large amount of grain to feed cows to the point that they gain enough weight to slaughter. Growing large amounts of grain, in turn, requires both bringing new land into production and using large amounts of chemicals to fertilize crops and protect them from infestation and disease. Rain forests and other delicate ecosystems have been destroyed to serve the planet's growing demand for beef, sparking concerns that humans are both driving some species to extinction and promoting global warming to satisfy their fast-food desires. McDonald's is not the only source of this pressure, of course, but it is the largest and most globally recognizable symbol of the global love affair with beef. It therefore takes a leading role in debates about human-caused environmental degradation and species extinction worldwide. Its demand for cheap chicken causes similar questions to be raised in terms of the mass-production chicken farms needed to satisfy its requirements.

In just fifty-four years, McDonald's has gone from a small number of restaurants offering quick meals at low prices to the symbol of global fast food. (As an aside, the restaurant only sells Coca-Cola soft drinks at its stores, further linking these two brands as global forces.) Today it has stores in 119 countries across six continents. It has annual revenues of over $24 billion.[25] It is a global symbol of America and a major force in contemporary globalization.

A BRIEF GLOBAL CULTURAL HISTORY OF BLUE JEANS

It is not strictly correct to say that Levi Strauss, a German-born entrepreneur who moved to San Francisco during the gold rush that hit California after the ore was discovered there in 1848, invented blue jeans. The fabric called "denim" existed before Strauss made pants from it, and in fact denim clothing existed when Strauss started to market the pants that now bear his name. Indeed, Strauss never intended to become a clothing maker: he went to California to sell mining supplies to hopefuls infected with gold fever. That business failed, however, and Strauss went into business with Jacob Davis, a local tailor who hit upon the idea of adding copper rivets to the pockets and other weak points of the denim pants he made. Thus were Levi's blue jeans born.[26]

Blue jeans quickly became a standard item for American workers. Cowboys wore them as they rode. Farmers wore them as they planted and reaped. Laborers relied on their sturdiness as they laid pipes, built roads, and worked in factories. Manufacturers produced women's sizes in World War II to accommodate the many women who moved into the war-production workforce. Jeans were reliable. They also signaled the wearer's status as working-class.

In an early example of the way popular culture fed on and reinforced itself, the film industry helped bring jeans to global consciousness. Cowboys were seen to wear them in generations of early movie Westerns. This established blue jeans as quintessentially American clothing. Whether good guys or bad guys, cowboys were American. So were jeans. (Notably, at a conference I attended in Istanbul in April 2017, titled "America at Home and Abroad," "America" as a concept was represented on the cover page of the conference program by a stack of blue jeans.)

Blue jeans began to move out of the world of work in the 1950s. Beatnik poets and cultural nonconformists adopted them as expressions of their rejection of mainstream culture, symbolized in their view by the gray flannel suit of the "organization man" who went to work in a big, anonymous office building to sell insurance or do some other apparently boring and soulless job. Beats and "bad boys," symbolized by actors like James Dean and Marlon Brando and movies like *Rebel without a Cause* and *The Wild Bunch*, expressed their refusal to conform to dominant norms and values by wearing tight jeans rolled up at the ankles, often with black leather jackets and white T-shirts with cigarette packs rolled up in the sleeves. Elvis Presley, too, became an early icon of jeans-wearing rebellion as he challenged the sexual mores of the times while performing hits like "Jailhouse Rock." Jeans were a way for wearers to publicly declare their unwillingness to comply with the values of McCarthyite, Cold War America.

Like most cultures facing challenge, 1950s America fought back against the perceived threat posed by the growing number of apparent deviants across society wearing blue jeans. Dress codes were instituted and aggressively enforced in schools: not only were jeans banned, but women were often denied the right to wear pants at all. Police treated bands of jeans-wearing youths as likely criminals and sought to break up any group as quickly as possible. Mainstream movies and television shows reinforced traditional morality by showing teenagers in conformist clothing behaving as their parents wanted them to. Wearing jeans was a political act with political consequences.

The 1960s shattered whatever efforts mainstream America had undertaken to limit the cultural spread of blue jeans. The social and political protesters of the decade wore blue jeans to signal their rejection of conventional American values. In part, this was a result of the attempts to control jeans wearing in the 1950s: wearing blue jeans after society tried to stamp them out was a clear declaration of resistance. The fact that the pants were made of denim cotton provided an additional statement of difference. Fashion in the 1950s had emphasized artificial fabrics like easy-to-clean polyester. Cotton was natural—the antithesis of the corporate-dominated, antinature ethos of the organization man. Jeans became as much a symbol of the counterculture and student activist movements of the period as did long hair, drug use, the sexual revolution, and what is today referred to as "classic" rock.

By the end of the decade, jeans were ubiquitous in the United States—especially among students. U.S. jeans sales doubled nationally in the three years from 1962 to 1965. They quintupled again from 1965 to 1970.[27] A decade that had begun with students wearing coats and ties, or at least khakis and button-down shirts, to their college classes ended with students in blue jeans, even if they did not intend to make a political statement. As often as not, their parents were wearing jeans too.

The 1970s saw jeans enshrined as a central symbol of American culture. The upscale department store chain Neiman Marcus gave Levi Strauss & Co. its Distinguished Service in Fashion Award in 1973. The American Fashion Critics gave the company a special award for making "a fundamental American fashion that . . . now influences the world." The now defunct American Motors Corporation, maker of the Gremlin and Hornet car lines, contracted with Levi Strauss to provide blue denim fabric for the interiors of its two automobiles. Denim was believed to signal both patriotism (an ironic reversal of the values of the 1960s counterculture activists) and optimism to consumers. These decisions were confirmed by 1977, when over 500 million pairs of jeans were sold in the United States alone. This was more than double the U.S. population.[28]

The degree to which jeans had emerged from the counterculture and entered mainstream society in the 1970s was reflected in the emergence of a large market for upscale, expensive, "designer" jeans. Fashion powerhouses like Calvin Klein, Givenchy, and Oscar de la Renta produced expensive jeans as fashion statements. Calvin Klein sold 125,000 pairs of these costly pants every week in 1979.[29] Jeans had evolved from workmen's staple to fashion essential.

Along the way, blue jeans became a global standard of fashion. Several different measures of their global popularity can be offered, but a particularly striking one derives from a study of consumer awareness of American brands in the Soviet Union. A 1989 survey of college students at Kharkov State University in Ukraine found that English-speaking students knew of a wide range of American brand names, including blue jeans companies. The students also recognized American automobile, cigarette, and soft drink brands.[30] (Jeans were heavily traded on the black market in the Soviet Union in this period.)

Other measures of the global success of blue jeans can be offered as well. One study found that in 2011 the average consumer worldwide owned seven pairs of jeans.[31] The average man owned six pairs, while the average woman owned seven.[32] Seventy-five percent of consumers reported that they "loved" or "enjoyed" wearing denim; 75 percent of women and 72 percent of men reported preferring to wear denim jeans to other casual pants.[33] In 2016, more than 1.2 billion pairs of jeans were sold globally, and jeans sales outside the United States made up nearly $43 billion of the $56 billion in jeans purchases worldwide.[34]

One of the more striking features of this global growth is that jeans sales are less dependent on franchised networks of suppliers than is the case with restaurants or soft drinks. There are major brands of jeans, of course: Levi Strauss and Wrangler are global icons. But blue jeans have been adapted and produced across the globe. In some cases, this production is explicit piracy, meaning that established brand labels are simply sewn directly onto pants made in factories and workshops not affiliated with the companies in any way. In many cases, however, the making of blue jeans is simply another domestic industry. It is possible to buy locally produced blue jeans in many places around the world; as one example, I found numerous denim shops in the Grand Bazaar in the heart of Istanbul. Jeans are a culturally transparent product, in Scott Robert Olson's phrase: they emerged from the American cultural milieu but offered images of comfort, freedom, and even nonconformist rebellion that resonated with customers worldwide.[35] It is possible to see people wearing jeans virtually anywhere on the planet regardless of, or perhaps in addition to, whatever the native standards of clothing might be.

As with Coca-Cola and McDonald's, any product that has global impact also generates social and economic concerns. The same is true for blue jeans, although in the absence of a central corporate brand on which to focus concerns, the issues raised regarding blue jeans and the blue jeans industry are more diffuse and indirect than those aimed at Coke and McDonald's.

One set of complaints targets the creeping casualism embedded in the very notion of wearing blue jeans. Fears that jeans cause cultural change have been common in both industrial democracies and emerging societies around the world. Numerous commentators have opined that blue jeans represent a threat to proper dress codes in the office, in schools, and even in public life. Blue jeans are seen to tempt people away from proper conduct precisely because they are comfortable and convenient: their casual use is believed to promote lack of care in relation to one's job, one's studies, and one's interaction with other human beings. Such concerns are particularly noteworthy in "new" areas of jeans' global expansion. Whether the style is infiltrating the boardroom or rural Asia, concerns are raised that the norms, values, ideals, and rituals associated with normal life in these cultural enclaves are likely to be changed under the casualism that emerges when blue jeans are common.

Another focus of concern in the globalization of blue jeans has been the politics of cotton. Cotton is a globally traded product that has the potential to be a major export in many developing countries. It is also, of course, the source of denim, the foundation material for blue jeans. Building on the notion of comparative advantage discussed in chapter 1, many countries around the world have excellent growing conditions for cotton. They also have low labor costs, meaning that cotton can be grown there relatively inexpensively. According to the theory of comparative advantage, these countries ought to dominate the global trade in cotton. These nations could then use any profits generated from growing cotton to support their national development, and consumers around the planet could enjoy high-quality cotton products at low prices. The United States, however, has a well-developed cotton industry that is not globally competitive under current trade conditions but has substantial influence in Congress and the rest of the U.S. political system. U.S. cotton farmers have used their political clout to gain national subsidies for their products, in effect using U.S. taxpayer dollars to subsidize the real price of U.S. cotton on global markets. American taxpayers pay some of their taxes to U.S. cotton producers so that these producers can sell cotton for the same price as international producers can.

This practice violates the theory of free trade in several ways. For example, it raises the actual cost of cotton goods for American consumers, since they are paying taxes to buy jeans at the same cost at which they could buy jeans made with cotton produced by international farmers without any tax subsidy. It also means that international producers do not have the opportunity to invest their profits into local economies, thereby stimulating local demand for goods and services—including those of U.S. companies and brands.

Regardless of the policy recommendations embedded in the theory of free trade and comparative advantage, U.S. cotton farmers use their political power to maintain the tax subsidies their products receive. This in turn causes significant challenges for advocates of free trade, especially when new international trade agreements are negotiated. Recent trade negotiations have been complicated by the desires of many countries to protect their politically powerful yet uncompetitive industries; one particularly contentious set of issues has been the international trade in cotton. Blue jeans manufacture by no means accounts entirely for the growth in cotton farming globally, but it is a central market for the cotton industry. Blue jeans are, consequently, indirectly at the center of global trade fights today.

There have been environmental complaints about blue jeans as well. Cotton fields might occupy lands that could be used for growing food. Alternatively, cotton fields might replace vital habitats for native species. Concerns have also arisen about the dyes used to make jeans blue or other colors, as well as the techniques like acid washing used to weather jeans into fashionable looks. Chemicals can leach—or be dumped—into local water supplies. Workers exposed to toxic fumes have experienced serious health consequences. And of course, the simple act of transporting cotton and cotton goods to markets around the world entails burning fossil fuels in trucks, trains, and ships. Global trade may well encourage global warming.

At least one other concern about the blue jeans industry deserves attention: how they are made. Most blue jeans are made in factories in the developing world, many of which are so-called sweatshops. This complaint is by no means unique to the blue jeans industry: most apparel is made in factories in places without the same standards for worker health, safety, comfort, and decent treatment that are common, if not universal, in countries across North America, Europe, and Japan. The low wages paid in many such factories stand in stark contrast to the hundreds of dollars some customers pay for designer jeans (or shoes, or jackets, or other apparel items). One of the consequences of low-priced clothing is exploitative labor practices in the parts of the world that actually make the jeans worn by people elsewhere.

As was the case with the analysis of the global/cultural position of Coca-Cola and McDonald's offered earlier, whether one thinks that blue jeans are wonderful or a profound symbol of globalization gone wrong, it is clear that what started as a technical solution to the problem miners had getting clothing strong enough to stand up to the demands they placed on it has become a central force in economic and cultural globalization. Blue jeans are an American phenomenon that has become a global one—and a local one at the same time. They express rebellion, Western individualism, and personal freedom even as they are marketed by global megacorporations to an increasingly interconnected world. This convergence of economics and culture is a central feature of globalization today.

THE EMERGING GLOBAL CULTURAL HISTORY OF THE NFL

Unlike Coca-Cola, McDonald's, and blue jeans, the National Football League (NFL) has not achieved anything like an iconic global status. American-born sports like baseball and basketball do have an international presence; Iran, for example, has a professional basketball league. So does China. And while Canada has its own national football league, populated mostly by expatriate Americans, far and away the most popular sport in the world is soccer—which is known in most countries as "football." Global sports commentators usually must say explicitly that they are referring to "American" football when describing the American game—otherwise their audiences will assume they mean soccer. By contrast, inside the United States it almost never occurs to anyone who hears the word "football" that one might be speaking about soccer. (This book uses the American terms for these two sports for the sake of simplicity.) Thus, while the world drinks American drinks and eats American foods and wears American clothing (all while watching

American movies and television shows and listening to American music), it does not, for the most part, play American football.

Despite the gap that exists between American sports and the global audience, the NFL has begun extensive efforts to take its sport worldwide. League leaders have recognized that the world exists and has money. They are trying to replicate the success of companies like Coca-Cola, McDonald's, and Levi Strauss in making their products an essential part of global life.

Notably, the NFL is organized on a version of the franchise principle. Power in the league really lies in the hands of each team's owner. Owners (who may be one person or a consortium of individuals) enter contractual relationships with each other to follow agreed-on bylaws governing schedules, rules, labor practices, and cost- and profit-sharing plans. The owners have created a central governing board to enforce rules and adjudicate disputes. This differs from the case of both Coca-Cola and McDonald's, in which a central company licenses and administers franchisees, but it has proved a successful model for increasing the size of profits for the NFL. The owners' association reserves the right to approve or reject new owners and new franchises, as other franchise operations do.

As a sport, football emerged in the mid-nineteenth century on American college campuses. Derived from rugby, early football lacked features like the forward pass that are common in the game today. A consortium of universities in the American Northeast negotiated the first set of rules governing football in 1876; over the next decade, many of the rules that define modern football, such as eleven-man teams, four downs per possession, and the requirement that the ball be moved a certain number of yards (at first five, then later ten) to start a new sequence of downs, were developed.[36]

While this early version of football was popular, especially on college campuses, it was also dangerously violent. Players ran into each other at high speed with little or no protective clothing or equipment, and formations developed that placed opposing players at high risk. Most notorious of these was the "flying wedge," in which players linked their arms together and charged into the opponent's ranks. Eighteen players died in 1905 alone.[37]

To protect the sport from its own violence, President Theodore Roosevelt asked football's governing body to create new rules to reduce the death and injury count. Innovations like the forward pass and the creation of a neutral zone separating teams by a yard before initiating each play were integrated to try to reduce the game's violence. When these innovations failed to prevent further deaths, teams were required to increase the padding and protection offered by their uniforms. Interlocking formations were also banned. The sport flourished.

Professional football developed in the early part of the twentieth century. The first player paid to perform was William Heffelinger, who earned $500 in 1892. The first game between two professional teams occurred in 1915. The first professional football league was established in 1920, with Olympian and semiprofessional player Jim Thorpe as its president. The league changed its name to the National Football League in 1921. It had eleven teams spread across the Midwest, often in relatively small towns. Today's Chicago Bears, for example, started life in 1920 as the Decatur Staleys in Decatur, Illinois. They moved to Chicago in 1921 and became the Chicago Bears in 1922.[38]

College football dominated fans' attention until World War II. After the war, professional football began to appear on American television screens, and the professional game, which was faster paced and higher scoring than the college version, grew in popularity. Stars like Johnny Unitas, Bart Starr, Paul Hornung, and Frank Gifford wowed audiences with their skills, and American marketers linked them with various products for advertising and promotional purposes. (It was, for example, common at the time for athletes to advertise cigarettes on the grounds that one brand or another was particularly good for calming the lungs and increasing performance.)

Professional football emerged in its contemporary form in the 1960s. A competitor league, the American Football League (AFL), was formed in 1960 to challenge the NFL's dominance of the sport. While NFL leaders at first dismissed the AFL as an upstart, the AFL had substantial success in recruiting and signing top college talent. The two leagues announced they would merge in 1966, and in 1970 the modern NFL was created with two conferences, the National Football Conference and the American Football Conference.

At the heart of the merger was a game that has become the linchpin of the NFL's global marketing efforts, the Super Bowl, billed—probably inaccurately—as the most watched single sporting event in the world. (Soccer's World Cup draws far more viewers worldwide; however, the

World Cup occurs only once every four years, while the Super Bowl is an annual event. The Super Bowl is the most watched television event in the United States every year.) The Super Bowl began as a competition between the winners of the NFL and AFL championships. While the game started as a relatively small affair, almost an afterthought to each league's regular season, the Super Bowl is now an international marketing extravaganza. The NFL uses the Super Bowl to try to garner global attention: the 2017 game was shown live in Australia, Canada, England, France, Germany, Italy, Mexico, New Zealand, and Spain, for example.[39] Streaming through social media and other platforms provided many other opportunities for global audiences to watch the game, although time differences make watching live problematic. I can attest that the 2008 game, Super Bowl XLII, was the first Super Bowl broadcast live in the United Kingdom. Given the time difference between the United States and the United Kingdom, the game began at about 11:30 p.m. local time. Meanwhile, in 2016, live streaming the game while I was living in Finland would have required starting to watch at 2:30 a.m.

Marketing the Super Bowl as an international game has been only part of the NFL's global strategy. The league also created a subsidiary in Europe. NFL Europa went by several different names from 1991 to 2007. Most of its teams were based in Germany. The NFL shut the league down in 2007 in favor of more aggressive efforts to market its primary product, the NFL, to a global audience.

In 1986, the league started to literally take its product on the road. It began playing at least one preseason game internationally each year. Tokyo and London have seen the most games, but the league has sent teams to Berlin, Mexico City, Barcelona, Dublin, Osaka, and Sydney as well. Starting in 2007, the league sent two teams to London to play a regular season game at Wembley Stadium. This game became a regular feature of the NFL's season, and in the 2017–2018 season the NFL is planning four games in London. (One of the London games was the only one I watched while living in Finland during the 2015–2016 season.) While this costs teams a home game and the home ticket sales associated with it, the NFL deems it an important part of increasing the league's international appeal.

There are significant barriers to the NFL's global spread, however. Among these is a marked lack of familiarity with football's rules and ethos worldwide. One small example can be found in the fact that kickers, who play an important but relatively small part in a football game, often receive the biggest cheers in arenas outside the United States. This makes perfect sense, of course: soccer players are, as a practical matter, kickers, and superstar David Beckham's kicking skills are of such international acclaim that the 2002 cult hit movie *Bend It Like Beckham* played off them to ground its soccer-based love-and-cultural-struggle story. But while points after touchdown, field goals, punts, and kickoffs can play a crucial, sometimes even determinative role in the outcome of a game, kickers and kicking occupy only a tiny amount of field time in football. The league emphasizes the aggressive, intense hitting and physicality of its players as the source of the game's energy and excitement, not the play of kickers—who usually avoid the most intense action unless they are compelled to join in during an emergency. Put another way, NFL superstars are usually quarterbacks, linebackers, and wide receivers. Kickers are specialists without broad appeal.

Football is also a team sport whose stars' faces are obscured by masks and helmets. Thus, the very equipment required to play the game in relative safety guarantees that as the players engage in their acts of courage, athleticism, and strength, they will not be seen except through the slotted gaps of a face mask or by the numbers they wear on their backs. This stands in stark contrast to soccer, basketball, and baseball: the crowd could see Brazilian soccer hall of fame legend Pelé kick his remarkable bicycle kick into the net; they now watch stars like Ronaldo, Messi, and Neymar, who are so globally famous they only need one name for everyone everywhere to know who they are—outside the United States, of course. Similarly, the National Basketball Association has made Chinese star Yao Ming a central part of its global outreach efforts, making him the face of the NBA in Asia. The NBA rode the shoulders of stars like Michael Jordan and Magic Johnson to global prominence in the 1980s—although it should be noted that even at the height of his popularity, Michael Jordan would not have had anything close to the global following of a modern soccer superstar. Neither would LeBron James. It is simply harder for football to duplicate the personality-based global marketing efforts that other sports have been able to utilize.

Football is also quite complex and expensive to organize. Soccer, after all, requires nothing more than some players, a mutually agreed-on spot to serve as a goal, and something to kick—as the monks of *The Cup* proved, a Coke can is sufficient. Basketball too requires little more than a ball, a couple of players, a flat space free of obstructions, and a hoop of some sort ten feet above the ground. Even shoes are optional. Moreover, the skills developed in these casual games can translate into national and international success: many stars of professional basketball learned the game in the rough-and-tumble world of pickup ball at an inner-city playground, for example. Indeed, it is possible to become a superstar in basketball through hard work, as NBA hall of fame player Larry Bird did through endless hours of practice in the barn next to his childhood home, regardless of the weather or the temperature.

None of this is true for football—in part because of things like insurance, uniform costs, and travel expenses. Organized football teams require a substantial amount of money to support players as they practice and play. NFL teams have forty-five active players on their rosters, for example, all of whom need to be transported to games, fed, insured, cared for when they get hurt, and, of course, paid. Some college teams have more than one hundred players with the same needs—other than getting paid. But even unorganized football is much harder to develop than is either soccer or basketball. A football field is 120 yards long and 53.5 yards wide—uncommon measurements in a world that has largely adopted the metric system. It takes eleven players on both offense and defense to play the game, and while it is possible to play both offense and defense, players usually need to specialize in one or the other (or a separate specialty like kicking) to advance. And while it is possible to play a version of football with less than a full complement of eleven players, a player usually needs to compete on a full-sized field against a full roster of talented opponents to have a chance to become a professional. These limitations make it harder for football to spread globally than for most other international sports.

Of course, the forces that limit the global spread of football are unlikely to deter the league's efforts to build a world of football fans. As suggested by the global success of franchises like Coca-Cola and McDonald's, as well as the spread of American styles like blue jeans, American manufacturers, franchisers, and marketers have demonstrated repeated success in taking their products to the world. The NFL today finds itself in the same position that McDonald's, Coca-Cola, and countless other global American businesses have in the past. Football may or may not become a global sport: the failure of NFL Europa points to the difficulties the league may face in spreading its product across the planet. That said, the track record of American goods and services, whether those discussed in this chapter or the movies, music, and television programs discussed in chapter 3, suggests that American football will likely become at least a much bigger sport around the world.

A BRIEF GLOBAL CULTURAL HISTORY OF FACEBOOK

The newest and arguably the most important force promoting the globalization of American popular culture is social networking. Originally conceived of as a way for friends—mostly college students at a few elite schools—to identify and interact with one another online, social networks have exploded into platforms for commerce, brand identification and loyalty, and even political revolutions.

Social networking barely existed when the first edition of this book was published in 2007. The first truly successful social network, Facebook, was created only in 2004. It followed from a programming exercise in which Harvard student Mark Zuckerberg hacked into the databases of each of Harvard's residence halls to create a web page on which fellow students could rate the relative attractiveness of Harvard's female students. "The Facebook," as it was originally titled, was intended to provide an online alternative to a hard copy book in which Harvard University pictured its students.

In its earliest iteration, The Facebook's users had to have a Harvard e-mail address to join the site. Soon thereafter, however, access to The Facebook was broadened to include students at other universities—most notably Stanford University in Palo Alto, California. Opening membership to Stanford students brought The Facebook to the attention of the technology professionals in Silicon Valley, centered in nearby San Jose, California. The company, now renamed Facebook, moved operations to California to be among the technology-savvy companies and programmers there. It opened to everyone with a valid e-mail address in 2006.

To say that social networking has been a growing phenomenon is like saying Mount Everest is sort of tall or the Pacific Ocean is kind of large. To anyone older than about thirty, social networking is a remarkable social innovation. They can remember a time "before Facebook."

To increasing numbers of younger people, however, social networking is just the way things are—and always have been. Meanwhile, social networks have proliferated. Twitter, Reddit, Tumblr, Instagram, and numerous other platforms have emerged to allow people to interact through digital space. Likewise, as platforms have multiplied, so have the ways site members use them to connect with ideas and people: users can tweet and pin and like and reblog and post and otherwise engage with groups, communities, individuals, and ideas in ways that were literally impossible even fifteen years ago. Social media is also in the process of profoundly disrupting whole industries, like taxicabs and hotels, as people use social network platforms to build the "gig economy" of people working for hire on demand, mediated through an application downloaded onto their ubiquitous smartphones. The social media revolution may be in its early phases, but it is transforming society as it develops.

Facebook stands at the center of the social networking revolution. While not the first, it is today far and away the most expansive, popular social network in the world. In December 2016, the company reported 1.23 billion active daily users worldwide; 1.86 billion people used the service at least monthly. That works out to about 25 percent of the population of the planet. If it were a country, Facebook would be by far the most populous country in the world. More than 85 percent of its users live outside the United States and Canada.[40]

There are significant regional gaps in Facebook's membership, however. The site has few members in China, for example, where the government seeks to control online access and has created competitor services like WeChat, Renren, Youku, and Weibo. (China's efforts to control its citizens' access to things like American popular culture and Facebook will be addressed in more detail in chapter 5.) Countries like Iran and Vietnam have also fought against Facebook and other social media. And, of course, the service is least likely to be used in places where people cannot afford access to smartphones or other digital media devices and the electricity to power them—although such limitations are becoming less significant as used mobile phones are increasingly available and as battery technology develops. These limitations aside, Facebook has the broadest membership of any social networking service in the world.

Whatever Facebook's charms as a place for people to rekindle friendships with high school friends or maintain relationships with distant family, for the purposes of this book what matters is the profound role Facebook and sites like it play in bringing American popular culture to a global audience. Facebook has provided marketers, sellers, producers, and proponents of American popular culture with multiple, reinforcing ways to push goods and services to a worldwide audience. A movie producer can release trailers for upcoming films and create a fan page for a film he or she is making. Facebook subscribers can "like" the page to receive updates about the movie, read comments from stars, and participate in interactive games or other activities related to the picture. Such fan pages can be created in multiple languages, or members can "like" a page in a language like English. In other words, the producer can build an audience for the movie by constructing an online community of support for it—a community that can be global because it is virtual. And what is true for a film can, of course, be just as true for music, television programs, or consumer goods like blue jeans, fast food, and sporting events. Facebook facilitates new kinds of interconnections among consumers and producers in digital relationships that could not exist otherwise.

Of course, much of Facebook's role in spreading American popular culture globally is not quite so marketed or directly transactional. That is, it is not necessary that a producer create a page that someone must "like" to connect a user to American popular culture content. Rather, Facebook has large numbers of fan pages constructed by ordinary users unconnected to the project at hand. Facebook hosts *Star Trek* fan pages and clothing-style fan pages and pages celebrating cultural events that are made and administered by persons-at-large, Facebook members who care about the issue/work/artifact and simply chose to express themselves on the matter, letting other users find them along the way. This user-driven content is, if anything, more authentic and meaningful to the member than producer-driven content. It exists as an expression of the fantasies and desires of people who have no financial incentive to promote the topic at hand. They engage the issue because they want to, finding a connection that is meaningful to them to sustain their interest in the topic.

Much of the content posted on Facebook by fans or producers is, importantly, exactly the kind of digitally extracted material that so concerns movie, music, and television producers, as discussed in chapter 3. Content, perhaps taken from sites like YouTube (owned by Internet search giant Google) or ripped from other sources, can be uploaded to Facebook's servers for display and advertising. Indeed, some opponents of restricting downloads, legal or not, point out that all such activity is a form of advertising for a given product: the person may not have paid for the rights to the song she has posted on Facebook, but when others hear it, they may well pay to download the album, movie, or television program. In either case, of course, American popular culture products end up being promoted.

Facebook, it should be noted, works hard to promote connections between users and content like that created by producers or fans. The company mines the data that users provide to it to refine both the advertisements users see and the messages the site sends to them. Facebook tracks users' connections with other users, assessing who a given member spends more time with and who receives less attention. Facebook also charts how much time its users spend on various sites and embeds cookies in the user's browser that report the member's "likes" of various persons, products, and services. Further, the company tracks what a member's friends "like" and how a member's friends interact with Facebook, on the theory that one's friends are like you in interests and experiences and so can serve as a proxy for your goals and desires. All this information, in turn, informs Facebook's ad placements and other "pushed" material, like the recommended pages that it presents to users. Facebook even shapes the e-mails its users see (or don't) according to the algorithms it employs to control the user's experience.

Facebook is trying to dominate its users' attention as part of what is being called the "attention economy": the idea that profits stem from keeping people focused on one social media platform (and its attendant advertising) rather than some other social media platform or website. Facebook wants to be its members' primary Internet portal and hopes its users move from Facebook-driven link to Facebook-posted advertisement in an endless cycle of Facebook-promoted content. Moreover, it offers a platform for users to play online games, take online quizzes, or participate in events with communities of like-minded people. Many people spend remarkable amounts of time playing games or otherwise engaging on Facebook and other social media, in part living in a Facebook-constructed artificial environment (all, of course, while Facebook examines their behaviors, seeking ways to better deliver specific types of users to specific advertisers). Indeed, if anything, Facebook might do even more to connect its users to its interface than it actually does: one former student of mine suggested that Facebook could alter a nation's sleep patterns and likely undermine its economic productivity simply by requiring that anyone playing one of its games wake up and interact with the game for at least ten minutes every three hours or immediately lose.[41]

To the degree that Facebook is successful in keeping its users connected to its servers and to each other, it also promotes what we can term a Facebook culture. The service encourages people to make numerous connections with other people, as well as products and services. I recently got a guilt-and-shame-laden notice on my account that if I had more friends, I'd have more updates—and, implicitly, more reason to spend more time on Facebook. In this way, Facebook promotes a kind of easy, casual conversational exchange among persons that may challenge established social conventions in many communities. Users are "friends" with people they may have never met and interact with them through casual forms like "text speak" or, increasingly, emoji language. Text speak is, notably, easier in a language like English than in, say, a pictographic language like Chinese and so may promote English as an international language. This is a recognizably American style of interpersonal exchange that, like learning to queue at McDonald's or to eat with one's hands, might reshape various cultural norms in "connected" societies.

Facebook can thus be seen as an engine for developing, curating, and promoting a vast array of cultural products to the broader world. People from almost everywhere who have enough political freedom and electricity infrastructure can engage with whatever material is posted on the site. And, of course, Facebook is not the only social networking platform. Others, like Twitter, are popular, as are photo-sharing sites like Instagram and Reddit, and blogging platforms like Tumblr, WordPress, and Blogger have proliferated. The ten or so years in which the world has grown increasingly wired together have brought with them the exponential growth of connections and linkages through which American cultural products can enter global use.

Inevitably, however, social networking has its critics. Facebook, in particular, has come under repeated criticism for its casual attitude toward users' privacy. The company assumes that members desire to share their information, and so it has regularly changed or otherwise created privacy settings that allow the maximum number of people to know what a given user is doing or sharing at a specific time. At one point, for example, Facebook planned to announce members' online purchases on their feeds if they logged in to a company through Facebook's site. Concerns that users might be buying presents or other items they wished to keep private led Facebook to cancel that function. Even today, however, users of the online music service Spotify have the option to log in to the site with their Facebook IDs—a feature that allows both companies to gather private information about users and potentially share it with others.

Additional concerns pertain to social networking's role in what might be termed "creeping Americanism" globally. Social networks empower technology-comfortable people with access to basic infrastructure like cell phones and electricity to connect in new and sometimes surprising ways, both locally and internationally. As a practical matter, therefore, younger people tend to congregate virtually on social networks. In other words, precisely those people who cultures typically fear will be corrupted by external influences (children and the relatively young, as discussed in chapter 1) engage most actively in global cultural exchanges through social networks. Likewise, precisely those people who are most worried about the cultural corruption of their children by alien and external forces—parents and social elders—are most disconnected from social networking. The tension is obvious. And notably, as parents and grandparents have joined Facebook, younger people have moved to services like Snapchat to escape parental oversight. The groundwork has been laid for a generational gap of unprecedented scope, a topic we will return to in chapter 6.

As discussed in more detail in chapter 5, social networking services have also faced criticism as tools of political rebellion and revolution, not to mention outright thuggery. The 2010–2011 Arab Spring protests were organized through sites like Facebook and Twitter. So too were the Occupy protests that began on Wall Street but rapidly spread around the world in the summer and fall of 2011. It is also clear that social networking services have abetted criminal activities like the London riots of August 2011. Notably, each of these events did not just cause social and political controversy. They also prompted government efforts to crack down and limit users' access to social networking sites. The technology may be neutral, but its use never is.

EVERYTHING, EVERYWHERE, ALL THE TIME

The five pop culture phenomena examined in detail in this chapter—Coca-Cola, McDonald's, blue jeans, the NFL, and Facebook—represent only a small slice of American popular culture beyond movies, music, and television programs. Many other companies, products, and practices might have been discussed to illustrate the global spread of American popular culture. Moreover, as the tie-in between McDonald's and Coca-Cola described earlier in this chapter suggests, the forces, products, ideals, values, rituals, and business practices embedded in American popular culture can work in intersecting and mutually supportive ways. American pop culture is a global behemoth.

The global ubiquity and interconnectedness of American popular culture can perhaps best be illustrated in a vignette offered by Robert J. Foster in the introduction to his book *Coca-Globalization*. Foster describes a night of entertainment he enjoyed in Papua New Guinea (PNG), arguably as far away from the bright lights and high-tech world of modern consumer culture as it is still possible to get today. As he puts it in this extended quote,

> On the last night of my brief visit in 2000, I did witness something that I had never before seen in these islands: a Pepsi commercial. As a fundraising event for the local community school, a video night had been organized. Dozens of school age children and a smaller contingent of adults of all ages poured into a gated enclosure on a perfect moonlit evening to watch a motley assortment of offerings—*Space Hunter, Jeremiah Johnson, Moses* and Michael Jackson's *Greatest Hits* (deliberately shown late in the program, after the younger children had fallen asleep). The worn cassettes were played on a television monitor hooked to a VCR and powered by a noisy diesel generator. The dusk to dawn marathon began with a compilation of music videos by Papua New Guinean pop bands, a stream of highly stylized song and dance routines almost invariably staged on a beach. Just before the tape ended, a brief promo for Pepsi-Cola, a sponsor of the recording company that produced the music, filled the monitor. Attractive young Papua New Guinean men and women cavorted together on screen in a speeding motorboat. In the audience, the adults clucked and the teenagers whistled at the spectacle. As the commercial's upbeat jingle finished, the warm night air moved to the hissed sounds of children

enunciating the word "Pepsi" or practicing their English by reading aloud the mellifluous slogan, "It's Pepsi in PNG."[42]

It's all there—absent, perhaps, a Facebook page announcing the event, which couldn't have been made because Facebook did not yet exist when this party occurred. American movies and music are tied to American products in a seamless whole. The PNG artists' work probably would be recognized as pop anywhere in the world because it flowed from forms generated in American pop culture. Advertising promoted not just a brand and lifestyle identity but English as well. There is even a brief glimpse of adult concern about the moral content of the programming on the docket: Michael Jackson's hits had to be played after the youngest children went to sleep, not before.

In some ways, what is remarkable about Foster's story is not that Papua New Guinean children were learning English from a Pepsi commercial but that Foster was surprised by it at all. Papua New Guinea is, admittedly, on the fringes of world trade and world politics, but the world is rapidly becoming smaller, and fewer and fewer places retain the kind of cultural isolation needed to avoid exposure to the various components of American popular culture. People worldwide report learning English from American movies, music, and television; there is no inherent reason why the people of Papua New Guinea should be any different. Foster's many travels to the region sensitized him to the changes that led to a small group of New Guinean fund-raisers watching American programming with a Pepsi commercial, but it is unlikely that anyone without such long experience would have been as surprised. One expects to see American popular culture products, styles, and values across the world, at least most of the time. (On my return from Istanbul in April 2017, for example, I noted that the airport shops were filled with Disney princesses—especially the *Frozen* characters—as well as Batman and Superman paraphernalia and the like, but other than Turkish candies, there was nothing definably Turkish for sale.)

Of course, American popular culture is not all about sodas and jeans and music. Movies show characters driving cars; these can be and often are obviously American. They show styles of dress, modes of behavior, and attitudes toward authority, religion, tradition, and sexuality that often manifest recognizably American perspectives on these contentious issues. In some cases, explicit placements of music or products are added to a film or television program, and numerous websites push Internet users to download ringtones, purchase items, or participate in social networks dedicated to various products and programming. Fast-food restaurants offer tie-ins with movies and music; the purchase of consumer items can bring coupons to some store or film. Social networks tighten these linkages by having consumers "like" products and establish brand and personal affiliations online. And consumers consume it all, in vast quantities, across the world in more and more markets.

CONCLUSION

American popular culture exists beyond its music, movies, and television programming. It exists in foods, dining experiences, clothing styles, and sports and in modes of human interaction as well. It emerged from specific historical contexts to become globally ubiquitous and culturally powerful both within and outside the United States. It is—or at least can be—an overwhelming, totalizing experience.

As suggested throughout this chapter, as well as in chapter 3, anything as globally pervasive, appealing, and potentially culturally transformative as American popular culture tends to generate concern, fear, opposition, and even anger. People worry that their children are adopting alien values shaped by a distant power over which they have no influence. Local producers worry that international conglomerates will drive them out of business. Local artisans, performers, critics, and artists worry that native, domestic cultural forms of music, art, and performance will be abandoned in favor of the whiz-bang wizardry of Hollywood productions. Yet others, both in the local community and elsewhere, worry that environmental degradation will destroy traditional ways of life and the natural environments that sustained them. In the end, all fear that unique, important, and distinctive lifestyles may be crushed and replaced by a washed-out, generic culture that political theorist Benjamin Barber once referred to as "McDisneySoft." Perhaps today that term should be expanded to "iMcDisneySoftBook."

Such concerns are not surprising. Nor are they irrational or panicked. As discussed in chapter 1, people usually respond in these ways when they perceive that their culture is under assault. This reaction is inevitably more intense when the agent of cultural change is distant and apparently untouchable. It is to be expected, then, that various communities worldwide have acted to protect or otherwise shield their cultures from the apparent onslaught of American popular culture. As discussed in detail in chapter 5, such reactions have been common worldwide. However, even as some communities have sought to limit the influence or power of American popular culture in their societies, most of the world's major economic powers have been working to lower trade barriers and enhance contacts among the world's communities. Popular culture has been a contentious and significant part of these efforts. It is to the question of how American popular culture intersects with the world of global trade policy that chapter 5 turns.

NOTES

1. The following discussion of the development of the franchise in the United States derives from Carrie Shook and Robert L. Shook, *Franchising: The Business Strategy That Changed the World* (Englewood Cliffs, NJ: Prentice Hall, 1993), 139–66; John A. Jackle and Keith A. Sculle, *Fast Food: Roadside Restaurants in the Automobile Age* (Baltimore: Johns Hopkins University Press, 1999), 139–62; and Thomas S. Dicke, *Franchising in America: The Development of a Business Method, 1840–1980* (Chapel Hill: University of North Carolina Press, 1992).

2. "World Motor Vehicle Production," OICA, http://oica.net/wp-content/uploads/ford-2010.pdf (accessed January 27, 2012).

3. "World Motor Vehicle Production."

4. "Our Business," Walmart, https://corporate.walmart.com/our-story/our-business (accessed May 9, 2017).

5. Orville Schell, "How Walmart Is Changing China (and Vice Versa)," *Atlantic Monthly* (December 2011): 80–98.

6. "Starbucks Coffee International," Starbucks, https://www.starbucks.com/business/international-stores (accessed May 9, 2017).

7. "Best Global Brands 2016 Rankings," Interbrand, http://www.interbrand.com/best-brands/best-global-brands/2016/ranking (accessed May 9, 2017).

8. This history is adapted from "125 Years of Sharing Happiness," Coca-colacompany.com, https://www.coca-colacompany.com/content/dam/journey/us/en/private/fileassets/pdf/2011/05/Coca-Cola_125_years_booklet.pdf (accessed July 14, 2017); "About Us," World of Coca-Cola, https://www.worldofcoca-cola.com/about-us/coca-cola-history (accessed May 9, 2017); and Mark Pendergast, *For God, Country, and Coca-Cola: The Unauthorized History of the Great American Soft Drink and the Company That Makes It* (New York: Scribner, 1993).

9. Pendergast, *For God, Country, and Coca-Cola*, 354–71; quote on 365.

10. See Cecil Munsey, *The Illustrated Guide to the Collectibles of Coca-Cola* (New York: Hawthorn Books, 1972), for a guide on such matters.

11. See Campaign to Stop Killer Coke, http://www.killercoke.org (accessed January 31, 2012).

12. Except where otherwise noted, the history of McDonald's presented here derives from numerous sources, including Shook and Shook, *Franchising*, 139–66; Jackle and Sculle, *Fast Food*, 139–62; "Our History," McDonald's, http://www.mcdonalds.com/us/en/our_story/our_history.html (accessed May 10, 2017); and "McDonald's Corporation," Funding Universe, http://www.fundinguniverse.com/company-histories/McDonalds-Corporation-Company-History.html (accessed May 10, 2017).

13. Jackle and Sculle, *Fast Food*, 135–36.

14. "12 McDonald's," Interbrand, http://interbrand.com/best-brands/best-global-brands/2016/ranking/mcdonalds (accessed May 10, 2017).

15. "McDonald's Sales Drop," *U.S. News & World Report*, January 23, 2017, https://www.usnews.com/news/business/articles/2017-01-23/mcdonalds-sales-rise-globally-but-dip-in-us (accessed May 10, 2017).

16. Francis Fukuyama, *The End of History and the Last Man* (New York: Free Press, 1992).

17. Jonathan Steele, "Muscovites Find Perestroika in a Restructured Cow," *Guardian*, February 1, 1990.

18. James L. Watson, ed., *Golden Arches East: McDonald's in East Asia* (Stanford, CA: Stanford University Press, 1997).

19. Amie Tsang and Sui-Lee Wee, "McDonald's China Operations to Be Sold to Locally Led Consortium," *New York Times*, January 9, 2017, https://www.nytimes.com/2017/01/09/business/dealbook/mcdonalds-china-citic-carlyle.html (accessed May 10, 2017).

20. Watson, *Golden Arches East*, 1–38.

21. Watson, *Golden Arches East*, 1–38.

22. Watson, *Golden Arches East*, 1–38.

23. Watson, *Golden Arches East*, 1–38.

24. Eric Schlosser, *Fast Food Nation: The Dark Side of the American Meal* (New York: Houghton Mifflin Harcourt, 2001).

25. "McDonald's 2016 Revenues to Decline YoY Despite Improvement; to Pick Up Pace Thereafter," NASDAQ, May 19, 2016, http://www.nasdaq.com/article/mcdonalds-2016-revenues-to-decline-yoy-despite-improvement-to-pick-up-pace-thereafter-cm623673 (accessed May 10, 2017).

26. This history derives from "The History of Blue Jeans," Jeans and Accessories, http://jeans-and-accessories.com (accessed May 10, 2017), and

"Blue Jeans History," Great Idea Finder, http://www.ideafinder.com/history/inventions/bluejeans.htm (accessed May 10, 2017).

27. Beverly Gordon, "American Denim: Blue Jeans and Their Multiple Layers of Meaning," in *Dress and Popular Culture*, ed. Patricia A. Cunningham and Susan Voso Lab (Bowling Green, OH: Bowling Green State University Popular Press, 1991), 34.

28. Gordon, "American Denim," 36.

29. Gordon, "American Denim," 37.

30. Virginia Wallace-Whitaker, "Awareness of American Brand Names in the Soviet Union" (paper presented at the annual meeting of the Association for Education in Journalism and Mass Communication, August 10–13, 1989).

31. "How Many Pairs of Denim Jeans Do Consumers Own?," Lifestyle Monitor, Cotton Incorporated, http://lifestylemonitor.cottoninc.com/LSM-Fast-Facts/001-How-many-pairs-denim-jeans-do-consumers-own/?category=denim&sort=viewall&mainSection=fastFacts&currentRow=3 (accessed January 31, 2012).

32. "How Many Pairs of Denim Jeans Do Men Own?," Lifestyle Monitor, Cotton Incorporated, http://lifestylemonitor.cottoninc.com/LSM-Fast-Facts/002-How-many-pairs-denim-jeans-do-men-own/?category=denim&sort=viewall&mainSection=fastFacts&currentRow=11 (accessed January 31, 2012); "How Many Pairs of Denim Jeans Do Women Own?," Lifestyle Monitor, Cotton Incorporated, http://lifestylemonitor.cottoninc.com/LSM-Fast-Facts/003-How-many-pairs-denim-jeans-do-women-own/?category=denim&sort=viewall&mainSection=fastFacts&currentRow=12 (accessed January 31, 2012).

33. "Percent of Consumers Who Love or Enjoy Wearing Denim," Lifestyle Monitor, Cotton Incorporated, http://lifestylemonitor.cottoninc.com/LSM-Fast-Facts/004-Percent-consumers-wearing-denim/?category=denim&sort=viewall&mainSection=fastFacts&currentRow=13 (accessed January 31, 2012); "Do Men and Women Prefer to Wear Denim Jeans or Casual Slacks?," Lifestyle Monitor, Cotton Incorporated, http://lifestylemonitor.cottoninc.com/LSM-Fast-Facts/009-Men-Women-Prefer-Denim-Jeans-Casual-Slacks/?category=denim&sort=viewall&mainSection=fastFacts&currentRow=17 (accessed January 31, 2012).

34. "Denim Jeans Industry Statistics," Statistic Brain, http://www.statisticbrain.com/denim-jeans-industry-statistics (accessed May 10, 2017).

35. Scott R. Olson, "Hollywood Planet: Global Media and the Competitive Advantage of Narrative Transparency," in *The Television Studies Reader*, ed. Robert C. Allen and Annette Hill (New York: Routledge, 2004), 114.

36. Except where otherwise noted, the following history is adapted from "A Brief History of the Game," Alameda High School, http://www.hornetfoot

ball.org/documents/football-history.htm (accessed May 10, 2017); "History of Football," Sports Know How, http://www.sportsknowhow.com/football/history/football-history.shtml (accessed May 10, 2017); "The History of American Football," Talk American Football, http://www.talkamericanfootball.co.uk/guides/history_of_american_football.html (accessed May 10, 2017); and "History of American Football," Wikipedia, http://en.wikipedia.org/wiki/History_of_American_football (accessed May 10, 2017).

37. Katie Zeima, "How Teddy Roosevelt Helped Save Football," *Washington Post*, May 29, 2014, https://www.washingtonpost.com/news/the-fix/wp/2014/05/29/teddy-roosevelt-helped-save-football-with-a-white-house-meeting-in-1905/?utm_term=.00ffac41d684 (accessed May 10, 2017).

38. "Tradition: History by Decades," Chicago Bears, http://www.chicagobears.com/tradition/history-by-decades/highlights-1920s.html (accessed May 10, 2017).

39. James Brady, "Super Bowl 2017 International Broadcasts: How to Watch Falcons vs. Patriots Abroad," SBNation, http://www.sbnation.com/nfl/2017/2/4/14496302/superbowl-51-international-tv-schedule-radio-streaming-patriots-falcons (accessed May 10, 2017).

40. "Our Mission," Facebook, https://newsroom.fb.com/company-info (accessed May 10, 2017).

41. Justin Thomson, personal communication, April 2011.

42. Robert J. Foster, *Coca-Globalization: Following Soft Drinks from New York to New Guinea* (New York: Palgrave Macmillan, 2008), x–xi.

CHAPTER 5

GLOBAL TRADE AND THE FEAR OF AMERICAN POPULAR CULTURE

This chapter explores the legal context of international trade in popular culture—a trade that is tightly linked to global fears of the power of American popular culture to corrupt societies and overwhelm competitors. It begins with an extended discussion of two competing schools of thought regarding trade in culture. One, advocated by the United States, holds that cultural products are like any other goods and should be traded freely to guarantee everyone across the globe the chance to enjoy entertaining programming at low cost. The other school, advanced by most of the rest of the world's nations but led by Canada and France, insists that cultural products are different from other goods and services and should not be subject to the free trade rules that have increasing influence over the global economy. These two schools of thought have shaped, and continue to shape, many international agreements in the post–World War II period.

This chapter analyzes the cultural features of these trade agreements and then offers a series of case studies of the ways several different countries have attempted to limit the influence and power of American popular culture within their borders. To the degree that people link American values with globalization as such, they tend to resist and reject those forces that promote globalization worldwide.

It should be noted here that the trade agreements examined in this chapter focus on measurable trade in products like movies, music, and television. The audiovisual industries are recognized around the world as having a profound and powerful ability to shape and define a culture. Accordingly, nations and communities tend to both jealously guard their domestic culture-producing institutions and to react to perceived threats to their local cultures from foreign sources. However, as discussed in chapter 4, culture operates at levels and in a manner not always directly expressed in the kinds of tangible, measurable ways that trade agreements can regulate. Because of this immeasurable dimension, the impact and fear of American popular culture is greater than a narrow focus on television programs, music, and movies might suggest. Discussions of global trade in culture matter for reasons beyond, or in addition to, those that can be calculated in the flow of audiovisual products around the planet. Thus, this chapter uses regulation of the global trade in movies, music, and television as a proxy for greater concerns about the ways in which American popular culture affects the global community. As will be seen, while people around the world enjoy the goods and services created by American pop culture makers, they and their governments fear these artifacts as well. This fact has shaped the way globalization has developed.

TRADING AMERICAN POPULAR CULTURE

As addressed in chapter 1, the process of globalization has been tightly bound up with a series of decisions made by several countries, led by the United States, to open their borders to (relatively) free markets, the easy exchange of capital, and new economic, political, and cultural systems. However, as this chapter will show, concerns that popular culture and other forms of mass communication may harm or destroy local cultures have been central to these agreements from their inception. Accordingly, restrictions on international trade in cultural products have been built into every trade agreement since the first General Agreement on Tariffs and Trade (GATT) was passed to promote freer trade in the Western world in 1947. In fact, today, other than enforcing restrictions on population migration, some of the strictest state regulations on global trade focus on cultural goods and services. Cultural matters have been both contentious and important from the very beginning of the modern era of globalization.

At the core of concerns about trade in culture lies a deceptively simple question: Is popular culture a commodity like rice or computers or automobiles, or is it an agent of socialization that shapes culture? If popular culture is a commodity, the logic of the free market suggests that few, if any, restrictions ought to be placed on its global exchange. If people like American popular culture products, and if enjoyable products can be created in the United States more effectively than they can be produced anywhere else, then people ought to be allowed to enjoy as many American popular culture products as they like without regulation. Anything less will guarantee that people will have access to fewer popular culture products, likely at higher prices, than they would have in a world of global free trade in culture.

By contrast, if popular culture is a meaning-bearing entity, if its products both manifest and shape culture, then an argument can be made that states and communities have an interest in limiting access to and the influence of a popular culture alien to their own. After all, as discussed in chapter 1, communities inevitably try to protect and pass down their cultures—that's how cultures persist. Thus, if American popular culture is, in fact, American, and its products might produce changed values and attitudes in its consumers, then local communities have reason to both fear American popular culture and to try to protect their own cultures from the influence of the American "other." Any society might fear that inviting American popular culture in through the front door might risk throwing its own, local culture out the back.

THE AMERICAN ARGUMENT

Unsurprisingly, the United States has been at the forefront of efforts to reduce barriers to the trade in cultural products since the era of contemporary globalization began in the 1940s. The U.S. position has been and remains that popular culture products are no different from any other commodity, and so no special rules or exemptions ought to govern cultural-product trading worldwide. In part, this position is grounded in simple economic interests. As shown throughout this book, the United States holds a unique, globally dominant position in trade in popular culture. This does not mean that all popular culture produced and enjoyed around the world is American; rather, it means that in global pop culture matters, the United States is the nation most likely to benefit from free or relatively free trade. Its products already have a worldwide audience, and its makers have various competitive advantages in producing popular culture that make it possible for American popular culture to succeed in global trade. Moreover, the corporations that shape American popular culture have proven able to use their power and influence and wealth to compete against foreign producers. They have likewise proven able to purchase rivals or drive competitors out of business. Finally, while much of the rest of the world consumes American popular culture, the reverse is much less true: Americans watch few foreign movies or television programs and do not listen to significant amounts of foreign-produced music. Americans also do not support many sports popular outside U.S. borders—most obviously the sport everyone else in the world calls "football." This means that even as American producers regularly outcompete global popular culture producers in their home countries, those foreign producers cannot outcompete American makers in the United States. This ensures a regular and profitable stream of income for U.S. producers that foreign producers lack. On purely economic grounds, then, free trade in culture makes sense to American policymakers and business leaders.

Yet the economic explanation is not the whole of the reason Americans advocate free trade in culture. U.S. policymakers and citizens alike tend to believe that free trade is a cultural necessity. Free trade, as an ideology, combines cultural values like individualism, capitalism, optimism, and entrepreneurialism in ways that reinforce American popular support for things like democracy, freedom, and human rights. As discussed in chapter 1, Americans might not always live up to the commitments their belief in free trade suggests they ought, but the underlying cultural norms are there nonetheless. Free trade is generally seen to be a component of the notion of freedom as such. Consequently, those who believe that allowing free trade in goods and services is a crucial part of promoting human freedom in all dimensions of life see limits on trade in culture as limits on freedom itself. For many American advocates of free trade, then, open trade in cultural products is a passionately held cultural belief, not only an economically advantageous one.

American trade negotiators and business leaders have adopted both economic and cultural explanations for their advocacy of free trade in culture. Speaking of efforts to liberalize the trade in movies in the late 1980s and early 1990s, for example, Peter Morici, who served as director of the U.S. International Trade Commission during the period, noted, "When we're talking about cinema, I think it's largely a commercial issue and not a cultural issue. Globally there's a preference for what Hollywood puts out. We have a very competitive industry, and that is certainly evidenced by the amount of film we sell worldwide." Similarly, a spokesman for the California Trade and Commerce Agency, Mike Marando, insisted, "Making movies is a market-driven product. We don't see it as cultural imperialism. We see it as a marketplace issue."[1]

Others have defended free trade in cultural products as enhancing global culture without undermining local ones. Tyler Cowen, an economist who represented the United States at the United Nations Educational, Scientific and Cultural Organization (UNESCO), agreed that globalization was bringing cultures closer together and shaping common cultural experiences for many of the world's peoples. "You can see a poster of [basketball star] Michael Jordan in Bali, Indonesia, in South America, in Scandinavia, and of course in Chicago in the United States," Cowen noted. But he argued that this common global experience does not necessarily lead to the destruction of local and distinctive cultures. Instead, he offered a broader understanding of diversity, one grounded in the choices people have available to them as they go about their lives: "Another notion of diversity is what I call 'diversity within society.' Diversity within society refers to the menu of choice. What do we have to choose from? What options do we have? What kinds of opportunities do we have with our lives? When we ask ourselves, 'Does globalization bring more of this kind of diversity?,' we find that the answer is usually yes."[2] Individual consumer choice, then, is seen as a manifestation of political, social, and economic freedom. Accordingly, limiting trade in culture limits the opportunities all people might have for self-expression and individual fulfillment.

THE COUNTER-AMERICAN ARGUMENT

One reason many nations oppose free trade in culture derives from their commitment to a concept that can be termed the *culture exception.* Countries that insist on exceptions for culture in free trade agreements make a series of linked arguments that, together, expose their collective fears that American popular culture products may lead to cultural corruption, cultural imperialism, and/or cultural homogenization. For them, restrictions decried by the United States are essential to their economic and cultural survival. Each may have a different basis for opposing unfettered trade in cultural artifacts, but they combine in alliances that seek to limit cultural globalization's potentially negative effects—even when they have agreed to free trade in other goods and services. In other words, the countries opposed to the free trade of culture have, for the most part, otherwise accepted the consequences of free trade in most aspects of international economic life. They simply exempt culture from such rules.

The culture exception argument is grounded in the reality that cultures, once lost, stay lost. Languages, religions, lifestyles, and orientations toward the shared community can die. Thus, free trade in culture is inherently more dangerous than free trade in other products. After all, while free trade in other products may cause one country's people to lose jobs in industries that produce goods that another country's people can produce more cheaply, those jobs can—hopefully—be replaced. Workers can be retrained into fields in which the nation has a comparative advantage—at least in theory. Moreover, free trade tends to make goods and services cheaper, thereby making it easier for people around the world, including the country that lost jobs in this globalized competition, to acquire goods and services at reduced cost. (Again, at least in theory.) In contrast, free trade in culture might threaten cultural death, and so many people seek to avoid it. Accordingly, advocates of the culture exception insist that cultural trade is different from trade in any other good or service.

In 1993, for example, French president François Mitterrand revealed his fears of American cultural destruction when he claimed that "creations of the spirit are not just commodities; the elements of culture are not pure business. What is at stake is the cultural identity of all our nations—it is the freedom to create and choose our own images. A society which abandons the means of depicting itself would soon be an enslaved society."[3] Similarly, in 2002, a Canadian government group, the Cultural Industries Sectoral Advisory Group on International Trade, opposed free trade in cultural products on the grounds that such trade would tend to create cultural homogeneity:

> The underlying principle and overall objective of the instrument is to ensure that cultural diversity is preserved in the face of the challenge posed by globalization, trade liberalization and rapid technological changes. Although new information technologies, globalization and evolving multilateral trade policies offer indisputable possibilities for the expression of cultural diversity, they may also be detrimental to ensuring cultural diversity. This is particularly the case when, for example, domestic cultural content is not accorded reasonable shelf space in its own domestic market, when the over-concentration of production and distribution of cultural content contributes to the standardization of cultural expression, or when developing countries, because of lack of resources, run the risk of being excluded from the international cultural space as it is currently being constructed with new information and communications technologies. There is an urgent need to address these new developments to ensure that cultural diversity, as a factor of social cohesion and economic development, is preserved and enhanced.[4]

In commenting on a proposed free trade agreement between the United States and Australia, the Music Council of Australia, in a report to the Australian government's Department of Foreign Affairs and Trade's Office of Trade Negotiations, likewise insisted, "The larger context for this discussion is the need to maintain and foster cultural diversity. The rationale for trade liberalization depends upon the doctrine of comparative advantage which, in the cultural sphere, leads to cultural homogeneity. The two objectives are basically opposed. But in the cultural sphere, cultural diversity is more important than economic efficiency."[5]

The European Commission has likewise argued, "Cinematographic and televisual programmes are goods unlike any other: as *privileged vectors of culture*, they retain their specific nature amid the new types of audiovisual product which are currently multiplying; as living witnesses to the traditions and of the identity of each country, they merit encouragement; only a strong European industry will be able to guarantee both the diversity of programmes and an increase in the international influence of European cultures. Given the position of the image in our society, much is at stake in cultural terms."[6] Culture, the argument goes, must be exempted from free trade.

Opponents of free trade in culture also make a business case for their position. Advocates of the business case for regulating free trade in culture focus on issues like jobs, their nation's balance of trade with other nations, and even national security in insisting that there are reasons to maintain limits on trade in certain industries—including popular culture products. For example, as discussed later in this chapter, when the new Western bloc negotiated the 1947 GATT in the aftermath of World War II, the United States specifically exempted the European film industry from free trade demands. The United States agreed that the nations of Western Europe, which had been devastated by the war, needed time to recover before they would be able to compete with American products. In other words, the United States agreed that the shattered nations of Western Europe had an economic interest in protecting their domestic audiovisual culture industries from American competition so that the European industries could rebuild their facilities, hire new employees, and try to level the global playing field before facing competition from the international American popular culture powerhouse.

Since 1947 other nations have claimed that their nascent, infant industries needed time to grow before facing American competition—including, notably, the prospect of being bought on the open market by the global corporations centered in the United States. Others have insisted that the jobs created by workers in the AV industries are important and require protection.[7]

Whether for business or cultural reasons, then, trade in culture and cultural artifacts is very controversial and contentious. This is true even for nations that otherwise seem to embrace free trade. Culture is different, at least for most of the nations of the world.

POPULAR CULTURE IN INTERNATIONAL AGREEMENTS (1947–2017)

This section explores the ways in which international efforts to create free trade among at least some of the world's nations have been affected by issues associated with trade in culture. While globalization is not driven only by free trade policies, global laws regarding how goods and services should be traded have been central to the ways in which globalization has unfolded at least since the end of World War II. As will be seen, the controversy about whether culture should be subject to free trade rules has been manifest in many of the global trade agreements passed since 1947. Indeed, some of the most contentious issues that free traders have had to address have been those involving trade in cultural artifacts.

GATT/WORLD TRADE ORGANIZATION

Concerns and questions about trade in culture date from the first agreement that promoted free trade in the modern era, the General Agreement on Tariffs and Trade adopted in 1947. Written for both economic and political reasons, GATT was conceived of as a way to build a strong and productive international economy among the world's major industrial powers. It was also viewed as a tool for building new, cooperative political relationships among countries that had recently been at war with one another. Policymakers expected that creating patterns of mutual trade and dependency on various partners for important goods and services would reduce the chances that the nations that had just unleashed the horrors of World War II on each other, and indeed had suffered through World War I in the living memory of many people at the time, would go to war again. They sought to cement an alliance of Western, democratic powers against the newly emerged threat represented by the Soviet Union and the growing Communist bloc. GATT was expected to provide both economic benefits and political legitimacy for the new Western alliance.

The first GATT agreement created a special exemption for cultural artifacts. Specifically, Article 4 addressed European fears of American cultural imperialism in that it allowed European countries still recovering from the devastation of World War II to impose quotas on the number of foreign films—usually American—that could be distributed and shown in their countries. In addition, it allowed European governments to use tax revenues to fund and otherwise subsidize the production of movies in their countries. These subsidies served to supplement the costs associated with producing and distributing movies, meaning that the filmmakers did not need to generate enough money to produce movies only from ticket sales in theaters or other market-based mechanisms, like product placements. Cumulatively, these supports were intended to give the European film industry time to rebuild itself with the revenues generated from domestic audiences without competition from American movies.

In addition, Article 20 of the 1947 GATT allowed nations to protect their "national treasures" variously defined.[8] It allowed European governments to designate some cultural artifacts as crucial to their national identity and thereby to exempt such items from sale to individuals and companies (or museums) in foreign countries. Cultural products were not necessarily available for ordinary purchase.

The 1947 GATT agreement protected culture industries for other reasons as well. France, in particular, insisted that culture be exempted from free trade in order to protect French culture as such. French policymakers believed (and still do) that American films and other audiovisual programs have a unique capacity to shape and undermine French culture. American policymakers agreed, but they believed that the cultural changes that might follow from free trade in culture would be good for the Western alliance. As Irwin Wall put it,

> One of the more curious aspects of the postwar period is the enormous amount of acrimony expended by both Americans and French over ostensibly superficial questions. Films and Coca-Cola . . . are a case in point. . . . At a time when basic essentials of food and coal were lacking, and the Americans were lending and then giving the French billions, both these nonessential items were pressed upon the French as exports for which they were expected to pay with their very scarce dollars. . . . Both items carried a symbolic importance as manifestations of the American "way of life," which magnified their importance far beyond the few millions they were expected to earn. Fitting symbols of the consumer society, both were symbols of anti-Communism as well.[9]

Little changed in matters of cultural trade after the original GATT was adopted in 1947. European nations consistently maintained their right to protect their culture industries through quotas and subsidies. Additionally, in an effort to avoid cultural homogenization, they also regularly declared their domestic movie, music, and television production companies and facilities to be national treasures not subject to purchase by international corporations. The United States has generally opposed this position and, during what was called the Uruguay Round of GATT talks, which began in 1986, insisted that cultural industries needed to be brought into the arena of free trade.

In the General Agreement on Trade in Services (GATS), negotiated during the Uruguay Round, signatories agreed to develop schedules for integrating their service and telecommunications industries into a global economy. As in 1947, however, France continued to insist that audiovisual industries be exempted from free trade rules. This demand was a central sticking point in what turned out to be seven years of negotiations during the Uruguay Round and very nearly led to the collapse of the GATT negotiations as their December 15, 1993, deadline approached. In the end, the United States relented and agreed to pursue the question later. Culture, again, was treated separately from other forms of trade as fears of American imperial or homogenizing culture became front and center in the talks.[10]

While cultural issues served as a point of contention in the Uruguay Round, they also stimulated new areas of international agreement. From the U.S. point of view, GATS took an important step toward creating a global marketplace of ideas by strengthening international copyright laws governing creative works (including television programs, movies, and music, as well as items like computer software and pharmaceutical drugs). American negotiators had insisted for years that without strong copyright protections, individuals and organizations had little incentive to publish their ideas for the world to use, develop, and implement. (The digital pirates discussed in chapter 3 violate precisely these copyright protections when they illegally copy or download movies, music, and television programming.) Some negotiators resisted the American call for strong copyright protections on the argument that copyright enforcement could be used to quash local creative industries, as well as to exclude some goods and services from developing markets, but the American position basically prevailed, and GATS contained provisions seeking to protect copyrights around the world.

GATS also set in motion the global concentrations of ownership of television, music, and movie production and distribution described in chapter 3, making it easier for international corporations to buy and own telecommunications companies around the world. Prior to GATS, under the standards enshrined in Articles 4 and 20 of GATT, ownership of such facilities had been more restricted.[11] GATS set legal conditions under which it became possible for telecommunications companies to become transnational corporations. It was thus a key step in encouraging the kind of corporate centralization of the entertainment industry described in chapter 3.

The World Trade Organization (WTO) supplanted GATT in 1995. In 2001, the WTO initiated the Doha Round of trade talks to try to come to further agreements about international trade in various products and services, including popular culture products. The Doha Round has never produced an agreement. Indeed, negotiations have been essentially frozen since 2008. The global economic crisis of that year sent numerous nations into severe recessions, and as a practical matter it made nations far less open to free trade policies.

The biggest sticking point is trade in agriculture. As noted earlier in this book, nations like the United States have tried to protect their domestic agriculture industries from competition from cheaper international sources, which has had the effect of reducing those nations' abilities to translate their agricultural and resource wealth into growth and development projects at home. However, trade in goods like patented pharmaceutical drugs and copyrighted artifacts like movies, music, and television programming has also been part of the talks and proven hard to come to agreement on. U.S. negotiators continue to insist on maximum market freedom for cultural products (even as they defend agricultural subsidies at home) and on maximum enforcement of trademark rights for producers of copyrighted material. Other nations continue to insist on limits on trade in culture and less rigorous enforcement of copyright law. As a practical matter, these issues are likely to remain unresolved for the foreseeable future.

UNESCO

As a comprehensive global agreement on trade has grown elusive, advocates for—and those concerned by—global trade in culture have sought other venues in which to advance their interests. Globalization today, after all, is not the same as it was in 1947, and its effects are felt in more and more countries, whether they signed the GATT and WTO agreements or not. Increased trade and other contacts placed continuing and intensifying pressures on cultures around the world. For example, in the early part of the twenty-first century, UNESCO found that 50 percent of the world's languages were in danger of extinction. It further found that 90 percent of the world's languages had no meaningful Internet presence. Only five countries monopolized the world's culture industries, while eighty-eight others had never had their own domestic film-production facilities.[12] Globalization had global effects beyond the parameters of specific trade agreements.

The changed nature of the issue encouraged a changed response to it. Rather than focusing on the narrow confines of international trade agreements to which they might not have been privy anyway, many of the nations that were worried about the potentially negative effects of globalization on culture used their membership in the United Nations to push for a new way to address trade in culture around the world. They worked through the auspices of UNESCO to develop and ultimately adopt a new treaty that seeks to protect culture from most free trade rules.

In 2001, UNESCO passed the Universal Declaration on Cultural Diversity. In that document, the United Nations and the declaration's signatories insisted that cultural diversity is a "common heritage of humanity." They then called for the development of a treaty to promote and protect cultural diversity on a global scale.[13]

A draft treaty followed in 2005. It clearly illustrated the tension between the integrating and fragmenting forces of globalization as it related to fears of American popular culture corruption, imperialism, and homogenization. Passed on October 20, 2005, the draft was intended to empower states to protect their interests in their cultural industries. As the specific language states, the objectives of the Convention on the Protection and Promotion of the Diversity of Cultural Expressions were

(a) to protect and promote the diversity of cultural expressions;

(b) to create the conditions for cultures to flourish and to freely interact in a mutually beneficial manner;

(c) to encourage dialogue among cultures with a view to ensuring wider and balanced cultural exchanges in the world in favour of intercultural respect and a culture of peace;

(d) to foster interculturality in order to develop cultural interaction in the spirit of building bridges among peoples;

(e) to promote respect for the diversity of cultural expressions and raise awareness of its value at the local, national and international levels;

(f) to reaffirm the importance of the link between culture and development for all countries, particularly for developing countries, and to support actions undertaken nationally and internationally to secure recognition of the true value of this link;

(g) to give recognition to the distinctive nature of cultural activities, goods and services as vehicles of identity, values and meaning;

(h) to reaffirm the sovereign rights of States to maintain, adopt and implement policies and measures that they deem appropriate for the protection and promotion of the diversity of cultural expressions on their territory;

(i) to strengthen international cooperation and solidarity in a spirit of partnership with a view, in particular, to enhancing the capacities of developing countries in order to protect and promote the diversity of cultural expressions.

These goals, in turn, were to be met with respect to principles 2 through 8 of the convention:

- Sovereignty, or the right of a community to support and protect expressions of cultural diversity in their territory (principle 2)
- Equal dignity and respect for all cultures, including minority and indigenous communities (principle 3)
- International solidarity and cooperation, especially in making it possible for less advantaged, less developed communities to build and strengthen their culture-producing institutions and practices (principle 4)
- Complementarity of economic and cultural development, meaning that peoples have the right to support both direct economic activities and cultural, expression-oriented norms (principle 5)
- Sustainable development, linking today's cultural activities to future enterprises and values (principle 6)
- Equitable access—the principle that persons should have the opportunity to enjoy cultural artifacts from societies outside their own (principle 7)
- Openness and balance, meaning that the signatories to the UNESCO treaty would promote free expression and free exchange of ideas and values across the world (principle 8).[14]

Interestingly, the vote on this draft was 148 for, 2 against, with 4 abstentions. As would be expected given its historical position on free trade in culture, the United States offered one of the no votes, joined by its close ally Israel. Every other nation either supported the treaty draft or refused to commit.

Once drafted, the treaty went to UN member states for approval. The convention needed to be ratified by thirty nations before going into effect. In a sign of international skepticism about and fear of the power of the international, American-driven industries that dominate global trade in culture, the treaty was ratified by December 2006. UNESCO director general Kōichirō Matsuura noted that the "rapidity of the adoption process is unprecedented. . . . None of UNESCO's other cultural conventions has been adopted by so many States in so little time."[15] It went into international effect in March 2007. As of December 2016, the treaty has 145 signatories, including the European Union as a bloc.

As a practical matter, the UNESCO treaty has not stopped or even appreciably slowed the spread of American popular culture globally. Rather than a tool of enforcement, then, the treaty is more a symptom of global skepticism about the trade in culture that is central to contemporary globalization. Regardless of the positions taken by U.S. trade negotiators in these matters, most people around the world both enjoy the products produced by the American popular culture industry and fear that these products are so suffused with the values, ideals, norms, rituals, behaviors, and styles of American life that they will overwhelm local, non-U.S. cultures. These fears are only intensified when economic livelihoods are put on the line, as happens when American goods and services compete with locally produced ones. Moreover, as is clear from chapter 4, American popular culture can influence social and political life in many ways beyond those detailed in this chapter. Cultural concerns generate some of the most intense reactions from people around the world who fear their ways of life are passing, only to be replaced by a new, essentially American one. The UNESCO convention expresses this concern through the auspices of the world's primary institution of collective representation, the United Nations.

NORTH AMERICAN FREE TRADE AGREEMENT

The tension between a desire for free trade in most goods and services and fear of cultural competition can also be examined in detail in the context of Canadian-U.S.-Mexican relations as defined in the North American Free Trade Agreement (NAFTA). This trio of relationships is among the most important in the world. The United States and Canada share the world's longest undefended border, for example, and each is the other's biggest trading partner. The two countries have a virtually unmatched history of cooperation and peace. Similarly, Mexico provides the United States with much of its oil, and the complex dynamics of South and Central American immigration (legal and illegal) into the United States have been the source of great controversy between the two nations, especially in the United States. Mexico is also a producer of large amounts of Spanish-language popular culture products sold and used in the United States.

NAFTA is premised on the insight that while relations among the United States, Canada, and Mexico are and ought to be close, both Canada and Mexico share certain problems in trade and cultural influence in their dealings with the United States. These are particularly acute for Canada. Canada, after all, has a small population: something over 35 million people inhabit that vast country, while California alone has more than 38 million people. Its most commonly spoken language is English (except in the province of Quebec), as is the case in the United States. It also has its own domestic popular culture industry. Its economy, while large in comparison with those of most nations around the world, is tiny compared to that of the United States. Canada might, therefore, be swallowed up, at least in economic and cultural terms, by its massive neighbor to the south.

Canada's policymakers believe that protecting its domestic popular culture industry is a crucial component of establishing and maintaining a Canadian national identity. They believe that Canadians will lose a certain sense of being Canadian if they fail to protect their culture industries. That they must do this while living next to the American cultural behemoth significantly complicates their efforts in this area.[16]

Mexico, of course, is larger in population than Canada: it has a population of at least 122 million. Moreover, the fact that it is a Spanish-speaking nation insulates it somewhat from the power of American audiovisual culture artifacts since these are usually produced in English. However, the economic power of the United States, combined with the global appeal of so much of American popular culture (both audiovisual and otherwise), works to make it harder for Mexico to maintain a cultural identity than it would be did the two countries not share a border.

Issues involving cultural trade were highlighted when the United States and Canada, along with Mexico, pursued and passed NAFTA in the 1990s. NAFTA lowered an array of trade barriers across North America. As was the case with trade negotiations elsewhere in the world, during the NAFTA talks U.S. negotiators sought to reduce restrictions both on international ownership of culture-producing institutions like movie studios and radio stations and on the exchange of goods and services traded across international borders. They also sought to reduce subsidies and other forms of government support for culture industries so that all nations would have to compete for business on purely free market grounds.

Canada and Mexico reacted to these American demands in ways that reflected their cultural vulnerability to the United States. Canadian negotiators, for example, resisted U.S. demands on much the same grounds as their European counterparts had. The Canadian Trade Negotiator's Office, for example, insisted, "It is critical to realize that open competition in a North American marketplace would threaten the ability (as well as the incentives) of our culture/communications industries to provide Canadian content to Canadian audiences. In this sense it would also threaten what gives us reason to call ourselves a sovereign nation."[17] Brian Mulroney, then prime minister, similarly noted, "Canadian cultural products are emphatically not the same as American cultural products. Cultural products express cultural identity, something individual to a given nation. Therefore, you cannot simply let American cultural products substitute freely for Canadian, unless you are willing to put open competition for its own sake ahead of maintaining our cultural heritage."[18]

Mexico took a starkly different position regarding trade in culture during the NAFTA talks. Its positions came closer to those professed by American negotiators. In part, this relative openness to free trade in culture derived from the fact that Mexico's economic and cultural relationship with the United States is very different from Canada's. Mexico has a popular culture industry that serves a much larger market than does Canada's, for example. Moreover, Mexico's movie, music, and television industries produce works in Spanish. This accords Mexican cultural products a degree of autonomy from American products not shared by Canadian works. Indeed, Mexican television shows, music, and movies have a substantial presence in Spanish-speaking populations in the United States itself—something that is not true of Canadian products created in English. American products are simply less competitive across the Mexico-U.S. cultural gap. As a practical matter, the Canadian popular culture industry is far more vulnerable to American products than is Mexico's.

NAFTA reflects these cultural concerns. Canada enjoys special privileges when it comes to cultural trade that Mexico did not seek. For example, Annex 2106 exempts Canadian audiovisual industries from the free trade requirements embedded in the treaty. It also empowers the Canadian government to review and limit any U.S. investments in what the annex calls Canada's "cultural heritage or national identity" facilities—terms that generally refer to television stations, film-production facilities, and the like.[19] Canada has thus been able to maintain its subsidies for film production and its ownership requirements for radio stations. As happened with other international trade negotiations, the United States consented to the culture exception to enhance the rest of the agreement on its terms.

In contrast, Mexican negotiators generally accepted the logic of free trade in their cultural exchanges with the United States. The major exceptions were that foreign ownership of Mexican audiovisual production companies was limited to 49 percent, and a quota of 30 percent was established for Mexican movies on theater screens. This quota, it should be noted, has never been enforced. Therefore, the percentage of Mexican movies shown in Mexican theaters decreased to 10 percent by 1997.[20] Otherwise, trade in cultural products between the United States and Mexico accords more with the American vision of free trade than with that of nations, like Canada, that advocate for a cultural exception.

Interestingly, in future negotiations Mexican officials may seek to undermine Canadian resistance to free cultural trade as regulated in NAFTA. U.S. popular culture providers, of course, continue to pressure the U.S. government to reject protectionist cultural trade clauses in trade treaties. Among other threats, major American popular culture corporations have urged the U.S. government to place import tariffs on other Canadian products, such as lumber, to force the Canadian government to eliminate barriers to the free exchange of cultural artifacts. However, Mexican authorities have recognized a large and growing market of Spanish speakers in Canada for whom Mexican-produced television programs and music might be particularly attractive. Consequently, Mexican negotiators are also pushing Canada to reduce its trade restrictions on popular culture products.[21]

More recently, U.S. president Donald Trump has suggested that the entire structure of NAFTA needs to be renegotiated, if not abandoned. His 2016 campaign for the presidency used claims that NAFTA was a "bad deal" for American industry to frame a promised effort to completely reform or reject it. While trade in popular culture played no role in Trump's campaign—he was focused almost entirely on industrial manufacturing enterprises—should such renegotiation occur, all the protocols and rules addressed in this analysis would be mooted. As of this writing, no move to suspend or transform NAFTA has been initiated, but given the central role concerns about NAFTA played in the Trump campaign, the future of NAFTA is not clear.

TRANS-PACIFIC PARTNERSHIP

The Trans-Pacific Partnership (TPP), negotiated among most of the world's major economies in countries that border the Pacific Ocean, was envisioned as NAFTA on a transcontinental scale. What NAFTA did for the United States, Canada, and Mexico in North America, the TPP was supposed to do for nations on the Pacific Rim. (China, the world's second-largest economy, was notably absent from the TPP.) A global common market valued at nearly $28 trillion would have been created in the process.

As with any major trade agreement, the details of the TPP were many. Core elements included setting common standards for the regulation of commonly traded products like automobiles, for mutually enforceable environmental regulations, and for workplace and labor rules. TPP advocates saw standardizing such rules as a central step toward creating a true free market: if all nations demand similar levels of regulation for workplace safety, for example, then labor costs might even out among societies. This, in turn, might make it financially sensible to build factories in so-called first world places like the United States or Japan instead of moving them to places with much, much lower workplace safety standards—and lower labor costs.

One significant plank in the TPP covered intellectual property, copyright, and patents. It strengthened protections for items like movies, music, and television programs, along with software and pharmaceutical products. It encouraged signatory nations to create the equivalent of U.S. patent offices and provided legal standards by which U.S. producers could sue if they believed their products had been pirated or otherwise abused. For the American popular culture industry, in any case, the TPP was a significant improvement over current international law.

Notably, the TPP was controversial from its inception. It was greeted skeptically by many non-U.S. actors, on much the same grounds as GATT/WTO agreements had previously generated concerns: that cultural and other products might get wiped out by foreign—American—competition, either overwhelmed in the marketplace or crushed by lawsuits filed by wealthy American corporations. It was also greeted skeptically in the United States itself: many political leaders and large numbers of their constituents had come to believe that NAFTA was a mistake—that it had, as candidate Donald Trump claimed in the 2016 presidential campaign, been a bad deal for Americans. For leaders like these, the promise that the TPP would be a NAFTA for the Pacific Rim was a slur, not a compliment. Thus, it was not at all clear that the TPP would ever be ratified by the United States, although President Barack Obama supported it despite the disagreement of a wide spectrum of both Republicans and Democrats. In any case, on January 23, 2017, just three days after becoming president, Donald Trump signed an executive order withdrawing from the unratified TPP. It is, accordingly, unlikely to be passed, whatever the desires of the popular culture and intellectual property industries.

As these discussions of GATT/WTO, UNESCO, NAFTA, and the TPP make clear, the desire to protect culture and culture-producing enterprises from alien values and norms is clearly central to contemporary globalization, as is the desire to eliminate such barriers in favor of a truly free market. These competing goals are likely to continue to clash in the future. If anything, conflicts among those who wish to leverage the cultural and economic power of American popular culture products and those who wish to defend or protect local communities against what they see as threats to their continued existence are likely to intensify as more and more people around the world find American popular culture on the Internet, in their restaurants, in their towns and villages, and on their bodies as clothing. The future is therefore likely to bring a continuing cycle of claims from those who insist that free trade promotes freedom and from those who insist that trade in culture threatens national and cultural identity. Cultural cleavages can be expected to remain central forces in shaping contemporary globalization.

AMERICAN POPULAR CULTURE IN FOUR COUNTRIES

The rest of this chapter explores the ways four countries—France, Iran, Hong Kong, and Finland—have responded to the challenges to their national identities and cohesion that they assert are posed by American popular culture. It also explores state efforts to control social networking as part of a broader campaign to retain sovereignty in a global age.

Notably, the four countries under study here have little in common. France, like the United States, is an advanced industrial democracy. France and the United States have a long, deeply interconnected history: France helped the United States win its independence from Great Britain and was, in turn, liberated by the United States and its allies in World War II. It has maintained an uneasy alliance with the United States in the years since. Regardless of their policy differences, however, the two nations share a common political and economic tradition.

Iran, by contrast, is a theocracy run by Islamic mullahs. Prior to 1979, Iran and the United States were close allies; however, after the Islamic Revolution of 1979, Iran's leaders declared the United States the "Great Satan," and the country became one of the most active enemies of the United States—in cultural as well as political affairs. Its current progress in enriching nuclear fuel has heightened tensions with the United States and other nations in the world as concerns grow that it is seeking to build nuclear weapons. Iran is, accordingly, an isolated nation overtly hostile to U.S. politics and culture.

Hong Kong was, for most of the twentieth century, a colony of Great Britain and so was a haven for American ideas and people. It was (and remains) a center of production of the associated products of American political culture—for example, T-shirts and other clothing, DVDs, and the like. In 1997, however, Hong Kong was returned to China, putting one of the world's economic powerhouses under the control of the world's largest avowedly Communist country.

Finland is a developed country that has held a unique position for most of the post–World War II era: capitalist and democratic, it was unaligned with the Western powers due to its close political and physical proximity to the then Soviet Union. (Finland was governed by Russia from 1809 to 1917, having previously been a colony of Sweden for approximately six hundred years.) Its people were free but constrained: free speech and other human rights were widely respected, but the nation's leaders could not afford to forge a foreign policy seen to challenge their giant neighbor. As such, it developed as a border nation—a place where the values, goods, and services of the capitalist world meshed with the demands of a regional power it could not afford to alienate.

The lack of a common political history or cultural tradition among these four countries is quite useful for this study. After all, it would not be all that surprising if groups and countries that share values and ideals reacted similarly to what might be alien concepts or demands. However, to the degree that disparate systems react in similar ways, the influence of the independent force can be assessed. As will be seen, American popular culture is a source of controversy in each of the four countries examined here. Its effects play along the three dimensions of globalization described in chapter 1: economic, political, and cultural.

FRANCE

As noted earlier, France was and remains one of the United States' closest allies in world affairs. While relations between them are often tense, theirs are the differences of family members: the two nations often disagree about how best to achieve their otherwise shared goals of democracy, human rights, and capitalism, but they do not doubt the goals themselves. Hence even as U.S.-French relations wax and wane from tight alliance (the American Revolution, World War I, and World War II) to skeptical and even wary distance (the Napoleonic years, France's post–World War II rejection of NATO membership, and its refusal to support the United States in its wars with Iraq and Afghanistan), the relationship endures for social, political, economic, and ideological reasons.

Today, France finds itself in a relatively difficult position in terms of its cultural identity. Indeed, much of the explanation for France's position as a leader of the opposition to globalization in cultural products derives from its status as a proud nation that has been a global leader for most of its history but now worries that its language and culture are slowly being lost. Comparatively few people worldwide now speak

French, after all, particularly in contrast with the growth of English as a global language. Likewise, many French people believe that deeply embedded traditions of secularism and nationalism are under challenge in France as religiously active Muslims immigrate to the country. In this context, French policymakers worry that American and other cultural products will push historically French products out of the marketplace and remake French culture at the same time.

Such concerns seem credible when the dominance of American products in the French market is recognized. As recently as 1980, 50 percent of movies shown in France were French, while only 31 percent were American. By 1990, the percentages were more than reversed: only 31 percent of movies shown in France were French in origin, while 59 percent were American. The 39 percent market share that French movies attained in France in 2001 was the highest in many years. In 1990, France exported only 35 million francs' worth of television programming to North America (which includes Canada's French-speaking province, Quebec), while importing 600 million francs' worth.[22] Judged by the metric of tickets sold, thirteen of the top-selling movies in France of all time are American: *Titanic* (number 1), *Snow White and the Seven Dwarfs, Gone with the Wind, Once upon a Time in the West, Avatar, One Hundred and One Dalmatians, Cinderella, The Aristocrats, The Longest Day, The Lady and the Tramp, The Lion King,* and *Bambi*.[23] France is similarly enamored of American television: in 2012, of the ten most popular TV shows in France, seven were American: *Criminal Minds* (number 1), *The Mentalist, NCIS, Cold Case, CSI, Law and Order,* and *Without a Trace*.[24]

French leaders have responded to these concerns with an array of rules and regulations that seek to protect France's distinctive culture. To protect the linguistic and cultural status of French, for example, France has passed a series of laws mandating use of the language. The most important of these has been a series of laws requiring the use of proper French in commercials, advertisements, and popular culture programming. Law 94-665, passed in August 1994, is typical. Article 1 notes the key position of the French language in French culture and goes on to state that French "shall be the language of instruction, work, trade and exchanges and of public services." Article 2 extended this requirement into the commercial sphere, insisting that French had to be used in the designation, offer, presentation, instructions for use, and descriptions of the scope and conditions of a warranty of goods, products, and services, as well as bills and receipts. It further required the same provisions be applied to any written, spoken, radio, and television advertisement.[25]

French authorities have used this law to cite and fine companies, individuals, and even websites for violating the requirement stipulating the public use of French. For example, just between January and April 1996, French-language advocate groups brought 1,926 allegations of violations of Law 94-665 to the attention of French authorities; thirty-three convictions resulted from these efforts. A French linguistic society sued the Walt Disney Company for violating Law 94-665 at one of its Disney stores in Paris. While Disney initially fought the case, it conceded in time and removed the offending merchandise from the store's shelves. Another group sued British cosmetics company The Body Shop for failing to translate the labels on products like pineapple face wash into French, and yet another linguistic society sued the Georgia Institute of Technology—usually known as Georgia Tech—for failing to advertise its programs in French in online ads it offered there.[26]

Concerns about the erosion of French culture extend to the realm of social networking. In May 2011 France banned radio and television stations from urging audience members to go to the stations' Twitter feeds and Facebook pages for more information or to "like" the station. French authorities argue that such requests violate a 1992 law that bans "secret" promotion of non-French cultural artifacts. Thus even the use of social networking platforms is problematic in France's cultural space.[27]

The success of France's efforts to protect its culture is hard to assess. For example, English has hardly disappeared from daily use in France regardless of what French laws might say, and while subsidies to the French film industry (which in the early 1990s ran over $350 million per year) have allowed the nation to maintain an active role in movie production, American movies dominate French screens.[28] (French-made movies have virtually no presence in the United States, of course.) Similarly, while the French government can ban radio and television stations from explicitly referencing Facebook and Twitter, such social networking platforms are pervasive in France—and thus French people, especially younger people, have extraordinary access to American popular culture. Moreover, considering French birthrates and the rate of immigration into France, it seems hard to believe that any restrictions on popular culture will ensure the survival of French culture as most French people think of it today. However, the fact that the French are so fixated on protecting their culture is itself indicative of the importance of culture to contemporary globalization. France's restrictions may well be misaimed and ineffective, but they are passionately upheld. For the French, concerns about creeping Americanism are central to their relationship with the world at large.

IRAN

Iran provides an interesting test case for the perceived influence of American popular culture on national and cultural identity for several reasons. From the mid-1950s through the end of the 1970s, Iran was one of the closest allies of the United States in the Middle East. However, in 1979, the pro–United States leader of Iran, Shah Mohammed Reza Pahlavi, was overthrown and replaced by an Islamist government that rejected the Western-oriented social and economic programs of the shah's regime. Whereas the shah had offered his people, including women, the opportunity to get an education and enjoy the benefits of a consumerist society (while savagely repressing any movement for political or social equality or democracy), the theocratic state imposed by Muslim mullahs led by the Ayatollah Ruhollah Khomeini sought to enforce what it believed were true Muslim values, like requiring women to cover their bodies and faces before going out in public and mandating that men should grow beards. Political control was centralized in Islamic councils that determined who could or could not become part of the government.

Tensions exploded between the United States and the new, theocratic Iranian government as soon as it came to power. Some of the reasons for this were immediate: a group of radical Iranian students occupied the U.S. embassy in Tehran starting in November 1979, for example, which is technically an act of war. They and a series of government supporters held more than fifty Americans hostage for the next 444 days, releasing them only after Ronald Reagan was inaugurated president of the United States on January 20, 1981. Other reasons emerged in time: later that year Iran sponsored an embargo of oil shipments to the United States that sent the U.S. economy into a deep recession. Iran also sponsored the growth of other Islamist political movements, like Hezbollah and Hamas, as one aspect of its effort to export its revolution and its anti-American sentiments. The United States considers these groups terrorist organizations and condemns Iran's support for them. More recently, former president Mahmoud Ahmadinejad of Iran put his nation on a path to enrich enough uranium to potentially build a nuclear bomb. The United States opposes Iran's acquiring nuclear weapons. Tensions grew accordingly. (In 2015, Iran agreed to reduce its uranium enrichment and to allow international monitoring of its program. This agreement has lessened but not eliminated tensions between the United States and Iran.)

Iran's revolutionary government has also attempted to transform domestic Iranian life. Iranian policymakers have tried to insulate their citizens, particularly younger people, from the supposedly corrupting influence of American popular culture on what Iranian youths see, think, and want. For example, postrevolutionary Iran passed laws outlawing satellite dishes, Western music, and Western movies. It further established standards of dress that forbade women from wearing Western clothing or makeup. Perhaps most famously, in 1989 Ayatollah Khomeini issued a fatwa, or religious order, that authorized any Muslim to kill the author of *The Satanic Verses*, an Indian-born ex-Muslim named Salman Rushdie. This act is generally recognized to signify Iran's radical rejection of the democratic value of human rights. Iran has tried to isolate itself from the effects of Western ideas and experiences, including those associated with American popular culture.

These efforts to isolate the country from American and Western culture have found supporters in Iran. More conservative members of Iranian society clearly link westernization and Americanization as the forces they are fighting to resist. One, a woman named Khaki, notes, "You as a person should never forget your country. Iranian people prefer to go out of the country and show themselves as American." Similarly, she notes, "My uncle has been in the U.S. for 25 years. I can never accept his ideas. Too much democracy."[29] Other social conservatives have come to believe that encroaching American popular culture is a dangerous consequence of globalization, one that threatens the stability and cultural integrity of Iran. As Ayatollah Ahmad Jannati put it, "The biggest vice facing us is the cultural offensive. . . . What are those seeking the opening of the way for the U.S. thinking about? Why are you betraying Islam?"[30]

It is not particularly surprising, of course, that social conservatives resist outside influence, especially outside influence that might change traditional ways of life in their society. Such resistance is, after all, a useful working definition of what it means to be a social conservative, regardless of one's country or community. However, many Iranians who might be expected to have more progressive or globalist attitudes have also expressed worry about the threat of an American cultural invasion in Iran. That is, in Iran some people have largely accepted the goods and benefits associated with Western life and American culture—*Titanic* and Nike, Levi's and rock and roll—yet are concerned that American popular culture will destroy Iranian culture. As an example, some Iranian filmmakers—even reform-oriented, progressive ones—have worried that the unleashing of restrictions on American movies will lead to American cultural imperialism and the destruction of the native film industry.[31] Thus, like French and other policymakers who are otherwise supportive of globalization, some Iranian progressives worry that American corporate power may undermine the economic environment in which some Iranians make their living.

It is not clear that Iran's efforts to isolate itself from the feared consequences of exposure to American popular culture are working, however. Younger women have begun insisting on the right to wear something other than the hijab and have spent years slowly amending the published dress code to allow exposure of more hair and more skin in what has been called the "pink revolution."[32] A social media site called My Stealthy Freedom encourages women to publish photos of themselves with their hair or bodies not covered by scarves or hijabs.[33] A bootleg Victoria's Secret store operates there: while the company has no official franchise in the country, entrepreneurs in Iran buy goods from mainline stores, import them, and sell them as Victoria's Secret products. While these actions are illegal, enforcement of the revolutionary dress code is spotty. Iranians are accessing and responding to an array of popular culture referents whatever the policy of the government is.

In addition, many young people are teaching themselves English through the Internet, as well as with imported Western music and satellite television. People are exposed and drawn to Western fashion, programming, and social styles. For example, the ban on satellite dishes is flouted openly, and satellite dishes are common there. Estimates are that 70 percent of Iranians have access to them.[34] Thus movies like *Titanic*, *Face/Off*, and *Air Force One* have been widely available through satellite services and bootleg videotapes for many years.[35] Something called the Toosheh Project is building Internet service through satellite dishes, seeking to bypass government restrictions on what Iranians can access.[36] (The Iranian government officially bans services like Facebook and Twitter in the country, for example.) For every restriction the government conceives, attempts are made to subvert government control.

American popular culture is thus at the heart of political and social tension in Iran. The demand for access to American movies, styles of dress, social networking, and so forth pits American popular culture against the traditionalist, authoritarian ambitions of the Iranian political leadership. Moreover, the leadership seems to understand this and takes active, if sometimes contradictory, steps to try to lessen or avoid what it sees as the negative effects of American popular culture in Iranian society. (Iran's president, Hassan Rouhani, has a Twitter account, for example, and the nation's religious leader, the Grand Ayatollah Ali Khamenei, has a popular Instagram account.[37] President Rouhani has also spoken about the need to eliminate the restriction on satellite dishes, even as his own authorities have undertaken campaigns to eliminate them.) The globalization of American popular culture is thus central to contemporary political and social life in Iran.

HONG KONG

The case of Hong Kong offers a very different example of the way American popular culture shapes contemporary globalization. Through much of the twentieth century, Hong Kong had one of the world's most powerful capitalist economies. Its status as a British colony with a unique combination of a large population of well-educated people, one of the world's most accessible and strategic ports, and very loose regulations on business encouraged many companies to set up operations there. So successful was this combination of forces that in the latter half of the twentieth century, Hong Kong became one of the so-called Asian tigers, the Asian economic superpowers like Japan, South Korea, and Singapore (another small island nation with a global economic presence far larger than its geographic position would predict). Hong Kong was a central hub in the emerging globalist capitalist order from at least the 1950s on.

Given Hong Kong's status as a British colony, English became the common language there. The colony also enjoyed relative political and social freedoms, including access to and widespread enjoyment of an array of popular culture entertainments from the United States, Thailand, Korea, Japan, and China.[38] Hong Kong's citizens were broadly integrated into the West's economic, political, and cultural systems throughout the twentieth century.

This integration was challenged in 1997, when, as required by treaty, Hong Kong reverted to Chinese rule. While this event would have always been significant, it was momentous for one reason more than any other: mainland China's government became Communist in 1949, meaning that once transferred, one of the world's most capitalist communities would come under the control of the world's largest Communist country. Accordingly, the reversion of Hong Kong to Chinese rule meant that one of the most productive, integrated capitalist economies in the world was to be administered by a nation whose formal political doctrine was anticapitalist. Moreover, China does not practice Western governing principles like democracy and legal respect for human rights. Many people wondered how—or whether—Hong Kong could survive the transition.

At one level, the concerns of those who doubted China could effectively manage a capitalist Hong Kong were misbegotten. By 1997, China had begun a large-scale process of turning significant areas of its countryside into havens for capitalist production and development. Shanghai had by 1997 grown into an enormous city in a region in which capitalism is encouraged both for international corporations wishing to trade with or manufacture products in China and for Chinese people who wish to engage in entrepreneurial capitalist business ventures themselves. It has only expanded its capitalist presence in the global economy in the ensuing twenty years. It is therefore not surprising that China promised to allow Hong Kong to continue to play its central role in international capitalist trade after the takeover and has largely done so in the years since it assumed political management of the former British colony.

On another level, however, concerns about Chinese rule seem appropriate. To return to the arguments described earlier in this chapter, it is worth remembering that many advocates of globalization insist that capitalism and democracy are inextricably intertwined. The argument goes that nations must allow their people to be as creative and innovative as possible to compete in a global economy. This, in turn, is expected to compel a capitalist nation to adopt a democratic government that respects human rights. Chinese policy, by contrast, is grounded in the assertion that capitalist economic growth can be separated from democracy and demands for human rights. Shanghai, for example, remains under strong political control, and individual rights are not protected there. China's governance of Hong Kong has not been as strict as its governance of its mainland communities, but it has not allowed open democracy either. This is a profound challenge.

Given the linkages among capitalism, globalization, and American popular culture, there is inevitably a connection between American popular culture and the way China manages Hong Kong. For example, large numbers of the actual consumer goods people enjoy that are based on popular American movies, music, and television programs (e.g., action figurines, CDs, DVDs, clothes, T-shirts, bags, dolls, and everything in between) are manufactured in Hong Kong. Hong Kong is also one of the world's largest producers of illegal bootleg copies of American popular culture products, many of which are bought and sold across mainland China. This fact poses a problem for Chinese authorities, who want their citizens to participate in a capitalist system but also wish to avoid the political and social ideas embedded in the items they produce: if American popular culture tends to corrupt or replace indigenous values, Chinese policymakers who seek to maintain the status quo must figure out how to make people capitalist without also making them democratic or even American.

One particularly interesting example of China's efforts to limit what it sees as the potentially pernicious threat of American popular culture can be seen in the relationship the Chinese government has established with the Walt Disney Company. Disney has built a theme park in China, Disneyland Hong Kong. However, the Hong Kong government invested almost 80 percent of the cost of building the park and owns 57 percent control of it. Therefore the government can control what does or does not go into the park.

From the perspective of the Chinese government, Hong Kong was "special"—a community already integrated into the politics and economics of the wider world. This did not mean, however, that China would inevitably support bringing American popular culture products to the mainland. In fact, China later resisted the Disney Company's request to build a theme park in Shanghai. This resistance resulted from Disney's insistence that it would need to broadcast the Disney Channel in China to introduce its characters to the nation's population. China's leaders were unwilling to have such blatantly American programming on their airwaves.³⁹ Disney subsequently opened a theme park in Shanghai in 2016.⁴⁰

The Internet provides a particularly challenging environment for the Chinese government to act to limit the effects of Western ideas or entertainments on Chinese life. The rise of Facebook and other social networking services, along with Google's seemingly inescapable grasp of Internet searches, offers a strong challenge to any government that seeks to control its citizens' access to information it does not want them to see. From the perspective of an authoritarian government, if citizens can access Google or Facebook or any other social media/search engine in an unfettered way, then the government cannot control what its citizens see and know. This is particularly true for a nation like China, which is deeply embedded in the global economy and has a rapidly growing class of wealthy, technologically engaged citizens. For example, as noted in chapter 4, China has embraced American fast food. It seems to desire the commercial aspects of American popular culture while fearing the political and social implications of an open society. So how does a nation promote McDonald's and KFC but not allow its citizens to explore news and audiovisual programming as well?

China regulates Internet content quite heavily, banning many sites related to democracy, human rights, or religious groups and ideas forbidden in China. Facebook, Google, and Instagram are among the banned sites. Indeed, China's efforts to control the information its citizens get through the Internet are collectively known as the "Great Firewall of China." For example, China runs its own social networking sites. These are monitored and edited by government officials. Likewise, Internet searches and download traffic are routed through government-controlled servers so that authorities can use state-managed content filters to refuse to show citizens the information they have requested. They have also compelled international corporations to agree to filter their search responses in China: both Microsoft and

Google have at times agreed to comply with Chinese law and limit various banned search terms. (Google withdrew from its agreement and as of April 2010 no longer legally operates in China.[41])

It should be noted that it is not clear that China's efforts to restrict its citizens' Internet access are entirely successful. Use of virtual private networks to log directly onto servers based outside China and access the Internet openly and freely is common. Additionally, Chinese Internet users have become skilled at using code words to avoid censors. For example, the phrase "empty chair" has no inherent offensive meaning. However, Chinese users know that it refers to Nobel Peace Prize–winning dissident Liu Xiaobo, who was not allowed to travel to Oslo, Norway, to receive his award and whose absence from the ceremony was symbolized by an empty chair on the central dais. Other code words and phrases exist. To be "harmonized" is to be censored, since "harmony" is one of the goals of official Chinese policy used to justify censorship in the first place. Chinese Internet users have even found a way to swear online: the words for "grass mud horse" sound, when spoken together, like a Chinese swear word. Websites marked with this word are advertising their status as sites opposing China's censorship practices.[42]

In sum, as was the case with both France and Iran, even a nation as powerful and prominent as China shapes its policies and actions in tension with American popular culture. China is open to, and indeed participates significantly in making and distributing, many of the products that shape the global market in culture artifacts. Yet it shies away from embracing the political and social values embedded in much of American popular culture and seeks to prevent its people from experiencing these ideas and attitudes. It is, like much of the rest of the world, both attracted to and wary of the American popular culture juggernaut.

FINLAND

Finland is the one outlier in this group of case studies: it places almost no controls on its citizens' access to and use of American popular culture products. In some ways, this is not surprising: Finland is a liberal parliamentary democracy that is capitalist, rights respecting, and dominated by the rule of law. In such conditions, support for a population's right to enjoy whatever entertainments it wishes should not seem unusual.

France, however, is also a liberal parliamentary democracy and, as was discussed earlier, it has enacted numerous laws and policies aimed at protecting French society and culture from outside—often American—influence. Finland might do the same. Many of the conditions shaping France's efforts to insulate itself from American popular culture also exist in Finland. For example, only a little more than 5 million people speak Finnish worldwide. It is unrelated to most European languages and is particularly difficult to learn: I, for one, barely progressed past "hello," "good-bye," and "no, I don't have a rewards card" (at grocery stores and the like) in the ten months I lived there from August 2015 to May 2016. Accordingly, there is little likelihood that Finnish will grow in international usage over time. In fact, given that most Finns speak English well—formal English-language instruction begins in school by age ten, but most Finns have been exposed to English by friends, family, and popular culture well before then—there is reason to suppose that English might well supplant Finnish even in Finland itself. To the degree that language is an agent of cultural transmission and persistence, the uncertain survival of Finnish as a language might be a source of national concern (as it is in France).

Finland also has long occupied a unique geopolitical position, one that has led it to construct a distinctive culture that its citizens are proud of while not being nationalistic or boastful. As noted earlier in this chapter, the land that is modern Finland was occupied by Sweden for the better part of six hundred years—from sometime in the thirteenth century until Sweden lost control of it in 1809. During this time, Swedish rulers converted Finns to Christianity, imported Swedish people to settle Finnish territory, and established a Swedish-speaking hierarchy that managed the territory's affairs. These efforts to systematically remake local Finnish society led to Finnish resistance, albeit limited, to Swedish rule. However, Finnish reaction to the Russian takeover of Finland after Russia beat Sweden in the Finnish War of 1808–1809 offers some insight into the resentment Finns felt toward their Swedish rulers: Finns remember the Russian victory as a positive thing since the Russian Empire treated Finland as a largely independent grand duchy and left it to mostly manage its own affairs. This era allowed the first expressions of Finnish nationalism, most notably through the music of composer Jean Sibelius.

Finns' sense of their unique culture was further deepened after they won their independence in 1917 during the chaos that followed the Russian Revolution of that same year. After a brief civil war, Finland went on to fight two intense, if brief, wars with the Soviet Union: the Winter War of 1939–1940 and the Continuation War of 1941–1944. While it technically lost both—in each case, Finland sued for peace, lost territory, and had to pay war reparations to its opponent—Finns do not generally view these wars as defeats. Rather, they point out that although in the 1930s and 1940s the Soviet Union reabsorbed much of the territory of the former Russian Empire lost in the years after the 1917 revolution, Finland survived. Indeed, Finland didn't just survive, it prospered: it built a very safe, very stable society with excellent schools, a dedication to human rights, and a strong focus on using resources in an environmentally sensitive way. Finns are, accordingly, quite proud of the society they have built even if they are not likely to shout out loud about their successes.

Taken together, the mix of newly emerging national pride, fear that their language might disappear, and other cultural challenges could have induced the Finns to seek to protect their culture from outside influences, as it seems to have encouraged the French, Iranians, and Chinese to do (for different reasons). However, Finland places no restrictions on its people's use and enjoyment of American popular culture goods. American music, television programming, and movies are widely available and, with one exception (addressed below), broadcast in the language in which the product was made. (Finns don't dub movies into Finnish: they watch American movies in English, Russian movies in Russian, and so forth.) Jeans are popular, McDonald's and other fast-food places are common (albeit less so than in the United States), and Finns are as sensitive to the trends and fads of the moment as any other people. Disney is so popular that a student informed me that until I taught an article about Disney as an international representative of American culture, it had never occurred to her that Disney was American. Finally, given that the former mobile phone giant Nokia was Finnish and that Finland has some of the cheapest broadband and mobile rates in the world, its society is fully integrated into the web of cultural connections in which American popular culture operates.[43]

The one exception Finns make to allowing its citizens full and unfettered access to popular culture products in their original form is children's programming, which is usually dubbed into Finnish. This is not surprising, however: young Finnish children likely do not speak English (yet) and so need programming in a language they can understand. Once they learn English, however, they will have effectively unlimited access to English-language popular culture programming and artifacts for the rest of their lives.

There is no obvious reason why Finns are sanguine in the face of American popular culture, while people in France are worried about it. The nation lacks the sense of international status and deserved attention that seems to shape French policymaking: Finns have no illusion that people around the world should want to speak Finnish or be Finnish, so they seem to have less concern about "protecting" Finland's culture and language. In addition, Finland's long history of colonial occupation and political struggle for independence has combined with the country's harsh environment to instill in Finns what they call *sisu*. While there is no direct translation, *sisu* is usually explained as the sense that one simply works hard, endures, and keeps moving forward. It encompasses both the reality that Finnish culture has endured and Finns' confidence that it will continue to do so. As one student put it when I asked why Finns were so open to American popular culture (given the pressures discussed earlier in this section), "What choice do we have?" Finns seem to believe that they can fret about threats to their cultural way of life but, as with the weather, can't do anything about them. So, *sisu*.

Fear of American popular culture is not, as the Finnish case shows, inevitable. But the unique details of the Finnish experience in shaping that country's relatively open relationship with American popular culture suggest that fear may be a more common reaction than confidence. In either case, the globalization of American popular culture is shaping the way the world moves toward globality.

SOCIAL NETWORKS, POLITICAL REVOLUTIONS? THE CASE OF THE ARAB SPRING

One reason nations like Iran and China might be particularly worried about the political and social content of American popular culture can be seen in the central role that social media platforms played in the so-called Arab Spring, the series of political uprisings that swept across much of the Arab world from Tunisia to Syria from the winter of 2010 through the spring of 2012. Starting with a wave of protests in Tunisia that led to the ouster of Zine El Abidine Ben Ali, the longtime dictator of that country, and continuing through ongoing violent uprisings in Syria, numerous countries—Egypt, Libya, Yemen, Bahrain, Saudi Arabia, Jordan, Kuwait, and Algeria among them—have faced revolutions and rebellions that brought about end of the dominant regime (Tunisia and Egypt); a civil war that led to the death of one of the world's longest-ruling leaders (Libya); a coup that replaced another authoritarian ruler (Yemen); and political violence that has been viciously suppressed (Bahrain, Algeria) or is ongoing (Syria). Change happened or was attempted across multiple regimes that had previously been notable mostly for their stability and cruel repression of their citizens' freedoms.

For the purposes of this book, what matters about these rebellions and revolutions is that they were for the most part organized through social networking services like Facebook and Twitter. (The revolutions are obviously more important than the means by which they were undertaken. However, this is not a book about the Arab Spring.) The Tunisian revolution, for example, is now recognized to have started when a young Tunisian street vendor, Mohamed Bouazizi, set himself on fire after being abused by a Tunisian government official. As horrible as this act of self-immolation was, in and of itself it was unlikely to set off a political revolution: terrible things happen all over the world all the time, and for the most part life continues as usual. In this case, however, antiregime activists in Tunisia used Bouazizi's case as a symbol of political protest. They turned to Twitter and Facebook to both publicize the abuses that led to Bouazizi's suicide and to recruit and organize new activists to protest the authoritarian Tunisian regime. Essentially, tech-savvy protesters mobilized a resource they understood but the state did not to draw in large numbers of Facebook and Twitter users to work to overthrow the Tunisian regime. And, notably, this strategy worked: Bouazizi burned himself to death in mid-December 2010; President Ben Ali fled the country after the Tunisian army abandoned him just a month later.

The tactics that worked in Tunisia were tried elsewhere, most notably in Egypt, through the spring of 2011. While the Egyptian revolution took longer and was much bloodier than the Tunisian one, the outcome was the same: a dictator of long standing was deposed in favor of a regime the people hoped would take steps to build a democracy in their country.

Egypt attempted to stop the use of social networks as a tool of political revolution by quite literally pulling the plug on the nation's Internet service. The idea was to sever the link between the revolution's leaders and the users of social networking services and thereby to quell the growing protests. After all, regardless of the protesters' desires for democracy, human rights, and economic opportunities, the regime wished to keep its privileged, authoritarian position. However, organizers and activists managed to cobble together landline telephones, fax machines, and access to Internet servers outside Egypt to continue their protest-planning activities. In the end, the ubiquity and decentralized nature of the digital world defeated the regime's efforts to quash online organizing.

The success of these two revolutions, along with the ouster of autocrats in Yemen and Libya, led some commentators to suggest that these were "Facebook revolutions." The notion was that Facebook was the key to the uprisings—that without it, and Twitter as well, the revolts in Tunisia and Egypt would not have been possible. Indeed, Egypt's revolution was undoubtedly facilitated when Wael Ghonim, an Egyptian-born Google executive living in Dubai, set up a Facebook page to commemorate the death of an Egyptian man named Khaled Said at the hands of Egyptian government officials. As happened in Tunisia, this act of commemoration inspired passion among those angry with the regime; Ghonim reported that just two minutes after he created his tribute page to Khaled Said, three hundred people had joined it.[44] Social networks certainly provided platforms on which revolutions could be built.

That said, calling such uprisings "Facebook revolutions" seems profoundly tone-deaf to the sacrifices and bravery of the people of Tunisia, Egypt, Syria, Bahrain, and elsewhere as they sought political and economic freedom. They, not Facebook, deserve credit for the risks they took and the goals they achieved. Social networking platforms provided a readily accessible tool that protesters could use to organize challenges to regimes that were well established and seemed quite stable, but they did not undermine the regimes themselves.

Whether the Arab Spring was made up of "Facebook revolutions" is not, of course, really the issue here. Instead, the prominence of Facebook and Twitter in these revolutions serves to highlight the profound role that American popular cultural artifacts can play in social and political affairs. Put another way, while it is wrong to assert that Facebook caused the Arab Spring, it is also hard to imagine how the revolutions and rebellions that have swept the Arab world would have happened without such social networks. As such, these platforms played an important role in world affairs, albeit one never anticipated by their creators. Similarly, in the years since the Arab Spring, rulers in places like Turkey have either periodically cut off or greatly slowed their citizens' access to services like Facebook and Twitter in times of political and social unrest. They clearly fear the ability of these new forms of communication to remake the traditional power structures in their communities.

CONCLUSION

The relative success that antigovernment forces had in using Facebook, Twitter, and similar services to manage their revolutions highlights the reasons that governments like those of Iran and China seek to control and manage such platforms. After all, whether or not you or I approve of the ways governments may abuse their citizens' rights and dignities, the governments themselves wish to retain power. Accordingly, whether for fear that citizens will use a social network to organize a revolution or that the Internet (and even Disney) will expose them to values and ideals that a regime thinks will challenge its authority, governments all over the world seek to control and limit the effects of American popular culture.

In addition, whether in individual cases or as a matter of international law, American popular culture has been and remains one of the most divisive-but-attractive forces shaping contemporary globalization. Fears of both the economic and the cultural power of American popular culture are central to international efforts to restrain its effects on people's lives around the world. While this chapter has explored these tensions only in the arenas of the global audiovisual industry, the scope of popular culture is broad and deep. American pressures to make cultural artifacts mere commodities of exchange as part of the larger process of globalization may well be encouraging the fragmentation that globalization seems inevitably to stimulate. It is central to the way globalization has developed and is likely to develop.

NOTES

1. Quoted in Simona Fuma Shapiro, "The Culture Thief," *New Rules*, November 5, 2000, 10, http://www.newrules.org/publications/new-rules -journal-fall-2000.

2. Quoted in Patricia M. Goff, *Limits to Liberalization: Local Culture in a Global Marketplace* (Ithaca, NY: Cornell University Press, 2007), 142–43.

3. Quoted in Shapiro, "Culture Thief."

4. Cultural Industries Sectoral Advisory Group on International Trade, *An International Agreement on Cultural Diversity: A Model for Discussion*, September 2002, 4–5.

5. Music Council of Australia, *Submission to the Department of Foreign Affairs and Trade's Office of Trade Negotiations*, January 28, 2003.

6. Goff, *Limits to Liberalization*, 90 (emphasis added).

7. Goff, *Limits to Liberalization*, 24–35.

8. Hernan Galperin, "Cultural Industries in the Age of Free-Trade Agreements," *Canadian Journal of Communications* 24, no. 1 (1999): 49–77.

9. Quoted in Goff, *Limits to Liberalization*, 120.

10. Galperin, "Cultural Industries."

11. Galperin, "Cultural Industries."

12. "New UN Treaty to Preserve World's Rich Cultural Diversity to Come into Force in March," UN News Centre, December 19, 2006, http://www .un.org/apps/news/story.asp?NewsID=21046&Cr=UNESCO&Cr1 (accessed May 10, 2017).

13. "Convention on the Protection and Promotion of the Diversity of Cultural Expressions," UNESCO, October 20, 2005, http://portal.unesco.org/en/ ev.php-URL_ID=31038&URL_DO=DO_TOPIC&URL_SECTION=201.html (accessed May 10, 2017).

14. "Convention."

15. "New UN Treaty."

16. See Goff, *Limits to Liberalization*, 36–56, for an extended discussion of the issues facing Canada in relation to the United States.

17. Quoted in Goff, *Limits to Liberalization*, 44.

18. Quoted in Goff, *Limits to Liberalization*, 55.

19. Galperin, "Cultural Industries."

20. Galperin, "Cultural Industries."

21. Galperin, "Cultural Industries."

22. Goff, *Limits to Liberalization*, 85.

23. "List of Highest-Grossing Films in France," Wikipedia, https://en.wikipedia.org/wiki/List_of_highest-grossing_films_in_France (accessed May 10, 2017).

24. "French Prefer US TV Series," Tootlafrance.ie, http://www.tootlafrance.ie/features/french-prefer-us-tv-series (accessed May 10, 2017).

25. Christine Vanston, "In Search of the *Mot Juste*: The Toubon Law and the European Union," *Boston College International and Comparative Law Review* 22, no. 1 (1999), http://lawdigitalcommons.bc.edu/cgi/viewcontent.cgi?article=1217&context=iclr (accessed July 14, 2017).

26. Vanston, "In Search of the *Mot Juste*."

27. "France Bans Facebook and Twitter Promotion on TV," France 24, June 6, 2011, http://www.france24.com/en/20110606-business-technology-france-regulators-ban-facebook-twitter-promotion-on-tv (accessed May 10, 2017).

28. Benjamin R. Barber, *Jihad vs. McWorld: How Globalism and Tribalism Are Reshaping the World* (New York: Ballantine Books, 1996), 92.

29. "Iranian Youth Divided on Future," *Toronto Star Newspapers*, June 8, 2003.

30. John Lancaster, "Barbie, 'Titanic' Show Good Side of U.S.," *Washington Post*, October 27, 1998, http://www.washingtonpost.com/wp-srv/inatl/longterm/mia/part3.htm (accessed March 2, 2012).

31. Lancaster, "Barbie."

32. Barbara Slavin, "New Attitudes Color Iranian Society, Culture," *USA Today*, February 28, 2005, http://www.usatoday.com/news/world/2005-02-28-iran-pink_x.htm (accessed May 10, 2017).

33. My Stealthy Freedom, http://mystealthyfreedom.net/en (accessed May 10, 2017).

34. "Iran Destroys 100,000 'Depraving' Satellite Dishes," AlJazeera, July 25, 2016, http://www.aljazeera.com/news/2016/07/iran-destroys-100000-corrupting-satellite-dishes-160724202722493.html (accessed May 10, 2017).

35. Lancaster, "Barbie."

36. David Murphy, "Toosheh Uses Satellite TV to Sneak Content Past Iranian Censorship," *PC*, April 24, 2016, http://www.pcmag.com/news/343972/toosheh-uses-satellite-tv-to-sneak-content-past-iranian-cens (accessed May 10, 2017).

37. Max Fisher, "Iran's Supreme Leader Joined Instagram—Here's His First Photo," *Atlantic*, August 1, 2012, https://www.theatlantic.com/international/archive/2012/08/irans-supreme-leader-joined-instagram-heres-his-first-photo/260607 (accessed May 10, 2017); Mohammad Reza Azali, "Rouhani's

Government Is Trying to Remove the Ban on Twitter," *Techrasa*, April 11, 2017, http://techrasa.com/2017/04/11/rouhani-government-remove-ban-twitter (accessed May 10, 2017).

38. For a fuller discussion, see Wai-Chung Ho, "A Cross-Cultural Study of Preferences for Popular Music among Hong Kong and Thailand Youths," *Journal of Intercultural Communication* 7 (September 2004).

39. Keith Bradsher, "Disney Takes Exception to China's Media Rules," *New York Times*, September 12, 2005, http://www.nytimes.com/2005/09/12/business/worldbusiness/12disney.html (accessed March 2, 2012).

40. "Shanghai Disney Officially Opens: A Peek Inside," *Los Angeles Times*, June 17, 2016, http://www.latimes.com/business/la-fi-shanghai-disney-opening-htmlstory.html (accessed May 10, 2017).

41. "Roundup: Google Pulls Out of China," *Guardian*, March 23, 2010, https://www.theguardian.com/media/pda/2010/mar/23/google-china (accessed May 10, 2017).

42. Paul Wiseman, "Cracking the 'Great Firewall' of China's Web Censorship," ABCNews.com, http://abcnews.go.com/Technology/story?id=4707107&page=1 (accessed May 10, 2017).

43. Gordon Kelly, "Finland and Nokia: An Affair to Remember," *Wired*, October 4, 2013, https://www.wired.co.uk/article/finland-and-nokia (accessed May 10, 2017).

44. Jose Antonio Vargas, "Spring Awakening," *New York Times Book Review*, February 19, 2012, 12.

CHAPTER 6

AMERICAN POPULAR CULTURE AND THE FUTURE OF GLOBALIZATION

As this book has shown, there is something different about the products of American popular culture. The early transnational corporations that produced movies, music, and television programs took advantage of permissive laws, an open culture, a diverse audience, and ideal filmmaking weather to build global empires of audiovisual entertainment—empires that gave American producers an advantage in competing for the mass international entertainment audience that exists today. As a result, American movies, music, and television programming, whether produced in the United States or derived from forms of entertainment created by Americans, largely dominate world trade in popular audiovisual culture.

We have also seen that American influence in popular culture goes beyond the audiovisual industry. People around the world wear American styles of clothing, eat at American restaurants, drink American concoctions, and even enjoy distinctively American forms of sport. They connect through social networking services that are grounded in American styles of social interaction and serve as access points to multiple components of American popular culture—and potentially as platforms on which to build political and social revolutions. Chapters 3 and 4 chronicled a small number of these American cultural products, but it is worth remembering here that Coca-Cola spawned countless competitors and copycats, as did McDonald's and blue jeans—and Facebook, for that matter. Football is only the most recent American sport to go global: baseball and basketball have had audiences around the world for decades. These forms of popular culture, along with the audiovisual industries and many others, have spread American business styles, American cultural practices, and even American English as a mode of seemingly universal communication across the planet. American popular culture is a global juggernaut.

The popularity of American cultural products derives, at least in part, from the transparency and flexibility they embody. In creating works to satisfy an American audience, U.S. producers learned to appeal to a broad audience. They also grew into powerful companies that could take advantage of global economic and political changes to build a worldwide market for their goods. This business synergy made American products attractive around the world. American products and styles emerged from a U.S. context into a global community whose individual cultures were remarkably open to integrating American goods and services.

The transparent appeal and corporate power that gave American producers of popular culture a comparative advantage in world trade have not only brought American popular culture products to a world audience but instilled fear in the hearts of many people and communities worldwide. Some groups fear that members of their communities will abandon their traditional, local cultures in favor of an Americanized, global one. Others fear that American companies will use their power and wealth to drive local producers out of the market. Yet others fear both. Ways of life, after all, are found not only in cultural products but in the means of making them in the first place. American popular culture can challenge both.

The twentieth and early twenty-first centuries have seen American popular culture spread globally hand in hand with international efforts to restrict its influence. Global trade agreements have sought to both protect local culture producers and cultural forms and to allow large numbers of people worldwide to seek American movies, music, television, clothes, food, sports, and other cultural artifacts. If nothing else, globalization has made American popular culture a flashpoint across the world.

This chapter assesses the likely future of American popular culture as an agent of globalization. It argues that those who fear the global trade in American popular culture have reified and sanctified current cultural orders into eternal "cultures" that need protection from the prevarications of cultural "others." This chapter challenges this frozen vision of cultures in conflict. Culture is a more flexible concept than is generally recognized, a fact that will shape the globalization of American popular culture going forward. However, fears of corruption, imperialism, and homogenization will likely persist as long as human beings seek to inculcate their children with their values and to live in communities of like-minded people—in other words, as long as there are cultures. But the nature and terms of the debate will shift over time as both the products of American popular culture and the audiences that enjoy them change. This change will subsequently alter the way American popular culture affects globalization as a process toward globality. Just as true globality will likely never be achieved, American popular culture cannot and will not utterly corrupt, overwhelm, or wash away all diversity in cultures across the globe.

CULTURAL CHANGE, HYBRIDITY, AND AMERICAN POPULAR CULTURE

The discussions of Canada, France, Iran, Hong Kong, Finland, and the Arab Spring offered in chapter 5 showed that policymakers across these countries and regions often, but not always, fear that American popular culture could remake local ones. French and Canadian leaders, for example, worried that American culture would replace a distinctively French or Canadian culture. They also feared that American corporations would drive domestic companies out of business. As a consequence, they promoted policies intended to keep their culture-production capacity strong and independent of American control. Iran's leaders, in contrast, sought to keep its people free from the temptations of American popular culture and enacted policies intended to limit Iranians' access to American products—albeit incompletely. While China favored Disney's operations in Hong Kong, it worried that Disney might undermine local values elsewhere in the country—even in Shanghai, one of the most globalized cities on earth. And, of course, Arab rulers now overthrown or confronting rebellion did not want to face such upheavals—even if those of us outside the region might think the Arab Spring is a politically good thing. Only Finland was seen to be relatively open to American popular culture regardless of any potential threats American culture poses for Finnish life.

These reactions are grounded in a common concern that transcends even the obvious economic reasons why some nations oppose free trade in American products. They stem from the sense that American popular culture can transform local cultures into something different. American popular culture is seen as an agent of change in the local culture that replaces what is distinctive and unique at home with a globalized, American social and political order.

TYPES OF CULTURAL CHANGE

The fear that American popular culture can remake local cultures rests on the notion that cultures are basically fixed and immutable and so do not change easily over time. In this view, "culture" exists in a unified whole in which values, practices, and rituals reinforce one another. If cultural change occurs, it is likely to be disruptive, even coerced—and very probably illegitimate. Change is seen to result from the imposition of one set of cultural values on another, such that the weaker culture loses its identity and is effectively wiped out.

The sense that cultural change is inevitably coercive derives in part from cultures' basic stability. After all, cultures can be said to exist as definable and recognizable things only if they persist long enough for some group or community to develop a set of ideals, attitudes, rituals, norms, and behaviors that distinguish it from some other group or community. Since cultures are relatively stable, changes, particularly dramatic changes, are generally seen as unlikely.

The fact that cultures seek to replicate and sustain themselves informs the belief that cultural change must be coercive. Every culture, after all, defines itself in terms of both what its members believe/feel/do and what they do not believe/feel/do. By definition, aliens and strangers stand in some degree of tension with the local culture. If cultural changes occur while the local group is in contact with some stranger or strangers, it is common for native people to assume that the changes are the result of the work of the alien group. Moreover, if members of the local community believe that the changes are harmful to their way of life, they will commonly blame, fear, resent, and even scapegoat the outsiders. Any changes are believed to result from some external, alien force imposing a new order on a subordinate community.

Notably, this fear of a cultural other that imposes unwanted and dangerous changes on the local community exists in tension with the ways that change actually occurs in cultures. As will be seen, cultural change is ongoing, and while change might happen because one culture destroys another, that is not the only reason cultures change. Instead, at least three types of cultural change can be expected over time. Two of these—pattern-maintaining change and change toward flexibility—generally reinforce existing cultural patterns, beliefs, institutions, and behaviors. Only the third—cultural disruption—tends to undermine established structures.[1] Each type of change must be analyzed to understand if the kinds of changes feared by those opposed to cultural globalization are likely to happen.

Culturally disruptive change occurs when the existing institutions, values, norms, and practices of a society are overwhelmed in the face of some challenge. Existing patterns of life are profoundly disrupted when changes come too quickly to be assimilated effectively. An obvious example would be the changes that may follow when a society is conquered in a war. The winning group has the opportunity, if it wishes, to try to remake the culture of the loser by reorganizing schools, retraining teachers, barring local religions, and numerous other acts. Similarly, mass disease or a severe environmental crisis may make it impossible for a society to maintain its beliefs and practices. In such conditions, ordinary life cannot sustain itself, and unanticipated cultural consequences are likely to follow. Change in such circumstances is likely to be both painful and destructive.

Those groups and individuals who fear the spread of American popular culture typically associate its effects with this kind of sudden, shocking change. They view its coming to their communities as a plague: older, established, stable lives are disrupted and destroyed as people, especially young people, adopt the cultural styles found in American products. What is true for individuals can also happen in business: those who fear the coming of American popular culture assume and assert that established industries are vulnerable to the American plague, likely to be replaced by global corporate titans. Entire ways of life might be destroyed quickly. For such people, their societies must resist the American onslaught if they wish to retain their cultural identities.

Pattern-maintaining change is more common than disruptive change. It is also much less controversial. Indeed, after the fact it hardly seems like change at all. Pattern-maintaining change happens when new technologies, ideas, attitudes, norms, and values enter a culture and are integrated into it in ways that strengthen or reflect established forms of social organization. An obvious example is the American adoption of the automobile. The car transformed America in numerous ways: it moved people off farms and out of inner cities into suburbs, for example, even as it sped up the pace of American life by making trade and travel across large distances convenient for most people. It also destroyed numerous existing industries like stable/livery services and profoundly undermined the blacksmith trade. Moreover, cars were not popular when they first hit America's roads; in fact, many towns and villages passed laws restricting their use. Farmland gave way to tarmac, and pollution spread, as more and more people took their cars on the road. All of this, and much more, changed American culture dramatically. Whatever the modern consensus about the innate Americanness of the automobile, the gap between what America was like before it adopted the automobile and what it grew into afterward is profound.

Despite the changes the car caused in America, in time most Americans came to see owning a car as core to American identity. Automobiles came to represent freedom and independence, and they allowed Americans to express their innate individualism. The car changed America, but it is generally seen to have reinforced rather than shattered American culture.

The story of the integration of the automobile into American life offers useful insights into how changes caused by American popular culture might be experienced around the world. After all, car ownership only seems pattern maintaining in retrospect. It took many years before a consensus developed that automobile ownership was an important indicator of American identity: the modern American car culture of most adults owning cars they use regularly is largely a product of the post–World War II period. By extension, while the use and integration of American popular culture products may be disruptive in many cultures across the world, it does not follow that these disruptions will ultimately destroy local communities. Instead, they may be recognized as promoting local cultural values and opportunities. The Internet, for example, flows both ways: it is possible for people around the world to download American music and other products, but it is also possible for Americans to download materials from other cultures. Any analysis of the cultural future of globalized trade in American popular culture needs to recognize this fact.

Similar analysis can be offered of the third type of cultural change going on around us: change that enhances a culture's flexibility. Change toward flexibility occurs as societies grow more complex, or what sociologists refer to as "differentiated." Agrarian societies, for example, are relatively nondifferentiated: most people in a given community grow their own food with the intent of feeding their families, and while political, religious, military, or other leaderships usually exist, their sizes are constrained by the amount of food the community can grow. The culture of such societies is usually quite simple. Roles are well defined, taboos are clear, and social practices are typically tightly controlled. As societies differentiate, however, their cultures need to grow more flexible. For example, if some people are trained and supported as full-time health-care workers (whether medical doctors or medicine people), society needs to create and define a role and a place for them. It also needs to develop systems through which such people can satisfy their basic life needs (e.g., for food and shelter) even though the persons do not work in traditional subsistence jobs. A similar process of cultural adaptation needs to occur if an industrial revolution takes place, science expands the realm of the known, or previously repressed groups are integrated into the workforce. The more functions, ideas, institutions, and values a society admits, the more flexibility it requires.

Changes toward flexibility, it should be noted, can be quite disruptive. New ways of life replace old ones. To return to the example offered above, now that cars predominate in America's transportation system, there are virtually no blacksmiths and livery stables in the United States. These once crucial elements of life have faded away. Yet these changes are generally recognized as necessary, at least in retrospect. To offer an extreme example, if one community organizes its military around armored, horse-riding knights and another buys fighter jets and tanks, those who rely on the former for their security are almost certain to lose to an army with modern weapons and training. In such a case, it is probably best for a society that wishes to survive to give up using armored knights for defense and to buy fighter jets and tanks— even if such a change requires a change of culture. Differentiation and complexity are important to cultural survival even if the new order is strikingly different from the old one.

On its face, change toward flexibility is the type of change least likely to be caused by American pop culture products. After all, differentiation is a long-term process. However, it is likely that people living in communities that are much less differentiated than the United States will be exposed to American pop culture products in this modern era of globalization. To the degree that American movies, music, television, clothes, food, sports, and other artifacts carry American values and styles to the world, they may challenge the norms and values of cultures much less complex than that of the United States. Such exposure may, in turn, promote cultural change in those societies that may induce cultural differentiation. These changes may seem like cultural disruption to traditionalists but instead comprise first moves toward building more complex societies that can survive in the new, global era. It simply does not follow that any cultural change at all constitutes the profound disruption of an established culture.

Cultures are not fixed or immutable. Pressures to integrate new ideas, technologies, and institutions (pattern-maintaining change) tend to make societies more complex (change toward flexibility) at the cost of undermining various members' livelihoods, ideals, and cultural identities (cultural disruption). What is pattern-maintaining change for some is cultural disruption for others. Change toward cultural flexibility disrupts the cultural values preferred by traditionalists who wish to maintain an established way of life. Consequently, cultures change over time and yet usually retain a sufficiently distinctive character that members of the community still think of themselves as "American" or "French" or "Thai."

When discussing the likely future of the globalization of American popular culture, then, it is not particularly useful to complain that

American culture changes—or might change—local ones and stop there. Change may occur, but what matters is what happens in the moment of cultural intersection. Points of cultural contact can bring both coercive and consensual changes that, while disruptive, may sustain or transform cultures. The question in any given moment of change, then, is whether the processes are forced on a community or not. Those that are coercive are likely to be met with resistance and resentment and will take root only if the force promoting the change can sustain pressure on the community over time. Those that result from more voluntary patterns of adoption may disrupt established traditions but are nonetheless more likely to be integrated into the local culture over time. For the purposes of this chapter, the central question is, Which type of change is more likely as American popular culture intersects with cultures around the world?

CULTURAL CHANGE AS CULTURAL HYBRIDITY

To anticipate the answer to this question, while it is certainly possible that changes to societies that integrate American popular culture products will be coercive, this is not likely. Instead, most cultural change derived from popular culture is likely to result from integrative and evolutionary developments. To return to a concept introduced in chapter 1, cultural change regularly results in the creation of hybrid cultures. Thus, while people across the world are likely to decry the changes to their culture that are occurring at any given moment, in time, most people will recognize the resulting hybrid as distinctively "their" culture.

In chapter 1, hybridity was roughly defined as "mixing," or "the ways in which forms become separated from existing practices and recombine with new forms and new practices."[2] Such communication and hybridization is a two-way process—Western societies may be as influenced by non-Western ones as non-Western communities are influenced by the West. While certain cultural forms may predominate—Western values may supersede local ones because of their market advantages or the soft-power appeal of American ideas and symbols, for example—there is nonetheless variation within "Western" culture, and non-Western cultures have influenced and continue to influence one another as well as Western culture itself. The final product of these interactions is not necessarily corruption, imperialism, or homogenization; it can instead be something entirely new. As noted in chapter 1, Jan Nederveen Pieterse has referred to this mixing of cultures as tending toward mélange—a system in which many hybridized cultures interact in a constantly evolving process.[3] Marwan M. Kraidy likewise noted that cultural hybridity is the likely endpoint of globalization.[4]

Why does cultural mixing occur? At least part of the answer lies in the population migrations that have led to the distribution of the world's peoples across the planet. As people move, they bring their cultures with them. Cultural contact, including mixing, is inevitable. Contemporary population migrations generally move from what is termed (awkwardly) the Global South toward what is called (again somewhat awkwardly) the Global North. While this terminology misses the fact that there are many underdeveloped areas in the North and, likewise, that there are developed areas in the South (e.g., Australia and Singapore), it does capture the essence of the contemporary flow: from less developed, less safe, less politically free areas toward safer, more developed, and more democratic regions. Such shifts can also occur within countries, as is happening in China: while the population of that country's largest cities exceeds the population of the United States (the world's largest economy), hundreds of millions of Chinese peasants still live in rural areas, many earning less than $2 a day. As rural people move to China's major cities they, too, are effectively moving from the Global South to the integrated, globalized North, even if they never leave their home nation. Finally, such shifts can occur across nations, as people leave one region for another. Regardless of the physical direction of travel, these movements are toward globally integrated regions and away from rural, less connected ones.

As discussed in chapter 1, scholars like Samuel Huntington and Benjamin Barber argued that conflict of one form or another would inevitably rise among different cultural groups at such points of cultural contact. These authors predicted cultural clashes would result as one group tried to impose its worldview on the other, while the latter resisted. Contact was expected to cause conflict, not consensus.

The empirical record, however, suggests that culture war is not the inevitable result of cultural contact. The interaction of the "other" and the known might lead to cultural conflict, but such contacts can also bring adaptation, learning, shading, and subtlety rather than brute force and the thoughtless imposition of alien values on a hapless, innocent population. For example, what is understood to be the distinctive culture of the United States today (as described in chapter 1) is clearly the result of many changes over time. Core components of American culture are in fact hybrids of earlier forms. Consider the following:

- The American English in which this book is being written is an evolved combination of Anglo-Saxon and Norman French that began developing well over a thousand years ago. That Anglo-Saxon/ Norman hybrid language has continued to evolve with considerable influence and loaned words from classical Latin and Greek, as well as from modern French, Italian, Spanish, Arabic, Turkish, Persian, and numerous other languages. (Even Finnish makes an appearance, having donated the word "sauna," among others, to English.)
- Most Americans did not drink beer regularly until large numbers of Germans moved to the central United States in the latter half of the nineteenth century and established, among other breweries, what became the Anheuser-Busch brewery in St. Louis, Missouri. Americans integrated beer drinking into their culture rather than preserving it as an essential element of "original" American culture.
- The strong presence of Irish Catholics in the politics of cities like Boston, New York, and Chicago only emerged after large numbers of that group immigrated to the United States due to the potato famine of the 1840s. Prior to that time, there was a strong anti-Catholic bias among mostly Protestant Americans. Indeed, Catholic immigration during the Irish potato famine encouraged many Americans to join the Know-Nothing Party, a political party formed with the explicit intent of stopping Catholic immigration. In time, however, cities like Boston, long controlled by a Protestant aristocracy, eventually transformed into Irish Catholic–run communities.

Because of changes like these (and many others), few people born in the United States in 1825 would recognize the way Americans live today. Yet, as discussed in chapter 1, the resulting hybrid culture is recognizably American. Hybridity emerges as different ideas, practices, values, and norms intersect. Its final form is rarely if ever predictable.

What is true in the history of the United States is true globally as well. There are countless examples of the ways in which one set of cultural practices ultimately informed and shaped ideas and values that are later seen as intrinsic to another culture. Judaism, Christianity, and Islam share a common ideological and theological tradition grounded in the teachings of Abraham. The profound political, economic, and social tensions that separate many adherents of these faiths today have resulted from the ways in which each has interpreted its heritage and its history, not because they emerged from different religious roots. Coffee is not native to Europe, even though Europeans arguably turned it into a global drink. Potatoes and tobacco came from the Western Hemisphere before being transplanted and adopted around the world. Horses did not exist in the Americas until Spanish conquistadors brought them in the 1500s; the iconic image of horse-riding American Great Plains tribes galloping across the West chasing bison was made possible only after Spanish conquerors came to the Western Hemisphere and set about the literal destruction of many native cultures—leaving horses in their wake. Thus, something that seems intrinsic to an indigenous American culture—horses for the Plains tribes—was in fact an unintended consequence of brutal colonialism and near genocide. (Given the topic of this book, it is interesting that perhaps the most vivid and beautiful presentation of this image appears in a Hollywood movie: Kevin Costner's 1990 Academy Award–winning global hit *Dances with Wolves*.)

Even these few examples suggest that human beings are exceptionally skilled at meeting groups and individuals of other cultures, learning from them, and adapting to their values. When we assess the impact of any cultural form on globalization, then, it is important to assess whether (and how) specific ideas, images, values, and norms embedded in the cultural artifact are perceived and responded to by the societies and groups experiencing the "other" culture.

GLOBAL CULTURAL HYBRIDITY AND AMERICAN POPULAR CULTURE

If nothing else, the global ubiquity of American popular culture suggests that it is an important source of the ideas, values, styles, behaviors, attitudes, and rituals that can promote cultural changes around the world. Indeed, as the discussions of the cultural changes caused by the introduction of McDonald's into Japan or the spread of blue jeans across the world showed in chapter 4, American popular culture has in fact caused changes in other cultures. Other brief examples can be offered. In 2005, for example, the long-running American television hit *The Simpsons* was adapted and shown in the Arab world as *Al Shamshoon*. Homer's name was changed to "Omar," while Bart became "Badr."[5] There is now a thriving global hip-hop music industry, one in which local performers sing in indigenous languages about cultural themes meaningful to their communities. A McDonald's opened in Zacatecas, the last Mexican state without one, in 2004.[6] Many of these changes have been highly controversial, of course: in Turkey in 2008, for example, I had a conversation with a student who acknowledged his own grandparents' deep skepticism of Turkish rap music, even though he insisted that many Turkish performers use it to shape and reinforce Turkish identity. But however popular or unpopular these cultural transitions have been, they are ongoing and important features of global politics today.

Cultural hybridity is not a one-way street, however. American pop culture products are dominant in global trade, but they do not emerge from a fixed cultural context any more than any cultural artifact of any other culture does. American popular culture continues to develop as life and culture in the United States grow and change. American pop culture therefore may offer something of a model of what may happen as globalization moves forward. For example, consider the following:

- In 2010, sales of Tostitos salsa made it the number two condiment brand in America (behind Hellman's mayonnaise); it sold $7 million more in salsa than Heinz did in ketchup.[7]
- Large numbers of Asian, Indian, and Arab workers hired by American contractors to load trucks, staff military bases, and perform manual labor for American units participating in Operation Iraqi Freedom regularly came together to watch Bollywood movies; some American soldiers and contractors watched as well.[8]
- Cricket leagues have formed across the United States, bringing a game popular in former British colonies like Pakistan and India to American shores.[9]
- The movie *Crouching Tiger, Hidden Dragon* was a breakaway hit in the United States even though it was in Chinese, starred Chinese actors, and was in the style of traditional Chinese martial arts films, not an established American genre. Westernized variants of Chinese martial arts films, like *The Matrix* trilogy and the two parts of *Kill Bill*, have become major hits as well.

- The American singer-songwriter Paul Simon used the music of Ladysmith Black Mambazo, a group that performs traditional South African music, in a collaboration that produced a world-wide hit.
- Caribbean reggae and Cuban musical forms enshrined in movies like *Buena Vista Social Club* have become popular across the United States.

At first glance this is a pretty unremarkable list. Various pop culture entertainments are popular both in the United States and across the globe. Indeed, the list seems little more than a reflection of realities of the entertainment industry in a globalized world. Yet the very unremarkableness of this list is in fact profoundly meaningful. In contrast with the predictions offered by Huntington or Barber, none of these essentially hybrid cultural artifacts has stimulated strong opposition, either in the United States or elsewhere.

For example, no American cultural or political leaders are currently engaged in a campaign to stamp out salsa eating as dangerous to American national pride or cultural integrity, even though salsa now outsells ketchup in America's grocery stores. This is, in fact, quite remarkable given that salsa's rise as a condiment has been associated with the growing importance of Hispanic immigrants to the United States. Large and increasing populations of people from Latin and South America have been legally and illegally immigrating to the United States in the last several decades. This, in turn, has been linked to an expansion of Hispanic political influence in the United States: in the 1970s, the Frito-Lay company was forced by Hispanic economic and social action to eliminate its "Frito Bandito" character at about the same time that Cesar Chavez was able to unionize itinerant Hispanic farm laborers under the auspices of the United Farm Workers. In the 1980s, Taco Bell's Chihuahua faced a similar fate. Subsequent political activism has brought one Latino politician, Bill Richardson, to several elected offices, including the governorship of New Mexico. Most recent presidential elections have seen major-party candidates go out of their way to speak Spanish at several points in the campaign. This political presence has been mirrored by an increasing Hispanic presence in American social and cultural consciousness. Many Americans now celebrate Cinco de Mayo (May 5) as an informal holiday (Mexican Independence Day), even though Mexican Independence Day is September 16. Spanish is now among the most sought-after language skills among employers and job seekers in the United States.

The noncontroversial integration of foods associated with Hispanic culture into "American" political and social life is perhaps even more striking given the election of President Donald Trump in 2016. As a candidate, Trump emphasized the risks and dangers of Hispanic immigration. In his speech announcing his decision to run for president, for example, Trump emphasized that Mexico was not "sending their best" to the United States, arguing that many Mexican immigrants were murderers, drug dealers, and rapists. His campaign hinged on a plan to build a border wall to physically separate Mexico from the United States and thereby eliminate illegal migration into the United States. He claimed that Mexico would pay for the wall and went on to repeatedly threaten the deportation of as many as 11 million Hispanics from the United States. Yet, on Cinco de Mayo 2016, Trump dutifully tweeted a picture of himself eating a taco bowl allegedly made at a restaurant at the eponymous Trump Tower in New York City. The caption read, "The best taco bowls are made in Trump Tower Grill. I love Hispanics!" Everything Hispanic was dangerous, Trump seemed to say—except the food.

Salsa did not cause these changes, of course; nor have all these changes happened smoothly and without resistance. They have, however, largely occurred without the kind of violence and cultural warfare expected by those pessimistic about cultural globalization. Cultural intersection need not lead to cultural conflict.

There is reason to think that similar changes can take place in other countries. Among other things, while people may protest rock music or Coca-Cola plants worldwide, rock songs and Coke remain popular. As noted in chapter 1, even as controversies about U.S. policies in global politics have intensified, American music, movies, television programs, social media, clothing styles, fast-food chains, and other artifacts have spread across more of the world. Jake Silverstein reported one small example: when he asked his Mexican contacts if going to McDonald's instead of making their own lunch over a fire was not likely to undermine or transform Zacatecan culture, he found that "without exception . . . [they] seemed to think I was insane to suggest that it might be preferable to build a small wood fire and reheat a taco when there was a possibility of visiting McDonald's for a burger and fries. . . . After all, a man could still build a fire and reheat his wife's cooking if he wanted to."[10] American pop culture products do seem to penetrate global markets without always causing obvious cultural disruptions. Instead, hybrid forms emerge both overseas and in the United States itself.

THE FUTURE OF AMERICAN POPULAR CULTURE AND GLOBALIZATION

Its global prominence places American popular culture in a unique position in world affairs. It is an agent of change in a world that is resistant to change, especially when that change is driven from far away and may well sweep away local cultures—and local jobs and businesses at the same time. It manifests values typically associated with American culture. These ideals are popular and appealing worldwide. They also induce fear and resentment at the same time.

Powerful forces drive the globalization of American popular culture. Some, like the advantages American manufacturers enjoy in areas like marketing, distribution, and technology, are asymmetrical. They are structural advantages that can make it relatively easy for the transnational corporations that produce American popular culture to impose their products on the rest of the world through free trade competition or the ruthless undercutting of local cultural products, while facing little competition from other culture makers. Other advantages, such as the natural evolutionary flexibility of culture and the transparent appeal of American values and products, are social, shaped by time and context. Both have favored the spread of American pop culture products around the world.

The insight that most cultural change creates hybrid forms is particularly important in the context of the global spread of American popular culture. As seen earlier in this chapter, American cultural products go out into the world at large and promote new cultural practices. It is also true that global artifacts come to the United States and reshape American culture. This reciprocal process leads to an obvious question: How will American movies, music, and television programs shape globalization in the future? While no complete answer to this question can be offered, several developments seem likely to emerge over time. The following takes each in turn as it seeks to frame a final answer to the question of how American popular culture will affect globalization for years to come.

- *American audiovisual products will continue to be a major force in global trade and entertainment well into the future.*

Because of both their established position and the increasing spread of communications technology, American movies, music, and television programming can be expected to retain their position as the most watched, most used, and most traded types of popular culture around the world. Indeed, the decline in numbers of restrictive authoritarian regimes that followed the end of the Cold War, combined with the movement of people from the less connected, underdeveloped Global South to the connected Global North, suggests that the market for American audiovisual entertainment and other cultural products is likely to expand at an escalating rate as new markets are identified and developed. Whereas the Global North has been largely saturated with American programming for nearly a century (at least in the case of movies and music), the Global South and its billions of people are a relatively untapped market. As a consequence of their established production, financial, distribution, and marketing capacities, the transnational corporations that control the American audiovisual industries are well positioned to take advantage of these new markets as they open. American audiovisual culture can therefore be expected to increase in global influence in the coming decades.

- *The global demand for other American products, like clothing styles and brands, restaurants, and sports is also likely to grow over time.*

The end of the Cold War brought many new opportunities for the expansion of American culture products. Corporations like McDonald's, Coca-Cola, and Starbucks have taken advantage of these opportunities to push their products all over the world. They have been able to do this both because they are large and wealthy companies that have the resources to pursue global expansion and because many of their products were well-established markers of American identity even before they entered foreign markets. These products were desired even before they were broadly available. The loosening of global trade restrictions has simply made it easier—or possible—for many American products to reach consumers who were well primed to accept them. Moreover, American producers now have extensive experience taking their brands global, suggesting that even if they enter markets not broadly exposed to American goods and services, they have the skills needed to introduce their products and create markets for them. These experiences suggest that American products will maintain and expand their presence across the world.

- *Social networking will continue to be a platform for the spread of information, products, cultural styles, and political and social change around the world.*

Facebook alone now boasts more than 1.23 billion daily users and 1.86 billion monthly users. It is, in other words, used by more than 16 percent of the people on the planet. Other social media platforms add even more connected users to the global network. Even if Facebook is eventually replaced, something else will certainly rise in its place. But whether it is Facebook or successor platforms, social networking services make it possible to tie large parts of the world together around shared ideas, values, practices, and, of course, cultural artifacts like movies, music, television programs, restaurants, sports events, and clothing styles (to name a few). Moreover, the creativity with which social networking services can be used to coordinate actions ranging from a marketing campaign to a revolution suggests that these sites are going to remain an integral part of the global community for the foreseeable future. They are, consequently, likely to be pivot points around which American popular culture engages the broader globe—and around which global cultural practices and artifacts enter the American cultural space. The interconnectedness of the world will expand the number and types of flash points for political and other controversies to emerge.

- *As social network platforms transmit information and entertainment across cultural and political boundaries, they will be the source of increasing tension as social and political conservatives seek to limit their power to affect local communities.*

In 2017, for example, a major Hollywood movie titled *The Promise* premiered. Starring A-list movie star Christian Bale, *The Promise* is set in World War I during the last years of the Ottoman Empire (centered in today's Turkey). The film depicts a love triangle set against a horrible act of violence that is generally referred to as the Armenian Genocide. From 1915 through 1923, the Ottoman government systematically worked to purge Armenians from Ottoman territory, executing, starving, and otherwise causing the deaths of approximately 1.5 million Armenians. One of the film's scenes takes place in a field filled with Armenian people recently killed by Turkish troops.

Whatever the merits of the film, the relevant point here is that while much of the world refers to the events framing *The Promise* as the Armenian Genocide, it is effectively against the law to refer to those events as genocide in Turkey itself. Article 301 of the Turkish penal code makes it illegal to insult Turkishness or otherwise denigrate Turkey as a nation. The Turkish writer Orhan Pamuk was brought to trial for making provocative statements about the Armenian Genocide, for example, although the charges were eventually dropped. Other writers and historians have also been charged with violating this law.

The Promise is, then, more than just a film. It is a vehicle with which various people and institutions can work to advance their agendas and preferences. So are lots of other popular culture artifacts. Popular culture is not, as Matthew Arnold once put, "chewing gum."

- *The YouTube-ification of entertainment is likely to expand.*

At least three hundred hours of video are uploaded to YouTube every minute.[11] Once "released" onto YouTube's servers, videos can transmit images as mundane as a child playing with a ball or as intense as a political or military conflict to any of YouTube's 1.3 billion worldwide users, who collectively watch more than 5 billion videos a day. Moreover, some of those videos can go viral, meaning that for some reason or another, people get excited by what they see, more and more people view it, and indeed whole cultures of copycats and parodies can be spawned from the original source—or from the copies themselves. This viral process offers some challenge to established content makers, as people find ways to entertain themselves without accessing traditional sources of audiovisual entertainment. However, there is no practical reason that television and movie studios as well as radio, music, and other culture makers cannot develop content that they can post to YouTube and use to promote their products. YouTube might become a platform for distributing movies, music, and television like Netflix is, and given that 80 percent of YouTube's users are from outside the United States, it is a significant platform for exporting American popular culture worldwide.

- *American popular culture will continue to be a major source of controversy in global trade agreements.*

    Given the economic, political, and cultural dimensions of the globalization of American popular culture, it is likely that while the United States will continue to push for free trade in cultural artifacts, most of the rest of the nations of the world will resist. American popular culture products generate enormous profits worldwide and, by extension, limit the number of dollars any community can spend on locally produced culture. This provides economic incentives for states and competitor companies to try to limit the local scope of American popular culture. In addition, constituted as it is by culture-bearing and culture-generating artifacts, American popular culture is likely to raise concerns from cultural traditionalists who fear that their way of life is under attack. Whether because of economic or cultural pressures or for their own interests, then, political leaders around the world have made limiting American popular culture a central platform of their national and international agendas. Continued resistance to the globalization of culture is likely, as demonstrated by the passing of the United Nations Educational, Scientific and Cultural Organization treaty on cultural diversity. Likewise, the struggles with passing either the most recent World Trade Organization treaty or the Trans-Pacific Partnership illustrate the uncertain linkage in various policymakers' minds of free trade and free trade in culture.

- *Challenges to American movies, music, and television programs will arise for a variety of economic, political, and cultural reasons, leading to new alliances seeking to limit the effects of American popular culture within their communities.*

    Given the multiple ways in which American popular culture intersects with and challenges cultures around the world, it is reasonable to assume that cultural groups, not just governments, will also work to limit its effects in their countries. New political alliances have formed among groups that otherwise share few interests. For example, some feminist groups in the United States have combined forces with evangelical Christian groups to fight the spread of pornography, whose makers have used new technologies like digital cameras and the Internet to create and distribute their products globally. Similar combinations can be expected to form as more and more places and people experience the political, economic, and cultural effects of American popular culture programming. The globalizing of American popular culture is thus likely to be a factor in creating resistance to it.

- *Increased exposure to American popular culture will encourage the development of hybrid forms that have value to local cultures.*

As addressed earlier in this chapter, exposure to the ideas, forms of entertainment, values, and social practices of one culture does not necessarily breed resentment, anger, and rejection. Rather, people can learn from each other. This has certainly happened with American music. The band that many people consider the greatest rock group of all time, the Beatles, was British, after all, and rap music has become local in many cultures around the world. Similarly, many stars of American country music today are from Australia. Television programs, too, can sponsor copycat products: a version of the American game show *Wheel of Fortune*, for example, is popular in Russia. In addition, *The Simpsons* has spread across the world despite its inherent irreverence and antiauthority spirit. Blue jeans and fast food are popular not just because they are American but also because they have been integrated into local cultures as meaningful and important parts of those communities' identities. There is no logical reason to presume that similar results will not follow when new people and new communities engage with American popular culture in the future.

- *Just as other cultures can adopt and integrate American programming, American culture can adapt and integrate entertainment forms that originated elsewhere.*

As their acceptance of salsa suggests, Americans are no more likely to automatically reject everything from somewhere else as "alien" and "other" than are people around the world. Moreover, the megacorporations that produce American popular culture have an economic interest in surveying world markets in search of programming that might be popular in the United States. In fact, reality shows like *Big Brother*, *American Idol*, and *Whose Line Is It Anyway?* originated in Great Britain before coming to America. Humiliation TV—such as *Fear Factor* and similar American programs in which people engage in dangerous stunts or subject themselves to "gross-out" eating or endurance contests in pursuit of various prizes—was pioneered in Japan. As more pleasant examples, the success of the Colombian pop singer Shakira has occurred across language boundaries, and it is worth noting that many subscribers to Telemundo are not native Spanish speakers. The international hit television show *Who Wants to Be a Millionaire* originated in the United Kingdom before becoming the narrative frame for the 2008 Academy Award–winning film *Slumdog Millionaire*. *Slumdog*, notably, was set in Mumbai (Bombay), India, and ended with a much-loved dance scene that evoked similar scenes common in Bollywood movies. Such cultural learning constitutes a two-way street, with each side informing the other.

- *Pop cultural interchanges can create economic and cultural bonds among people that may not be represented by political institutions.*

Whether as producers, consumers, or participants in shared entertainments that develop subcultures, diverse people around the world will likely develop relationships of mutual interest around the products of American popular culture. An obvious example of such linkages has been the worldwide spread of *Star Trek* fan clubs. *Star Trek* is literally a global phenomenon, and millions of people worldwide collect paraphernalia, attend conferences, and assert the IDIC (infinite diversity in infinite combinations) creed at home and abroad. Likewise, golfers can recognize each other globally by what they wear and carry; similar subcultures exist around the world, covering "sk8ters," rappers, and coffee aficionados. Such common bonds may not be expressed in the political system, however, for a variety of reasons, ranging from the rules of the system being written to advantage cultural conservatives (Iran) to sheer democratic inertia—both sk8ters and rappers lack either the numbers or the desire (or both) to challenge American policy toward specific countries. When we analyze the effects of American popular culture on globalization, then, it is important to look beyond the public statements of political leaders.

- *American popular culture may facilitate the emergence of a global culture, at least to a limited extent.*

As American popular culture reaches larger and larger audiences, as local cultures adopt and integrate American forms, and as American culture itself adapts to the ideas, norms, and values of other cultures for a variety of economic and pragmatic reasons, relatively shared vocabularies, concepts, and frames of reference will likely emerge to support the use of American movies, music, and television programming. The fact that most of American popular culture's products are presented in English, which is also a language of international global commerce, will only facilitate the rise of a common, if limited, global culture. Moreover, the fact that American popular culture is substantially "American" suggests that the general form and character of any emergent global culture is likely to be based on principles of choice, freedom, and consumption, at least in commercial affairs. It is easy to image Internet slang as a nearly universal language, for example. New contractions such as "btw," "u," "r," and others can be deployed by people with only limited understanding of English spelling or grammar to get their meaning across. Likewise, common cultural phrases now exist across the world. "OK" is perhaps the first truly global word, while phrases like "I'll be back" (*The Terminator*) spread around the world. Given these examples, it seems likely that at least some version of a consumer-driven, choice-filled culture will emerge, at least among the worldwide users and marketers of American popular culture.

- *Popular culture may influence political and social life in surprising ways.*

To take one example, the Israeli Labor Party was planning to hold a primary election on July 3, 2017, to choose its candidates for office. The election was scheduled to take place in Tel Aviv, the nation's largest city. However, pop star Britney Spears had previously scheduled a concert in Tel Aviv that same day. The result? The Labor Party moved its primary back one day to avoid the conflict with Spears's concert.[12]

- *Cultural integration is more likely within and among components of the Global North than within and among those of the Global South, thereby deepening the gap between north and south.*

The sharing of popular culture products is, by definition, more likely in areas with markets that have both an interest in and the capacity to consume a given product. Put another way, it makes little economic sense for Disney or any other transnational corporation to market a global blockbuster in rural India or rural China, since a ticket might cost $8 or more, and many people there make less than $2 a day. Thus, global exchanges of dollars, ideas, experiences, values, images, and technologies are likely to be concentrated in the globalized parts of the world. This, in turn, can be expected to encourage global migration from south to north as the gap widens between how one is living and how one might live. Indeed, the appeal of American popular culture should add energy to this migration, as people literally move "off the farm" to experience the world of possibilities manifested in the products of American popular culture—including the wealth, freedom, and lifestyles embedded in American culture. Accordingly, concerns of nations in the Global North about immigration, cultural cohesion, and the identity of their people can be expected to grow more intense for the foreseeable future.

- *Resistance to the spread of American popular culture, whether organized by states or by citizens, is likely to be hard.*

While numerous nations and social groups are attempting to limit the influence and power of American popular culture in their communities, three factors appear likely to limit the effectiveness of these efforts in the long run: (1) the spread of the technology through which American cultural artifacts can be accessed, (2) the global appeal of American culture in general, and (3) global population movements. As a practical matter, satellites and the Internet make gaining access to American popular culture relatively easy. Almost all national efforts to ban satellite dishes have failed for lack of enforcement, even in fairly restrictive regimes like Iran and China. North Korea may be the world's only exception, and even it is now facing the problem of smuggled Internet content that both exposes the regime's practices and allows its citizens access to the wider world. In addition, the products created within American popular culture are desirable and sought after worldwide. This does not mean that local forms need disappear, but it does suggest that efforts to ban appealing programming wholesale are unlikely to succeed, especially given easy technological access to it. Finally, the contemporary worldwide population migration from the Global South to the Global North (however conceived) means that there will be increasing numbers of people in areas and communities in which American popular culture is already present and pervasive. Under such conditions, plans or hopes to ban American cultural products are doomed to failure.

- *Nothing is inevitable about globalization and American popular culture.*

  Among other things, the analysis of the ways in which American popular culture has affected the process of globalization offered in this book ought to, at the least, provide an empirically based challenge to those scholars and pundits who insist that globalization is inevitable. As chapter 5 made clear, states still actively work to limit what they deem the pernicious economic, political, and cultural effects of American popular culture on their communities. Whatever the advocates of total globalization say about how people ought to behave in the marketplace, many peoples and governments are quite happy to accept less American programming, however enjoyable or inexpensive it might be, in favor of higher-priced, tax-subsidized local products. Nothing about globalization can be inevitable in such a world.

  Resistance need not lead to culture war, however. As addressed earlier in this chapter, cultures learn, change, and adapt. It is possible for cultures to integrate new ideas and experiences without necessarily experiencing corruption, imperialism, or homogenization. Accordingly, the interchange of American popular culture and cultures around the globe may encourage the emergence of new hybrid forms that accommodate new identities and opportunities for literally billions of people worldwide. While this process will inevitably displace or distort some ideas and practices, the cumulative effect may be seen as beneficial rather than harmful. To the degree such change occurs, the world's movement toward globality will be enhanced.

CONCLUSION

This book began by addressing the role American popular culture played in the Cold War. It has concluded with a consideration of how American cultural artifacts may influence the future of globalization. The evidence offered here shows that as one of the central components of contemporary global trade, American popular culture both encourages integration and promotes fragmentation as it shapes the way contemporary globalization is unfolding. The long-term course of globalization is, therefore, likely to progress much as Manfred Steger has suggested: toward globality without ever actually achieving it.[13]

American popular culture is one important component of this process, and it is likely to remain so for a long time to come. It is through popular culture that the rest of the world learns what "American" means, and any attempt to understand globalization without attention to the central role played by global interest in and fear of American popular culture is necessarily incomplete. In large measure it is through American popular culture that the rest of the world may decide whether to fear or favor the promise of a globalized planet.

NOTES

1. The following discussion of the three types of cultural change derives from Harry Eckstein, "A Culturalist Theory of Cultural Change," *American Political Science Review* 82, no. 3 (1988): 789–804.

2. William Rowe and Vivian Schelling, *Memory and Modernity: Popular Culture in Latin America* (London: Verso, 1991), 231.

3. Jan Nederveen Pieterse, *Globalization and Culture: Global Mélange* (Lanham, MD: Rowman & Littlefield, 2004), 69–71.

4. Marwan M. Kraidy, *Hybridity, or the Cultural Logic of Globalization* (Philadelphia: Temple University Press, 2005).

5. Jake Tapper, "'The Simpsons' Exported to Middle East," ABCNews.com, October 18, 2005, http://abcnews.go.com/WNT/story?id=1227362&page=1#.T05KLEprovo (accessed May 10, 2017).

6. Jake Silverstein, "Grand Opening: Ronald McDonald Conquers New Spain," *Harper's* (January 2005): 67–74.

7. Jeremy Olshan, "Hellmann's Mayonnaise America's Best-Selling Condiment," *New York Post*, September 17, 2011, https://nypost.com/2011/09/17/hellmanns-mayonnaise-americas-best-selling-condiment (accessed May 10, 2017).

8. Sgt. Tammy Johnson, 1244th Transportation Company, deployed to Kuwait and Iraq, April 2003–August 2004, personal communication.

9. "USA Cricket—League and Associations," ESPN cricinfo, http://www.espncricinfo.com/usa/content/page/406579.html (accessed May 10, 2017).

10. Silverstein, "Grand Opening," 72.

11. "36 Mind Blowing YouTube Facts, Figures and Statistics—2017," Fortunelords, https://fortunelords.com/youtube-statistics (accessed May 10, 2017).

12. Peter Beaumont, "Oops! Britney Spears Gig Forces Israeli Labour Party to Delay Leadership Contest," *Guardian*, April 5, 2017, https://www.theguardian.com/world/2017/apr/05/britney-spears-gig-forces-israeli-labour-party-to-delay-leadership-contest-security-tel-aviv-concert (accessed May 14, 2017).

13. Manfred B. Steger, *Globalization: A Very Short Introduction* (New York: Oxford University Press, 2003), 8.

GLOSSARY

American Exception (the): the circumstances that shaped the early dominance of the U.S. movie, music, and television industries in global popular culture production.

Arab Spring: series of social and political revolutions that broke out across much of the Arab world in 2011; understood to have been aided by social networking platforms like Facebook and Twitter.

Civic culture: the values, ideas, and expectations of the people who live in the United States, including ideas like democracy, individual rights, tolerance, and so forth; a source of shared identity that frames political and social debate in the United States.

Cold War: the nearly fifty-year political and military standoff between the United States and the Soviet Union from 1945 to 1991. It entailed military, economic, and cultural competition between the two powers and their allies to establish the preferred system of life.

Comparative advantage: the advantage one country or culture holds over other countries or cultures in the production of some consumer good.

Convergence: the term used to describe the reduction of the many companies and individuals who used to make popular culture to the few corporations that control the trade today; alternately known as "consolidation."

Culture: the root values, ideas, assumptions, behaviors, and attitudes that members of different communities generally share in an unexamined, automatic way. Cultures provide the context in which economic, social, and political life makes sense to their members.

Cultural corruption: the process by which one culture imposes its values, ideas, and preferred lifestyles on another, particularly coercively or nonvoluntarily.

Cultural homogenization: the idea that cultural interaction tends to promote sameness as one culture's values, ideals, and practices replace another's; usually associated with economic interaction and change rather than direct military-style coercion.

Cultural hybridity: the idea that as cultures interact, each learns and integrates new ideas and values from the other, creating a new culture or value in the process.

Cultural imperialism: the idea that one culture inevitably seeks to impose itself on another, often violently.

Cultural transparency: the ability of cultural products to have appeal across cultural boundaries and contexts.

Divorcement: the result of the 1948 Paramount case, in which the movie production companies were forced to sell their movie theater chains on the grounds that, through their ownership of them, they enjoyed an illegal monopoly on filmmaking and distribution in the United States.

Federal Communications Commission (FCC): U.S. government agency charged with licensing and regulating broadcast radio and television stations and, to a lesser extent, cable and satellite services as well.

Fragmegration: the tendency of the forces that promote globalization to also promote fragmentation and separatism in political and social affairs.

Franchise: a business arrangement in which the vendor usually owns a store or service agency independently of an established company but

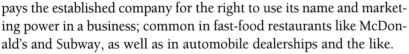

pays the established company for the right to use its name and marketing power in a business; common in fast-food restaurants like McDonald's and Subway, as well as in automobile dealerships and the like.

Free trade: the idea that goods and services should be traded across national boundaries with limited (if any) restrictions or impediments, such as taxes.

General Agreement on Tariffs and Trade (GATT): first efforts at establishing free trade among the world's industrialized economies. Originally negotiated in 1947, the treaty aimed to reduce barriers to cross-national trade to make for as free an exchange of goods and services as possible.

Globality: the goal of globalization; the end state of the process of eliminating barriers to interaction in human life across the globe.

Globalization: a process by which political, social, economic, and other spheres of human life grow increasingly interrelated regardless of governmental, cultural, economic, geographic, or other barriers that have historically separated groups of people.

Cultural globalization: the ways one culture's goods, services, ideas, values, and media affect other cultures once they enter the new exchanges opened by globalization.

Economic globalization: the linkage of the economic livelihoods of people living in many different countries through world trade, international finance, and the operations of transnational corporations.

Political globalization: the role that laws and other political actions play in creating contemporary globalization.

Global War on Terror (GWoT): U.S. military response after the terror attacks of September 11, 2001, involving the invasions of Afghanistan (2001) and Iraq (2003) and deploying resources globally to try to identify and stop terrorist acts before they take place.

Glocalization: the adaptation of international products to local conditions and the integration of local products into the global economy.

Hard power: the ability to coerce others, such as through military means, to follow your wishes.

Hays Production Code: a code of standards for making movies in the United States, created under the direction of former U.S. postmaster general Will Hays. Established in the 1930s to forestall regulation by government, its standards helped shape the stereotypical "American" movie.

High culture: works of art that, in contrast to popular culture products, are understood to exist as conscious acts of creation with no purpose other than their own existence.

McDonaldization: See cultural homogenization.

Nativism: resentment of immigration; a sense that people born and raised in a community are superior to others and that others pose a threat to the "native" way of life.

Negative liberty: the belief that liberty is the same thing as being left alone by the government. Americans generally believe that government should leave people alone so that individuals can think, believe, and act as they wish; adherents believe government should be as uninvolved in the lives of citizens as possible.

Networks: independently owned television and radio stations, or groups of stations, that share programming created by a central production company in exchange for fees and other goods, like advertising time (e.g., ABC, NBC, CBS, and Fox).

North American Free Trade Agreement (NAFTA): agreement on trade in goods and services among the United States, Canada, and Mexico, adopted in 1998.

Popular culture: anything used or engaged with by large numbers of people that was created primary to be consumed.

Populism: the belief that elites dominate the political and economic systems to their own benefit; thus, to protect their own interests, ordinary people need to challenge decisions and policies made by elites.

Positive liberty: the belief that real liberty is not possible until basic needs are met (e.g., enough to eat, personal security, basic, quality education). Adherents believe government should take a more active role in helping citizens fulfill these basic needs.

Protect Intellectual Property Act (PIPA): legislation proposed in the U.S. Senate in 2011 to punish Internet service providers that hosted illegally downloaded digital content or offered hyperlinks to illegally downloaded material; favored by content makers like movie, music, and television producers.

Public culture: the common terms of reference, symbols, rituals, and ideologies within which different groups and individuals press their claims for power, policy, and identity.

Soft power: the appeal of one group's cultural, social, intellectual, and ideological ideas, values, attitudes, and behaviors over another's.

Stop Online Piracy Act (SOPA): legislation proposed in the U.S. House of Representatives in 2011 to punish Internet service providers that hosted illegally downloaded digital content or offered hyperlinks to illegally downloaded material; favored by content makers like movie, music, and television producers.

Synergy: the vertical and horizontal integration of entertainment companies and the products they market; enhanced when a company can place a song in a popular television program it produces or make it the theme song for a movie it has financed. Multiple marketing outlets reach different audiences to hopefully increase sales, concentrate profit in the controlling company, and spread the risk of creating a movie, album, or television program across an array of businesses.

Trans-Pacific Partnership (TPP): proposed free trade treaty intended to create a NAFTA for most of the world's major economic powers with Pacific Ocean coasts; included strong protections desired by American popular culture producers for intellectual property and copyright enforcement rules. China was not in the TPP.

United Nations Educational, Scientific and Cultural Organization (UNESCO): UN organization dedicated to preserving, protecting, and advancing knowledge of cultures and cultural diversity through dialogue, respect, and mutual exchange.

World Trade Organization (WTO): successor to GATT (in 1995); broadened efforts to create free trade agreements among a larger set of countries than GATT addressed. It has largely been unable to make a deal since the failure of the so-called Doha Round of negotiations that started in 2001.

RECOMMENDED READINGS

Adams, Francis, Satya Dev Gupta, and Kidane Mengisteab, eds. *Globalization and the Dilemmas of the State in the South*. London: St. Martin's, 1999.

Adorno, Theodor. *The Culture Industry: Selected Essays on Mass Culture*. London: Routledge, 1991.

Allen, Robert C., and Annette Hill, eds. *The Television Studies Reader*. New York: Routledge, 2004.

Almond, Gabriel, and Sidney Verba, eds. *The Civic Culture*. Princeton, NJ: Princeton University Press, 1963.

Anderson, Benedict. *Imagined Communities: Reflections on the Origin and Spread of Nationalism*. London: Verso, 1983.

Appadurai, Arjun, ed. *Globalization*. Durham, NC: Duke University Press, 2001.

———. *Modernity at Large: Cultural Dimensions of Globalization*. Minneapolis: University of Minnesota Press, 1996.

Axford, Barrie. *The Global System: Economics, Politics, and Culture*. Cambridge, UK: Polity, 1995.

Baran, Stanley J., and Dennis K. Davis. *Mass Communication Theory: Foundations, Ferment, and Future*. 5th ed. Boston: Wadsworth Cengage Learning, 2009.

Barber, Benjamin R. *Jihad vs. McWorld: How Globalism and Tribalism Are Reshaping the World*. New York: Ballantine Books, 1996.

Barker, Chris. *Global Television: An Introduction*. Malden, MA: Blackwell, 1997.

Barney, D. *The Network Society*. Malden, MA: Polity, 2004.

Barry Jones, R. J. *The World Turned Upside Down? Globalization and the Future of the State*. Manchester, UK: Manchester University Press, 2000.

Beck, Ulrich. *What Is Globalization?* Oxford, UK: Blackwell, 2000.

Bellah, Robert N., et al. *The Good Society*. New York: Knopf, 1991.

——. *Habits of the Heart: Individualism and Commitment in American Life*. Berkeley: University of California Press, 1985.

Benedict, Ruth. *Patterns of Culture*. Boston: Houghton Mifflin, 1934.

Bercovitch, Sacvan. *The American Jeremiad*. Madison: University of Wisconsin Press, 1978.

——. *The Puritan Origins of the American Self*. New Haven, CT: Yale University Press, 1975.

Berger, Peter L., and Samuel P. Huntington, eds. *Many Globalizations: Cultural Diversity in the Contemporary World*. New York: Oxford University Press, 2002.

Berlin, Isaiah. *Two Concepts of Liberty*. Oxford, UK: Clarendon Press, 1958.

Boorstin, Daniel J. *The Genius of American Politics*. Chicago: University of Chicago Press, 1953.

Boyd, Todd. *Young, Black, Rich, and Famous: The Rise of the NBA, the Hip Hop Invasion, and the Transformation of American Culture*. New York: Doubleday, 2003.

Bryan, Lowell, and Diana Farrell. *Market Unbound: Unleashing Global Capitalism*. New York: Wiley, 1996.

Burnett, Robert. *The Global Jukebox: The International Music Industry*. New York: Routledge, 1996.

Calhoun, Craig. *Nations Matter: Culture, History, and the Cosmopolitan Dream*. London: Routledge, 2007.

Carver, Terrell, and Jernej Pikalo, eds. *Political Language and Metaphor: Interpreting and Changing the World*. London: Routledge, 2008.

Chalaby, Jean K. *Transnational Television Worldwide: Towards a New Media Order*. New York: I. B. Tauris, 2005.

Christensen, Terry, and Peter J. Haas. *Projecting Politics: Political Messages in American Films*. Armonk, NY: M. E. Sharpe, 2005.

Collins, Patricia Hill. *Black Sexual Politics*. New York: Routledge, 2004.

Combs, J. *Polpop: Politics and Culture in America*. Bowling Green, KY: Bowling Green State University Press, 1984.

Condry, Ian. "Japanese Hip-Hop and the Globalization of Political Culture." In *Urban Life: Readings in the Anthropology of the City*, edited by George Gmelch and Walter Zenner, 357–87. Prospect Heights, IL: Waveland Press, 2001.

Cornell, Grant H., and Eve Walsh Stoddard, eds. *Global Multiculturalism.* Lanham, MD: Rowman & Littlefield, 2001.

Cox, Harvey. "The Market as God: Living in the New Dispensation." *Atlantic Monthly,* March 1999, 18–23.

Crothers, Lane. *Rage on the Right: The American Militia Movement from Ruby Ridge to Homeland Security.* Lanham, MD: Rowman & Littlefield, 2003.

Crothers, Lane, and Charles Lockhart, eds. *Culture and Politics: A Reader.* New York: St. Martin's, 2001.

Cunningham, Patricia A., and Susan Voso Lab, eds. *Dress and Popular Culture.* Bowling Green, OH: Bowling Green State University Popular Press, 1991.

Curtin, P. D. *Cross Cultural Trade in World History.* Cambridge: Cambridge University Press, 1984.

Dallmayr, Fred. *Achieving Our World: Toward a Global and Plural Democracy.* Lanham, MD: Rowman & Littlefield, 2001.

Devine, Donald. *The Political Culture of the United States.* Boston: Little, Brown, 1972.

Diamond, Jared. *Guns, Germs, and Steel: The Fates of Human Societies.* New York: Norton, 1999.

Dicke, Thomas S. *Franchising in America: The Development of a Business Method, 1840–1980.* Chapel Hill: University of North Carolina Press, 1992.

Dicken, Peter. *Global Shift: Mapping the Changing Contours of the Global* Economy. 7th ed. New York: Guilford Press, 2015.

Douglas, Mary, and Baron Isherwood. *The World of Goods.* New York: Basic Books, 1979.

Dowmunt, Tony, ed. *Channels of Resistance: Global Television and Local Empowerment.* London: BFI Publishing, 1993.

Eagleton, Terry. *The Idea of Culture.* Oxford, UK: Blackwell, 2000.

Easton, David. *The Political System: An Inquiry into the State of Political Science.* 2nd ed. Chicago: University of Chicago Press, 1981.

Eckstein, Harry. "A Culturalist Theory of Political Change." *American Political Science Review* 82, no. 3 (1988): 789–804.

Edelman, Murray. *The Symbolic Uses of Politics.* Urbana: University of Illinois Press, 1964.

Eisenstadt, S. N. "Cultural Traditions and Political Dynamics: The Origins and Modes of Ideological Politics." *British Journal of Sociology* 32, no. 2 (1981): 155–81.

Ekachai, Daradirek, Mary Hinchliff-Pelias, and Rosechongporn Komolsevin. "Where Are Those Tall Buildings: The Impact of U.S. Media on Thais' Perceptions of Americans." In *Images of the U.S. around the World: A Multicultural Perspective,* edited by Yahya R. Kamalipour, 265–78. Albany: State University of New York Press, 1999.

Elazar, Daniel Judah. *American Federalism: A View from the States.* 3rd ed. New York: Harper & Row, 1984.

————. *The American Mosaic: The Impact of Space, Time, and Culture on American Politics.* Boulder, CO: Westview, 1994.

Ellis, Richard. *American Political Cultures.* New York: Oxford University Press, 1993.

Ellis, Richard, and Michael Thompson, eds. *Culture Matters: Essays in Honor of Aaron Wildavsky.* Boulder, CO: Westview, 1997.

Emmerson, Donald K. "Singapore and the 'Asian Values' Debate." *Journal of Democracy* 6, no. 4 (1995): 95–105.

Enloe, Cynthia. *Bananas and Bases: Making Feminist Sense of International Politics.* Berkeley: University of California Press, 1989.

Falk, R. *Predatory Globalization.* Malden, MA: Polity, 1999.

Fanon, Franz. *The Wretched of the Earth.* Harmondsworth, UK: Penguin, 1967.

Fischer, David Hackett. *Albion's Seed: Four British Folkways in America.* New York: Oxford University Press, 1984.

Foster, Robert J. *Coca-Globalization: Following Soft Drinks from New York to New Guinea.* New York: Palgrave Macmillan, 2008.

Freedman, Estelle B. *No Turning Back: The History of Feminism and the Future of Women.* New York: Random House, 2002.

Friedman, Jonathan. *Cultural Identity and Global Process.* London: Sage, 1994.

Friedman, Thomas. *The Lexus and the Olive Tree: Understanding Globalization.* New York: Picador, 1999.

Fukuyama, Francis. *The End of History and the Last Man.* New York: Free Press, 1992.

Gabler, Neal. *An Empire of Their Own: How the Jews Invented Hollywood.* New York: Crown, 1988.

Galperin, Hernan. "Cultural Industries in the Age of Free-Trade Agreements." *Canadian Journal of Communications* 24, no. 1 (1999): 49–77.

Gans, Herbert. *Popular Culture and High Culture: An Analysis and Evaluation of Taste.* New York: Basic Books, 1974.

Gaventa, John. *Power and Powerlessness: Quiescence and Rebellion in an Appalachian Valley.* Urbana: University of Illinois Press, 1980.

Geertz, Clifford. *The Interpretation of Cultures.* New York: Basic Books, 1973.

Gellner, Ernest. *Encounters with Nationalism.* Cambridge, MA: Blackwell, 1994.

————. *Nations and Nationalism.* Ithaca, NY: Cornell University Press, 1983.

Giddens, Anthony. *The Consequences of Modernity.* Stanford, CA: Stanford University Press, 1990.

Goff, Patricia M. *Limits to Liberalization: Local Culture in a Global Marketplace.* Ithaca, NY: Cornell University Press, 2007.

Goodman, Barak, dir. *Merchants of Cool.* PBS *Frontline*, 2001. http://www.pbs.org/wgbh/pages/frontline/shows/cool.

Greenfield, Liah. *Nationalism: Five Roads to Modernity.* Cambridge, MA: Harvard University Press, 1992.

Greenstone, J. David. *The Lincoln Persuasion: Remaking American Liberalism*. Princeton, NJ: University of Princeton Press, 1993.

Grewal, David Singh. *Network Power: The Social Dynamics of Globalization*. New Haven, CT: Yale University Press, 2008.

Guins, Raiford, and Omayra Zaragoza Cruz, eds. *Popular Culture: A Reader*. Los Angeles: Sage Publications, 2005.

Gusfield, Joseph. *Symbolic Crusade: Status Politics and the American Temperance Movement*. Urbana: University of Illinois Press, 1966.

Hafez, Kai. *The Myth of Media Globalization*. Cambridge, MA: Polity, 2007.

Hannerz, Ulf. *Cultural Complexity: Studies in the Social Organization of Meaning*. New York: Columbia University Press, 1992.

———. *Transnational Connections: Cultures, People, Places*. London: Routledge, 1996.

Hanson, Ralph. *Mass Communication*. 6th ed. Thousand Oaks, CA: Sage Publications, 2017.

Harrison, Lawrence E., and Samuel P. Huntington, eds. *Culture Matters: How Values Shape Human Progress*. New York: Basic Books, 2000.

Hartz, Louis. *The Liberal Tradition in America*. New York: Harcourt, Brace, 1955.

Havens, Timothy. "The Biggest Show in the World: Race and the Global Popularity of *The Cosby Show*." In *The Television Studies Reader*, edited by Robert C. Allen and Annette Hill, 442–56. New York: Routledge, 2004.

Hayden, Patrick, and Chamsy el-Ojeili, eds. *Confronting Globalization: Humanity, Justice, and the Renewal of Politics*. New York: Palgrave Macmillan, 2005.

Hebidge, D. *Subculture: The Meaning of Style*. London: Methuen, 1979.

Held, David, Anthony McGrew, David Goldblatt, and J. Perraton. *Global Transformations*. Cambridge, UK: Polity, 1999.

Hines, Colin. *Localization: A Global Manifesto*. London: Earthscan, 2001.

Hobsbawm, Eric. *Nations and Nationalism since 1780*. Cambridge: Cambridge University Press, 1992.

Hofstadter, Richard. *The American Political Tradition and the Men Who Made It*. New York: Vintage, 1974.

———. *The Paranoid Style in American Politics, and Other Essays*. New York: Knopf, 1965.

Hopper, Paul. *Understanding Cultural Globalization*. Malden, MA: Polity, 2007.

Hunt, Linda. *Politics, Culture, and Class in the French Revolution*. Berkeley: University of California Press, 1984.

Huntington, Samuel P. *American Politics: The Promise of Disharmony*. Cambridge, MA: Belknap, 1981.

———. *The Clash of Civilizations and the Remaking of World Order*. New York: Simon & Schuster, 1996.

———. *Who Are We? The Challenges to America's National Identity*. New York: Simon & Schuster, 2004.

Inglehart, Ronald. *Modernization and Postmodernization: Cultural, Economic, and Political Change in Forty-Three Societies*. Princeton, NJ: Princeton University Press, 1997.

———. *The Silent Revolution: Changing Values and Political Life among Western Publics*. Princeton, NJ: Princeton University Press, 1975.

Jackle, John A., and Keith A. Sculle. *Fast Food: Roadside Restaurants in the Automobile Age*. Baltimore: Johns Hopkins University Press, 1999.

Jameson, Frederic. *Signatures of the Visible*. London: Routledge, 1990.

Jameson, Frederic, and M. Miyoshi, eds. *The Cultures of Globalization*. Durham, NC: Duke University Press, 1998.

Johnson, Chalmers. *Blowback: The Costs and Consequences of American Empire*. New York: Henry Holt, 2000.

Katz, M. B. *The Undeserving Poor*. New York: Pantheon, 1989.

Keohane, Robert O. *After Hegemony*. Princeton, NJ: Princeton University Press, 1984.

Kingdon, John W. *America the Unusual*. New York: Worth, 1999.

Kivisto, Peter. *Multiculturalism in a Global Society*. Malden, MA: Blackwell, 2002.

Kluckhohn, Clyde. *Culture and Behavior*. New York: Free Press, 1962.

Kottak, Conrad Phillip. *Prime-Time Society: An Anthropological Analysis of Television and Culture*. Belmont, CA: Wadsworth, 1990.

Kraidy, Marwan M. *Hybridity, or the Cultural Logic of Globalization*. Philadelphia: Temple University Press, 2005.

Krasilovsky, M. William, and Sidney Shemel. *This Business of Music*. 7th ed. New York: Billboard Books, 1995.

Kuttner, Robert. *Everything for Sale: The Virtues and Limits of Markets*. New York: Knopf, 1997.

Lash, S., and C. Lury. *Global Culture Industry: The Mediation of Things*. Malden, MA: Polity, 2007.

Levine, Lawrence. *Highbrow/Lowbrow: The Emergence of Cultural Hierarchy in America*. Cambridge, MA: Harvard University Press, 1988.

Lewis, Bernard. *What Went Wrong? The Clash between Islam and Modernity in the Middle East*. New York: Oxford University Press, 2002.

Lockhart, Charles. *The Roots of American Exceptionalism: Institutions, Culture, and Politics*. New York: Palgrave Macmillan, 2003.

Lull, James. *China Turned On: Television, Reform, and Resistance*. New York: Routledge, 1991.

Luttwak, Edward. *Turbo-Capitalism: Winners and Losers in the Global Economy*. New York: Harper & Row, 1999.

Macedo, Stephen. *Liberal Virtues: Citizenship, Virtue, and Community in Liberal Constitutionalism*. Oxford, UK: Clarendon Press, 1990.

Madsen, Deborah L. *American Exceptionalism*. Jackson: University of Mississippi Press, 1998.

Maltby, Richard. *Harmless Entertainment: Hollywood and the Ideology of Consensus.* Metuchen, NJ: Scarecrow Press, 1983.

———. *Hollywood Cinema.* 2nd ed. Malden, MA: Blackwell, 2003.

McAnany, Emile G., and Kenton T. Wilkinson, eds. *Mass Media and Free Trade: NAFTA and the Cultural Industries.* Austin: University of Texas Press, 1996.

McBride, Allen, and Robert K. Toburen. "Deep Structures: Polpop Culture on Primetime Television." *Journal of Popular Culture* 29, no. 4 (1996): 181–200.

McCrisken, Trevor B. *American Exceptionalism and the Legacy of Vietnam: U.S. Foreign Policy since 1974.* New York: Palgrave Macmillan, 2003.

Mead, Sidney E. *The Nation with the Soul of a Church.* New York: Harper & Row, 1975.

Merelman, Richard. "On Culture and Politics in America: A Perspective from Structural Anthropology." *British Journal of Political Science* 19 (1989): 465–93.

Miller, Toby, Nitin Govil, John McMurra, and Richard Maxwell. *Global Hollywood.* London: BFI Publishing, 2001.

Mittelman, James H. *Globalization: Critical Reflections.* Boulder, CO: Lynne Rienner, 1996.

Moretti, Franco. "Planet Hollywood." *New Left Review* 9 (May–June 2001): 90–101.

Morone, James. *The Devils We Know: Us and Them in America's Raucous Political Culture.* Lawrence: University of Kansas Press, 2015.

Morris, Aldon. *The Origins of the Civil Rights Movement.* New York: Free Press, 1984.

Mukerji, Chandra, and Michael Schudson, eds. *Rethinking Popular Culture: Contemporary Perspectives in Cultural Studies.* Berkeley: University of California Press, 1991.

Munsey, Cecil. *The Illustrated Guide to the Collectibles of Coca-Cola.* New York: Hawthorn Books, 1972.

Neuhaus, Richard John. *The Naked Public Square: Religion and Democracy in America.* 2nd ed. Grand Rapids, MI: Eerdmans, 1984.

Noah, Timothy. *The Great Divergence: America's Growing Inequality Crisis and What We Can Do about It.* New York: Bloomsbury Press, 2012.

Nye, Joseph S. *Soft Power: The Means for Success in World Politics.* Cambridge, MA: PublicAffairs, 2004.

Ohmae, Kenichi. *The Borderless World: Power and Strategy in the Interlinked World Economy.* New York: HarperBusiness, 1990.

———. *The End of the Nation-State: The Rise of Regional Economies.* New York: Free Press, 1995.

Olson, Scott R. "The Globalization of Hollywood." *International Journal on World Peace* 17 (December 2000): 3–18.

———. "Hollywood Planet: Global Media and the Competitive Advantage of Narrative Transparency." In *The Television Studies Reader,* edited by Robert C. Allen and Annette Hill, 111–29. New York: Routledge, 2004.

Page, David, and William Crawley. *Satellites over South Asia: Broadcasting Culture and the Public Interest.* Thousand Oaks, CA: Sage, 2001.

Pendergast, Mark. *For God, Country, and Coca-Cola: The Unauthorized History of the Great American Soft Drink and the Company That Makes It.* New York: Scribner, 1993.

Pieterse, Jan Nederveen. *Globalization and Culture: Global Mélange.* 3rd ed. Lanham, MD: Rowman & Littlefield, 2015.

Putnam, Robert. *Bowling Alone.* New York: Simon & Schuster, 2000.

Pye, Lucien W. *Asian Power and Politics: The Cultural Dimensions of Authority.* Cambridge, MA: Belknap, 1985.

Quart, Alissa. *Branded: The Buying and Selling of Teenagers.* Cambridge, MA: Perseus Publishing, 2003.

Reich, Robert. *The Work of Nations.* New York: Vintage, 1992.

Ritzer, George. *The McDonaldization of Society 5.* 2nd ed. Thousand Oaks, CA: Pine Forge Press, 2008.

———. *The Blackwell Companion to Globalization.* Malden, MA: Blackwell, 2007.

Robertson, Roland. *Globalization: Social Theory and Global Culture.* London: Sage, 1992.

———. "Glocalization: Space, Time, and Social Theory." *Journal of International Communication* 1, no. 1 (1994): 25–44.

Rosenau, James N. *Distant Proximities: Dynamics beyond Globalization.* Princeton, NJ: Princeton University Press, 2003.

Ross, Marc Howard. "Culture and Identity in Comparative Political Analysis." In *Comparative Politics: Rationality, Culture, and Structure*, edited by Mark I. Lichbach and Alan S. Zuckerman, 42–80. New York: Cambridge University Press, 1997.

Rowe, William, and Vivian Schelling. *Memory and Modernity: Popular Culture in Latin America.* London: Verso, 1991.

Rupert, Mark, and M. Scott Solomon. *Globalization and International Political Economy: The Politics of Alternative Futures.* Lanham, MD: Rowman & Littlefield, 2006.

Said, Edward. *Culture and Imperialism.* New York: Knopf, 1993.

Sakr, Naomi. *Satellite Realms: Transnational Television, Globalization, and the Middle East.* New York: I. B. Tauris, 2001.

Sassen, Saskia. *Globalization and Its Discontents.* New York: Free Press, 1998.

Schatte, Hans. *Globalization and Citizenship.* Lanham, MD: Rowman & Littlefield, 2012.

Schiller, Herbert I. *Culture, Inc: The Corporate Takeover of Public Expression.* New York: Oxford University Press, 1989.

Schlosser, Eric. *Fast Food Nation: The Dark Side of the American Meal.* New York: Houghton Mifflin Harcourt, 2001.

Scott, Ian. *American Politics in Hollywood Film.* 2nd ed. Edinburgh: Edinburgh University Press, 2011.

Seagrave, Kerry. *American Television Abroad: Hollywood's Attempt to Dominate World Television.* Jefferson, NC: McFarland, 1998.

Shook, Carrie, and Robert L. Shook. *Franchising: The Business Strategy That Changed the World.* Englewood Cliffs, NJ: Prentice Hall, 1993.

Sklar, Robert. *Film: An International History of the Medium.* New York: Abrams, 1993.

Smart, Barry, ed. *Resisting McDonaldization.* London: Sage, 1999.

Smith, Rogers. *Civic Ideals: Conflicting Visions of Citizenship in U.S. History.* New Haven, CT: Yale University Press, 1997.

Sowell, Thomas. *Migrations and Culture.* New York: Basic Books, 1996.

Starr, Paul. *The Creation of the Media: Political Origins of Modern Communications.* New York: Basic Books, 2004.

Steger, Manfred B. *Globalism: Market Ideology Meets Terrorism.* 2nd ed. Lanham, MD: Rowman & Littlefield, 2005.

———. *Globalisms: The Great Ideological Struggle of the Twenty-first Century.* Lanham, MD: Rowman & Littlefield, 2009.

———. *Globalization: A Very Short Introduction* 3rd ed. New York: Oxford University Press, 2013.

———. *The Rise of the Global Imaginary: Political Ideologies from the French Revolution to the Global War on Terror.* New York: Oxford University Press, 2008.

Steger, Manfred B., Paul Battersby, and Joseph M. Siracusa, eds. *The SAGE Handbook of Globalization.* Vols. 1–2. Thousand Oaks, CA: Sage Publications, 2014.

Steger, Manfred B., James Goodman, and Erin K. Wilson. *Justice Globalism: Ideology, Crises, Policy.* London: Sage Publications, 2013.

Steigerwald, David. *Culture's Vanities: The Paradox of Cultural Diversity in a Globalized World.* Lanham, MD: Rowman & Littlefield, 2004.

Straubhaar, Joseph D. *World Television: From Global to Local.* Los Angeles, CA: Sage, 2007.

Sturmer, Corinna. "MTV's Europe: An Imaginary Continent." In *Channels of Resistance: Global Television and Local Empowerment,* edited by Tony Dowmunt, 50–66. London: BFI Publishing, 1993.

Tapp, Robert B., ed. *Multiculturalism.* Amherst, NY: Prometheus Books, 2000.

Taylor, Charles. *Modern Social Imaginaries.* Durham, NC: Duke University Press, 2004.

Thurow, Lester. *The Future of Capitalism: How Today's Economic Forces Shape Tomorrow's World.* New York: Morrow, 1996.

Tilly, Charles. *From Mobilization to Revolution.* Reading, MA: Addison-Wesley, 1978.

Tocqueville, Alexis de. *Democracy in America.* New York: Knopf, 1945.

Toll, Robert C. *The Entertainment Machine: American Show Business in the Twentieth Century*. New York: Oxford University Press, 1982.

Tomlinson, John. *Cultural Imperialism*. Baltimore: Johns Hopkins University Press, 1991.

———. *Globalization and Culture*. Chicago: University of Chicago Press, 1999.

Turner, Frederick Jackson. *The Frontier in American History*. New York: Holt, Rinehart, and Winston, 1962.

Wagnleitner, Reinhold, and Elaine Tyler May, eds. *"Here, There and Everywhere": The Foreign Politics of American Popular Culture*. Hanover, CT: University Press of New England, 2000.

Wasko, Janet. *Understanding Disney: The Manufacture of Fantasy*. Cambridge, MA: Polity, 2001.

Watson, James L., ed. *Golden Arches East: McDonald's in East Asia*. Stanford, CA: Stanford University Press, 1997.

Weatherford, Jack. *Genghis Khan and the Making of the Modern World*. New York: Crown, 2004.

Weiss, Linda. *The Myth of the Powerless State*. Ithaca, NY: Cornell University Press, 1998.

Whatmore, Sarah. *Hybrid Geographies: Natures, Cultures, Spaces*. London: Sage, 2002.

White, John Kenneth. *The Values Divide: American Politics and Culture in Transition*. New York: Chatham House, 2003.

Wildavsky, Aaron. "Choosing Preferences by Constructing Institutions: A Cultural Theory of Preference Formation." *American Political Science Review* 81, no. 1 (1987): 4–31.

Wolf, Naomi. *The Beauty Myth: How Images of Beauty Are Used against Women*. New York: Morrow, 1991.

Wood, G. *The Creation of the American Republic*. New York: Norton, 1969.

Young, Robert C. *Colonial Desire: Hybridity in Theory, Culture, and Race*. London: Routledge, 1995.

Zuberi, Nabeel. *Sounds English: Transnational Popular Music*. Urbana: University of Illinois Press, 2001.

INDEX

ABOUT THE AUTHOR

Lane Crothers is professor of politics and government at Illinois State University. His expertise lies in the fields of popular culture, social movements, and political culture and political leadership. From August 2015 to May 2016 he served as the Fulbright Bicentennial Chair in American Studies at the University of Helsinki; in the 2007–2008 academic year, he was the Eccles Centre Visiting Professor in North American Studies at the British Library in London. In addition to four editions of *Globalization and American Popular Culture*, he is author or coauthor of four other books, including *Rage on the Right: The American Militia Movement from Ruby Ridge to Homeland Security* and *Street-Level Leadership: Discretion and Legitimacy in Front-Line Public Service*, as well as several articles in the fields of social movements, political culture, and political leadership.

GLOBALIZATION

Series Editors
Manfred B. Steger
Royal Melbourne Institute of Technology
and University of Hawai'i–Mānoa
and
Terrell Carver
University of Bristol

"Globalization" has become *the* buzzword of our time. But what does it mean? Rather than forcing a complicated social phenomenon into a single analytical framework, this series seeks to present globalization as a multidimensional process constituted by complex, often contradictory interactions of global, regional, and local aspects of social life. Since conventional disciplinary borders and lines of demarcation are losing their old rationales in a globalizing world, authors in this series apply an interdisciplinary framework to the study of globalization. In short, the main purpose and objective of this series is to support subject-specific inquiries into the dynamics and effects of contemporary globalization and its varying impacts across, between, and within societies.

 Supported by the Globalization Research Center at the University of Hawai'i, Mānoa